Reconsidering the Insular Cases

Reconsidering the Insular Cases

The Past and Future of the American Empire

Edited by
Gerald L. Neuman
and
Tomiko Brown-Nagin

Human Rights Program Series
Harvard Law School

DISTRIBUTED BY HARVARD UNIVERSITY PRESS

Human Rights Program
Harvard Law School
6 Everett Street
Third Floor
Cambridge, MA 02138
United States of America

hrp@law.harvard.edu
http://www.hup.harvard.edu

ISBN: 978-0-9796395-7-9

Library of Congress Cataloging-in-Publication Data

Reconsidering the Insular cases : the past and future of the American
empire / edited by Gerald L. Neuman and Tomiko Brown-Nagin.
     pages cm. -- (Human rights program series)
  "This volume grew out of a conference held at Harvard Law School on
February 19, 2014, as a Francis Biddle Memorial Panel."
  Includes bibliographical references.
  ISBN 978-0-9796395-7-9
  1. Law--United States--Territories and possessions--Congresses. 2. United
States--Insular possessions--Congresses. 3. United States--Territories and
possessions--Congresses. I. Neuman, Gerald L., 1952- editor. II. Brown-
Nagin, Tomiko, 1970- editor.
  KF4635.A75R43 2015
  342.73'0413--dc23
                        2015000413

Printed by Signature Book Printing, http://www.sbpbooks.com

Contents

The Enduring Burdens of the Universal and the Different in the Insular Cases

Martha Minow*

Never during my three years as a law student or two years as a law clerk at federal courts did I hear of the "Insular Cases."[1] Yet the series of US Supreme Court decisions gathered under this name established a doctrine, in force to this day, determining that the US Constitution does not apply fully to territories acquired through conquest after the Spanish-American War and the signing of the Treaty of Paris in 1898.[2] When the Supreme Court reached its judgments in the Insular Cases, prevailing governmental attitudes presumed white supremacy and approved of stigmatizing segregation. But since that time, the court has rejected governmental actions predicated on intentional racism and the "separate but equal" doctrine of its 1896 decision in *Plessy v. Ferguson*.[3] The United States played a pivotal role in drafting and adopting the Universal Declaration of Human Rights.[4] And the Supreme

---

*   Morgan and Helen Chu Dean and Professor, Harvard Law School
1   I leave to the authors in this volume the task of determining which cases should be included in references to the Insular Cases.
2   Treaty of Peace between the United States of America and the Kingdom of Spain, U.S.-Spain, Dec. 10, 1898, 30 Stat. 1754.
3   Compare Plessy v. Ferguson, 163 U.S. 537 (1896), with Brown v. Bd. of Educ., 347 U.S. 483 (1954), and Loving v. Virginia, 388 U.S. 1 (1967).
4   Universal Declaration of Human Rights, G.A. Res. 217A (III), U.N. GAOR, 3rd Sess., at 71, U.N. Doc. A/810 (Dec. 10, 1948). See United Nations, "The Universal

Court has guaranteed even enemy combatants the essentials of due process.[5] Nonetheless, frozen in time, the Insular Cases stand. Their practical effect is to deny full application of the US Constitution within lands deemed by the government to be unincorporated, governing people who cannot participate in democratic elections, and refusing application of constitutional protections even to people recognized as US citizens.[6]

The Supreme Court did not devise the doctrine of the Insular Cases on its own. Among its sources were articles by distinguished scholars, including Abbott Lawrence Lowell, then a professor and later president of Harvard University, whose article in the *Harvard Law Review* articulated many of the ideas adopted by the Supreme Court.[7] Lowell contrasted arguments confining

---

Declaration of Human Rights: History of the Document," accessed Dec. 11, 2014, http://www.un.org/en/documents/udhr/history.shtml; Mary Ann Glendon, *A World Made New: Eleanor Roosevelt and the Universal Declaration of Human Rights* (New York: Random House, 2001).

5   Hamdi v. Rumsfeld, 542 U.S. 507 (2004) (relying on the Fifth Amendment for US citizens); Hamdan v. Rumsfeld, 548 U.S. 557 (2006) (relying on the Uniform Code of Military Justice and the Geneva Conventions for noncitizens). Note that US law makes the residents of many unincorporated territories citizens (see Jones Act, Pub. L. No. 64-368, 39 Stat. 951 (1917) (codified at 48 U.S.C. §§ 731 et seq. (2013)))—even while the Insular Cases deprive them of rights equal to those of other citizens.

6   See Harris v. Rosario, 446 U.S. 651 (1980). But see ibid., 652 (Marshall, J., dissenting); Juan R. Torruella, "One Hundred Years of Solitude: Puerto Rico's American Century," in *Foreign in a Domestic Sense: Puerto Rico, American Expansion, and the Constitution,* ed. Christina Duffy Burnett and Burke Marshall (Durham, NC: Duke University Press, 2001), 243.

7   Abbott Lawrence Lowell, "The Status of Our New Possessions: A Third View," *Harvard Law Review* 13 (1899): 155-76. He concluded:

The theory, therefore, which best interprets the Constitution in the light of history, and which accords most completely with the authorities, would seem to be that territory may be so annexed as to make it a part of the United States, and that if so all the general restrictions in the Constitution apply to it, save those on the organization of the judiciary; but that possessions may also be so acquired as not to form part of the United States, and in that case constitutional limitations, such as those requiring uniformity of taxation and trial by jury, do not apply. It may well be that some provisions have a universal bearing because they are in form restrictions upon the power of Congress rather than reservations of rights. Such are the provisions that no bill of attainder or ex post

constitutional rights to the states with arguments extending such rights wherever the nation has jurisdiction; he offered a third view extending only some limitations—such as ex post facto laws, no titles of nobility, and no bill of attainder—to the territories secured by the United States from Spain.[8] The *Harvard Law Review* published works by other scholars further developing these ideas.[9]

Especially for this reason, Harvard Law School has an obligation to bring attention and debate to the ongoing status of the Insular Cases. I am grateful to Andrés López for early conversations and to my colleagues Tomiko Brown-Nagin and Gerald Neuman for assuming leadership roles in crafting both a conference and now this book.[10] The contributors offer much-needed scholarship, legal analysis, and advocacy in hopes of garnering greater attention and dialogue for change. The status of Puerto Rico, other unincorporated territories of the United States, the rule of law in the United States, and the ideal of constitutional rights around the world are at stake. The status of people living in territories associated with other nations also presents crucial issues of constitutional law and human rights. Of course, these are matters of the first importance to those who are directly affected. It is my conclusion, though, that all are directly affected. In a 1979 case involving Puerto Rico, Justice William J. Brennan, Jr., joined by Justices Potter Stewart,

---

facto law shall be passed, that no title of nobility shall be granted, and that a regular statement and account of all public moneys shall be published from time to time. These rules stand upon a different footing from the rights guaranteed to the citizens, many of which are inapplicable except among a people whose social and political evolution has been consonant with our own.

Ibid., 176.

8   See ibid.

9   See, e.g., Simeon E. Baldwin, "The Constitutional Questions Incident to the Acquisition and Government by the United States of Island Territory," *Harvard Law Review* 12 (1899): 393-416; C. C. Langdell, "The Status of Our New Territories," *Harvard Law Review* 12 (1899): 365-92; Carman F. Randolph, "Constitutional Aspects of Annexation," *Harvard Law Review* 12 (1898): 291-315; James Bradley Thayer, "Our New Possessions," *Harvard Law Review* 12 (1899): 464-85.

10 The conference, "Reconsidering the Insular Cases," was held at Harvard Law School on February 19, 2014. For videos of the event, see Lana Birbrair, "The Insular Cases: Constitutional Experts Assess the Status of Territories Acquired in the Spanish-American War," *Harvard Law Today*, Mar. 18, 2014, http://today .law.harvard.edu/insular-cases-constitutional-experts-assess-status-territories-acquired-spanish-american-war-video.

Thurgood Marshall, and Harry A. Blackmun, pointed to these crucial words by Justice Hugo Black:

> The concept that the Bill of Rights and other constitutional protections against arbitrary government are inoperative when they become inconvenient or when expediency dictates otherwise is a very dangerous doctrine and if allowed to flourish would destroy the benefit of a written Constitution and undermine the basis of our Government.[11]

At a minimum, we mean to do our part so that no law students, law clerks, judges, or participants in our democracy remain uninformed about the Insular Cases and their continuing hold on our polity.

---

11   Torres v. Puerto Rico, 442 U.S. 465, 475 (1979) (Brennan, J., concurring) (quoting Reid v. Covert, 354 U.S. 1, 14 (1957)) (internal quotation mark omitted).

Acknowledgments

This volume grew out of a conference held at Harvard Law School on February 19, 2014, as a Francis Biddle Memorial Panel. We wish to express our gratitude to Dean Martha Minow and Andrés López for inspiring and encouraging the project, and to the Francis Biddle Memorial Lecture Fund for providing financial support. We are grateful to all the speakers at the conference, especially the keynote speaker, the Honorable Juan R. Torruella. We also wish to thank Patricia Merullo, Mindy Roseman, Cara Solomon, Yennifer Pedraza, Ellen Keng, Maureen Corrigan, and Kaitlyn Hennigan for their expert assistance in mounting the conference.

Elaborating the contributions of the conference in this book required further effort. We are grateful to all the authors for their smooth cooperation, and also wish to thank Mindy Roseman, Cara Solomon, and Gabriela Follett for their help in preparing the volume. We are grateful to Morgan Stoffregen for editorial support and to Catlin Rockman for the book's design.

Gerald L. Neuman and Tomiko Brown-Nagin
March 2015
Cambridge, MA

Introduction

Gerald L. Neuman

The US Supreme Court's decisions in the Insular Cases of 1901 provided the legal framework for the governance of a colonial empire in the Atlantic and the Pacific, loosening the constraints of constitutional principle in order to facilitate rule over the subjected areas and their inhabitants. In the wake of the Spanish-American War and the transfer of several of Spain's imperial possessions, the metaphorically expressed question "Does the Constitution follow the flag?" became newly urgent. The Supreme Court majority gave a new answer: not entirely.

The most important of the 1901 decisions was *Downes v. Bidwell*, in which the court divided five to four in favor of congressional power to discriminate between the mainland and the new territories in customs matters.[1] In retrospect, the crucial opinion was the concurrence of Justice Edward Douglass White. He accepted that the US Constitution governed the actions of the United States at any location, but he contended that it was still necessary to determine the appropriate geographical scope of each constitutional provision. The applicability of a constitutional limitation to a particular territory would depend on the situation of the territory and its relations to the United States. If the United States acquired a new territory and did not admit it as a state, then Congress could choose whether to "incorporate" the territory into the United States as an integral part or to treat it merely as a territory appurtenant to the United States. White thereby adopted a distinction that had been suggested by the political scientist Abbott Lawrence Lowell in an article in the *Harvard Law Review*,[2] although White added some elements of his own in elaborating the consequences. For incorporated territories, the Bill of Rights and other constitutional

---

1   Downes v. Bidwell, 182 U.S. 244 (1901).
2   Abbott Lawrence Lowell, "The Status of Our New Possessions: A Third View," *Harvard Law Review* 13 (1899): 155-76.

limitations would apply in the usual way. For unincorporated territories, only "fundamental" restrictions on government power would apply. Moreover, an unincorporated territory could be kept in subordination indefinitely, without the prospect of future statehood. The United States had to have the same power to acquire and govern overseas territories and populations as the European colonial powers were exercising under international law.

The four dissenters protested in vain that the majority's ruling departed from prior practice and constitutional values. In the years that followed, White's concurring analysis gained the support of a majority and then, after the death of the steadfast dissenter John Marshall Harlan, unanimity. The term "Insular Cases" may refer either to the original set of decisions from 1901 or to the entire series of decisions from *Downes v. Bidwell* (1901) to *Balzac v. Porto Rico* (1922) that solidified this jurisprudence.[3]

The doctrine of the Insular Cases has never been overruled, despite the tectonic shifts in constitutional law, international law, and human rights conceptions that have intervened since 1901. It continues to provide the foundation for governing inhabited territories and small islands without permanent populations.[4] The doctrine is peripheral to the interests of most constitutional law scholars, but highly consequential for the four million people who live in Puerto Rico, the US Virgin Islands, American Samoa, Guam, and the Northern Mariana Islands.[5] It affects their civil rights directly,

---

3   See Balzac v. Porto Rico, 258 U.S. 298 (1922). The decisions of 1901 also included *De Lima v. Bidwell*, 182 U.S. 1 (1901); *Goetze v. United States*, 182 U.S. 221 (1901); *Dooley v. United States*, 182 U.S. 222 (1901); *Armstrong v. United States*, 182 U.S. 243 (1901); *Huus v. New York & Porto Rico Steamship Co.*, 182 U.S. 392 (1901); *Dooley v. United States*, 183 U.S. 151 (1901); and *Fourteen Diamond Rings v. United States*, 183 U.S. 176 (1901).

4   I use "territories" as a generic term, without the intention of equating the status of different polities, and without implying a position about the extent of federal power over them.

5   The Commonwealth of the Northern Mariana Islands (CNMI) may be considered a special case because it negotiated its entry under US sovereignty while the United States was administering the islands as part of a strategic trust territory under the Charter of the United Nations. Lower courts have been willing to assume that the Covenant to Establish a Commonwealth of the Northern Mariana Islands in Political Union with the United States of America places judicially enforceable limits on congressional power over the CNMI and not merely obligations of good faith. See United States ex rel. Richards v. De Leon Guerrero, 4 F.3d 749 (9th Cir. 1993); Commonwealth of the Northern Mariana Islands v. United States, 670 F. Supp. 2d 65 (D.D.C. 2009). The Supreme Court has not addressed this issue; thus far, its only decision on the merits regarding the governance of the CNMI has

and it affects all their rights by limiting their political rights, which in turn reduces their ability to influence the laws that regulate them. The federal government has taken steps to reform territorial relations on a noncolonial basis, but relics of colonialism remain.

A doctrine that produces such effects must be continually reexamined, and that is why the Human Rights Program at Harvard Law School is publishing this volume. The book results from a conference that Tomiko Brown-Nagin and I organized at the initiative of Dean Martha Minow, which took place on February 19, 2014. The book includes the vivid keynote address delivered by Judge Juan R. Torruella of the United States Court of Appeals for the First Circuit, as well as other chapters based on presentations from the conference.

When legal rules have imposed injustice, it becomes necessary to contemplate both how the rules could be reformed and what additional measures should be taken in response to the injustice. This volume considers changes to the constitutional framework, which ultimately would depend on approval by the Supreme Court, and three strategies that could remove territories from the field of application of the Insular Cases doctrine. These strategies are admission to statehood, full independence, and the less widely known alternative of independence accompanied by a compact (i.e., a treaty) of free association. Each alternative has disadvantages and advantages in relation to the others and to the current status quo.

Most of the chapters emphasize the example of Puerto Rico, which was one of the original targets of the Insular Cases doctrine and is now where more than 90% of the insular citizens live. As several authors observe, the Commonwealth of Puerto Rico has suffered severe economic distress in recent years, and its recovery efforts have been hindered by the limits on its political power. A 2012 referendum demonstrated the paucity of support for the commonwealth's current governance framework. The path forward is complicated, however, by disagreements over the direction that reform should take and by the need to secure federal approval. Thus, recent events make the need to reconsider the doctrine and its alternatives particularly pressing.

The purpose of this volume is to provide a forum in which the authors speak for themselves. Nonetheless, the reader may be assisted by the following succinct overview.

The first three chapters discuss the historical context and legacy of the Insular Cases. Christina Duffy Ponsa explores the initial responses in Puerto

---

been a summary affirmance without opinion. See Torres v. Sablan, 528 U.S. 1110 (2000), aff'g mem., Rayphand v. Sablan, 95 F. Supp. 2d 1133 (D. N. Mar. I. 1999) (holding that the "one person, one vote" rule of equal protection law does not apply to the CNMI Senate).

Rico to acquisition by the United States, as well as how some political thinkers understood statehood as a vehicle for realizing autonomy. Efrén Rivera Ramos interrogates the meaning of the Insular Cases doctrine, unpacking a series of propositions that it has entailed, but indicating that fundamentally it has left Congress with the discretion to shape territorial governance. Bartholomew H. Sparrow examines the geopolitical context of the Insular Cases at their origin and through the course of the twentieth century into the present day.

The fourth chapter provides Judge Torruella's keynote address, which describes how the Insular Cases doctrine was originally—and remains—incompatible with US constitutional principles. In contemporary terms, he points to conflicts with international human rights norms of nondiscrimination and political participation.

The fifth and sixth chapters provide perspectives from international law and political theory. In contrast to the colonialist project that gave rise to the Insular Cases, as Chimène I. Keitner explains, the modern international law of decolonization and the right to self-determination provides for relationships of consent, including the option of two states linking themselves through a compact of free association. Rogers M. Smith explores how the differentiated constitutional regimes of the territories should be understood in the twenty-first century, when some variations in rights may be sought by territorial citizens as an accommodation to their cultural identities.

The last three chapters focus specifically on future status alternatives for Puerto Rico: free association (Rafael Cox Alomar), statehood (Andrés W. López), and independence (Carlos Iván Gorrín Peralta). None of the authors favors the status quo, and none of them suggests waiting for the political branches and the Supreme Court to revise their current understandings of congressional power over the territories.

CHAPTER ONE

When Statehood Was Autonomy

Christina Duffy Ponsa[*]

Over the past fifteen years, the Insular Cases of 1901 have been on a transformative journey. Once marginal judicial decisions that virtually no US constitutional scholar had ever heard of, they have come to be recognized as a watershed event in the constitutional history of American empire and as central doctrinal precedents in the US Supreme Court's jurisprudence on extraterritoriality and the war on terror. Nearly invisible for a century after they were handed down, the Insular Cases found their way into mainstream US constitutional scholarship as a result of the resurgence in interest in US empire that occurred in 1998—one hundred years after the United States annexed Puerto Rico, the Philippines, and Guam in the wake of the Spanish-American War. At the time, the annexation of these islands gave rise to a national debate over whether the United States could annex and govern the new "colonies" with a freer hand than it had used with previously acquired territories, and without eventually admitting them into statehood.

The Insular Cases answered both questions in the affirmative: holding that the newly annexed islands "belonged" to the United States but were not "a part of" it, the Supreme Court explained that fewer constitutional protections applied in the new territories and that a decision on their ultimate political fate could be indefinitely postponed. The islands came to be known as "unincorporated" because—as the court explained in the process of constitutionalizing their new status—they had not been fully "incorporated"

* I am grateful to Judge José A. Cabranes, Josep M. Fradera Barceló, Jody S. Kraus, Efrén Rivera Ramos, and the editors of this volume for their comments on earlier drafts of this chapter. A substantially longer, still-in-progress version of this piece has benefited from the feedback of many others recognized therein. All translations are my own.

into the United States. They were, in the court's memorable formulation, "foreign to the United States in a domestic sense."[1] The court thus relegated the unincorporated territories to an unprecedented status: confusing and ambiguous; constitutionally inferior to that of the United States' nineteenth-century territories; and denied even the implicit promise of statehood that earlier territories had always apparently enjoyed.

The Insular Cases left unanswered foundational questions of constitutional and national identity: Would Puerto Rico be independent? Would it be a state? Were its people US citizens as a result of the island's annexation by the United States? If not, would they ever be? If so, why weren't they on a path to statehood? Where, instead, were they headed? The Supreme Court's failure to answer these questions left Washington with unprecedented power to decide the fate of the United States' annexed territories. The court thus gave its imprimatur to policies devised by the US government with a view toward facilitating the United States' assertion of sovereignty and control over places and people it was not ready or willing to admit on a footing of equality into the Union.

The Insular Cases did their work, however, not merely by giving constitutional content and legitimacy to a novel category of second-class, "unincorporated" US territories. Equally importantly, they rendered these territories essentially invisible. The territories became, that is, doubly marginal: neither fully "domestic" nor fully "foreign," and devoid of both voting representation in the federal government and independent status on the international stage, they were at the top of nobody's agenda, and stripped of the power to set their own. Even more than formal legal subordination, it was their relative invisibility that trapped these places and their people in a second-class status with an uncertain future.

The Philippines briefly enjoyed a resurgence of attention when it came time in 1946 for its independence. But for Puerto Rico, a small island for which neither independence nor statehood had been taken seriously in Washington, invisibility remained a central feature of its daily political reality. Whereas the debate about what to do with Spain's former colonies had occupied the attention of officials at the highest levels of government during the brief period immediately surrounding the events of 1898, once it had been settled that Puerto Ricans remained subject to US sovereignty but without any promise of statehood, they quickly receded from the national view and, soon thereafter, from national memory.

It comes as little surprise, then, that the Insular Cases themselves were soon forgotten. As Sanford Levinson put it in an essay about their place in

---

1   Downes v. Bidwell, 182 U.S. 244, 341-42 (1901).

the canon of constitutional law, until the centenary of 1898, it was not at all embarrassing for a US constitutional scholar to admit that she had never even heard of the Insular Cases, much less read or taught or written about them.[2] One of the main aims of those who study the Insular Cases has therefore been, simply, to recover what was lost: to introduce constitutional lawyers and scholars to these decisions and to explain their significance for major issues of constitutional law and scholarship. As this volume attests, it is a project that has been notably successful.

Puerto Ricans, however, have never forgotten the events of 1898, so the renewed attention on the Insular Cases over the past two decades has not really been aimed at them. In Puerto Rico, the Insular Cases have always been part of the canon of constitutional law, and people have been reminded daily that their political fate remains unresolved. Yet even in Puerto Rico, there remains work to be done to achieve a better understanding of this critical turning point in our history.

The aim of this chapter is to contribute to that understanding by reexamining a brief but significant moment in the entwined histories of Puerto Rico and the United States. The moment in question is the nearly two-year period following Puerto Rico's annexation, during which there existed virtually unanimous support among the island's political leaders for Puerto Rico's admission into the United States as a state of the Union. This immediate and enthusiastic embrace of statehood has long struck Puerto Rican historians as puzzling, to say the least.[3] Mere months before the island's annexation,

---

2   Sanford Levinson, "Installing the *Insular Cases* into the Canon of Constitutional Law," in *Foreign in a Domestic Sense: Puerto Rico, American Expansion, and the Constitution*, ed. Christina Duffy Burnett and Burke Marshall (Durham, NC: Duke University Press, 2001), 123.

3   See, e.g., Fernando Picó, *1898: La guerra después de la guerra*, 2nd ed. (Río Piedras: Ediciones Huracán, 1998). After describing the switch in allegiance by the political elite of the town of Utuado from loyalty toward Spain to loyalty toward the United States, Picó wonders, "What is the historian to make of [this change of heart]? What could the Utuado elite be thinking, spilling patriotic prose in defense of Spanish territory in June and with the same fervor proclaiming adherence to the stars and stripes in August?" Ibid., 75. Rejecting the "simple reading" (which Picó describes as follows: "1) They were honest in June and hypocrites in August; 2) They were hypocrites in June and honest in August; 3) They were not honest in June or August; 4) They were honest in June and in August"), Picó offers the more subtle explanation that a range of interests brought together various segments of society—"young professionals educated in the United States and Europe, creole merchants and landowners most impatient with the [existing] political regime, and those popular classes in labor and social conflicts with managerial classes, [all of whom] had their own reasons for desiring political change"—in support of US

Puerto Ricans had been Spaniards, both in the legal sense (as subjects of the Spanish monarchy) and in terms of national identity. Unlike Cuba, which had been fighting for its independence for years, Puerto Rico had never produced an independence movement with realistic prospects of success.[4] Instead, for many decades Puerto Ricans had been struggling to obtain "autonomy" within Spain's constitutional framework. Puerto Rico's "autonomists" (*autonomistas*) wished for greater local self-government for the island, but as an integral part of the Spanish empire. Their motto was "the maximum decentralization compatible with national unity"—and the "nation" in question was Spain.

How, then, did Puerto Ricans switch allegiances so quickly? How could they transform themselves essentially overnight from loyal Spanish subjects into aspiring American citizens? Not only did Spain's withdrawal from the island fail to unleash an independence movement—it did the opposite, giving rise to a movement for US statehood. If Puerto Ricans were so ready to abandon their Spanish loyalties, why did they not embrace Puerto Rican nationality and independence? Why instead did they welcome the island's annexation into a foreign empire?

To understand what motivates these questions, imagine a spectrum on which one could align and match up ethnic identities and political statuses. On one end of the spectrum, Puerto Ricans would be a formal part of the Spanish empire, and authentically Spanish. On the other, they would be a formal part of the US empire, and authentically American. In between, we would find an independent Puerto Rico peopled by authentic Puerto Ricans. Reflecting this understanding, Puerto Rican intellectuals have long distinguished between "autonomy" and "statehood" as if the two were distinct

---

sovereignty. Ibid., 78. But that Picó finds the switch in allegiance puzzling cannot be denied—and he is not alone. Some historians have treated it as an embarrassing detour in what should have been a trajectory from Spanish colonialism to Puerto Rican national self-determination and independence. See, e.g., Eda Milagros Burgos-Malavé, *Génesis y práxis de la Carta Autonómica de 1897 en Puerto Rico* (San Juan: Centro de Estudios Avanzados de Puerto Rico y el Caribe, 1997), 305; Arturo Morales Carrión, *Puerto Rico: A Political and Cultural History* (New York: W. W. Norton, 1983), 140; Carmelo Rosario Natal, *Puerto Rico y la crisis de la guerra hispanoamericana (1895-1898)* (San Juan: Editorial Edil, 1989), 247-57. Others have offered less critical readings. See, e.g., Efrén Rivera Ramos, *The Legal Construction of Identity: The Judicial and Social Legacy of American Colonialism in Puerto Rico* (Washington, DC: American Psychological Association, 2001), 54; Ángel G. Quintero Rivera, *Patricios y plebeyos: Burgueses, hacendados, artesanos, y obreros; Las relaciones de clase en el Puerto Rico de cambio de siglo* (Río Piedras: Ediciones Huracán, 1988), 81-82 n.136.

4   It came closest in the Grito de Lares, an armed insurrection in 1868 that was quickly suppressed by Spain. See, e.g., Laird W. Bergad, "Toward Puerto Rico's Grito de Lares: Coffee, Social Stratification, and Class Conflicts, 1828-1868," *Hispanic American Historical Review* 60 (1980): 617-42.

and opposed constitutional alternatives suitable only for distinct and opposed ethnic identities—Spanish on the one hand, American on the other.[5] To make a transition from being Spanish to being Puerto Rican would be to make a natural transition, in terms of both formal political status and ethnic identity—self-respecting Spaniards born and raised in Puerto Rico may naturally come to see themselves as politically distinct descendants of Spain with a shared Spanish heritage. But to make a transition from being Spanish to being American—the transition Puerto Rico's autonomists seem to have tried to make in the wake of annexation—would be to make an unnatural transition, bypassing the possibility of achieving political independence and, with it, the culmination of Puerto Rican ethnic identity.

Whatever else one might say about this teleological way of thinking about the relationship between ethnic identities and formal political statuses, one can say this much: Puerto Rico's late nineteenth-century autonomists did not share it. The warm reception given by Puerto Rican autonomists to the United States in the period immediately following annexation cannot be explained away by dismissing it, as some have done, as an episode of temporary insanity among Spaniards who, under the circumstances, should have sought independence, or by tarring them as wannabe-Americans who sold out their own ethnic identity to a new and foreign empire, exposing a shocking lack of self-respect and pride in their distinct Spanish heritage. To do so is to indulge in a Puerto Rican version of the fallacy of the "great aberration," the historical interpretation according to which the United States' imperial adventures in the period surrounding 1898 were an unnatural departure from the past and a betrayal of true American constitutional principles. US historians have long ceased to think of 1898 this way, challenging the exceptionalist narratives that portray the events of the turn of the twentieth century as a deviation. Instead, they have revealed the continuities between the United States' imperial venture in 1898 and the century of continental expansion that preceded it, concluding that the turn of the century, while certainly a watershed constitutional moment in the history of US empire, was no deviation. An analogous account, however, has found adherents among those Puerto Rican intellectuals who see support for Puerto Rican statehood in the wake of annexation (and ever since) as its own "great aberration." According to this understanding, statehood represents an unnatural departure from the past and a betrayal of true Puerto Ricanness; to embrace it is to stray from the natural course of things.

In this chapter, I offer an alternative explanation for the autonomists' ready embrace of statehood following the island's annexation. Drawing on Puerto Rico's nineteenth-century constitutional history, I argue that the

---

5   But see, e.g., Gervasio Luis García, *Armar la historia: La tesis en la región transparente y otros ensayos* (Río Piedras: Ediciones Huracán, 1989), 98-99.

autonomists became supporters of Puerto Rico's admission into the Union immediately following the island's annexation because statehood was, quite simply, a highly desirable version of the political status they had been seeking from Spain for decades. Far from an unnatural departure from their Spanish heritage or a betrayal of their authentic ethnic identity as Puerto Ricans, to Puerto Rico's nineteenth-century autonomists, statehood *was* autonomy.

Today, statehood is seen by its opponents as anathema to Puerto Rican identity: if Puerto Rico were to become a state, they argue, Puerto Ricans would lose their culture, their language, their traditions. But the autonomists of the nineteenth century embraced a more fluid understanding of the relationship between sovereignty, territory, boundaries, and national identity than the one that subsequently prevailed and remains dominant to this day. They did not see their ethnic identity as an obstacle to statehood, or statehood as a threat to their ethnic identity, because they did not rigidly insist on a correspondence between ethnic identity, political status, and geographical boundaries. Instead, they believed they could become Americans without forfeiting or subordinating their distinct ethnic identity as Puerto Ricans—a belief arising out of a thoughtful engagement with the question of what relationship political status and ethnic identity should have. As stated in an autonomist newspaper on the eve of the US invasion, "because being Spanish is inherent in us, any kind of autonomy that is conceded to us cannot alter that condition."[6] "Postnational" long before that idea came into vogue, the autonomists saw the abandonment of their Puerto Ricanness as neither a prerequisite for nor a consequence of Puerto Rico's admission into statehood.

To be sure, their vision turned out to be overly optimistic. A more rigid understanding of the relationship between ethnic identity, political status, and geographical boundaries prevailed in the United States, where the idea of a Puerto Rican state of the Union turned out to be unthinkable, in large measure because of precisely the ethnic identity that the autonomists had wrongly believed would not stand in the way of statehood. They had underestimated the popularity of ideas of white Anglo-Saxon supremacy in the United States and the degree to which these ideas would shape US policies toward the new territories.

These developments proved bitterly disappointing in Puerto Rico. The autonomist consensus in favor of statehood fell apart; in its place emerged several coalitions embodying different reactions to the disappointment. One group would continue to pursue the goal of statehood but with an enthusiastically pro-American rhetoric that it hoped would lead the United

---

6   *El País*, Nov. 3, 1897.

States to offer statehood to Puerto Rico. Members of this group ceased to be viewed as autonomists, instead becoming known as "statehooders," or *estadistas*. Another group reacted by adopting a view that, in a sense, mirrored the view that had prevailed in the United States: in order for Puerto Rico to become a state of the Union, Puerto Ricans would have to cease being Puerto Rican. Among this group, some withdrew their support for statehood entirely, casting their lot with independence. Others, however, eventually embraced a third way: the idea that Puerto Rico should be neither a state nor independent, but should instead have a political status suited to its unique history, circumstances, and ethnic identity. Claiming the mantle of "autonomy," these latter-day *autonomistas* took up the pursuit of a relationship to the United States that would be equal to, but different from, that of the states of the Union: today, it is known as "commonwealth" status.

Today's *autonomistas* defend commonwealth status as the only way to achieve a sufficient degree of self-government for Puerto Rico and maintain a formal association with the United States while preserving Puerto Rican ethnic identity. Statehood, they argue, would not accomplish the same goal, because Puerto Ricans would lose their distinctive ethnic identity. Yet as I show below, the original autonomists saw no inconsistency between statehood and the preservation of their distinctive ethnic identity: in this sense, it is the statehooders who have remained true to the ideals of the late nineteenth-century autonomists.

That said, my goal is not to argue that statehooders are the "real" autonomists while commonwealth supporters are not. Rather, it is to challenge the opposite view: that commonwealth supporters are the "real" autonomists while statehooders are not. Neither group can monopolize the label and be accurate or faithful to the historical record. The view that treats commonwealth status as the sole legitimate heir to the autonomists' vision rests on precisely the rigid association between political status and ethnic identity that the nineteenth-century autonomists rejected; it rests on an unexamined and unsustainable account of the autonomists' views on ethnic identity. Properly understood, those views explain the autonomists' ready embrace of statehood following annexation and reveal a conception of Puerto Rican ethnic identity as inherently secure across a wide array of political arrangements.

When the late nineteenth-century autonomists greeted their new US sovereign, they brought with them the imaginative and unorthodox vision of imperial constitutionalism they had forged in the crucible of (Spanish) empire. The Insular Cases of 1901 dealt a fatal blow to this vision, which was soon forgotten. In this chapter, I attempt to recover it.

The Elusive "Special Laws"

Puerto Rico's quest for autonomy dates to Spain's first experiment with a written constitution in the early nineteenth century.[7] From 1808 to 1814, all but a corner of the Iberian Peninsula was occupied by Napoleon, who deposed and imprisoned the Spanish king, Ferdinand VII, and then installed his brother Joseph Bonaparte on the Spanish throne.[8] For his new conquest, Napoleon provided a constitution, the Constitution of Bayonne, which was formally adopted by a constitutional assembly convened under his control and which included delegates from the Spanish-American colonies and the Philippines.[9] The presence of delegates from Spain's colonies at the Bayonne assembly was a sea change: the Spanish Cortes, a legislative body that by tradition met when convened by the king, had never included representatives from the colonies. Responding to Napoleon's actions, the Spaniards who had formed a resistance government in the southern city

---

7   This chapter focuses on Puerto Rico's efforts at reform. For accounts focusing on analogous efforts in Cuba, see, e.g., Marta Bizcarrondo and Antonio Elorza, *Cuba/España: El dilema autonomista, 1878-1898* (Madrid: Editorial Colibrí, 2001); and Mildred de la Torre and Carmen Almodóvar Muñoz, *El autonomismo en Cuba, 1878-1898* (Havana: Editorial de Ciencias Sociales, 1997). Two helpful reviews of the literature focusing on Cuba are Antonio-Filiu Franco Pérez, "Cuba y el orden jurídico español del siglo XIX: La descentralización colonial como estrategia y táctica jurídico-política," *Revista Electrónica de Historia Constitucional* 5 (2004): 313-24; and Antonio-Filiu Franco Pérez, "*Vae Victis!* O, la biografía política del autonomismo cubano, 1878-1898," *Revista Electrónica de Historia Constitucional* 3 (2002): 257-79. See also Josep M. Fradera, "Why Were Spain's Special Overseas Laws Never Enacted?," in *Spain, Europe and the Atlantic World: Essays in Honor of John H. Elliott*, ed. Richard L. Kagan and Geoffrey Parker (Cambridge: Cambridge University Press, 1995), 334-49.

8   See Manuel Chust, *La cuestión nacional americana en las Cortes de Cádiz (1810-1814)* (Valencia: Centro Francisco Tomás y Valiente, 1999); Marie Laure Rieu-Millán, *Los diputados americanos en las Cortes de Cádiz: Igualdad o independencia* (Madrid: Consejo Superior de Investigaciones Científicas, 1990); María Teresa Berruezo, *La participación americana en las Cortes de Cádiz, 1810-1814* (Madrid: Centro de Estudios Constitucionales, 1986); Joaquín Varela Suanzes-Carpegna, *La teoría del estado en los orígenes del constitucionalismo hispánico* (Madrid: Centro de Estudios Constitucionales, 1983); Christina Duffy Burnett, "The American Delegates at the Cortes de Cádiz: Citizenship, Sovereignty, Nationhood (MPhil thesis, Cambridge University, 1995).

9   Carlos Sanz Cid, *La Constitución de Bayona: Labor de redacción y elementos que a ella fueron aportados, según los documentos que se guardan en los Archivos Nacionales de París y los Papeles Reservados de la Biblioteca Nacional del Real Palacio de Madrid* (Madrid: Editorial Reus, 1922).

of Cádiz, Spain's last remaining stronghold, convened a competing session of the Cortes on behalf of the absent king. Desperate for all the support they could muster—and not wanting to be outdone by Napoleon—they too invited delegates from the colonies.

The "American delegates," as they came to be known, traveled to this Cádiz Cortes bearing instructions from their respective local jurisdictions to seek governmental reforms: the unrest that would soon lead to the wars of Latin American independence was already in its early stages, and the Cádiz convention offered Spain's American subjects an opportunity to present their demands for reform to a Spanish government under siege and in need of their support. Yet upon their arrival, the American delegates realized they faced a more basic challenge: although the colonies had finally been granted representation in the Cortes, it soon became clear that the peninsular delegates would resist making it *equal* representation. Despite the roughly equal populations of Spanish domains on the peninsula and in the colonies, the Cádiz convention assigned the colonies a mere twenty-six delegates, and the peninsula over two hundred. This imbalance prompted the American delegates to demand that the Cortes formally declare the equality of the colonies. They eventually got their declaration, but only after being forced to submit to a compromise that deprived the statement of any real effect: the Cortes issued a decree describing Spain as "one, single nation" consisting of Spanish domains in both hemispheres, and declaring that the inhabitants of both hemispheres enjoyed "equal rights." The decree limited itself to declaring equality "in principle," expressly postponing its implementation in practice, and as a result, the number of American delegates remained a fraction of the number of peninsular delegates throughout the proceedings at Cádiz. The practice of declaring principles without then putting them into effect would become a recurring theme in Spain's treatment of the colonies throughout the nineteenth century.

The final text of the Spanish Constitution of 1812 reiterated the declaration that "[t]he Spanish Nation consists of all Spaniards in *both* hemispheres," thus giving formal constitutional sanction to the inclusion of Spain's colonies in the drafting and adoption of this constitutional text and in the legislative body of the Cortes.[10] However, the full effect of this opening declaration was yet again undermined in practice: although the 1812 Cádiz Constitution arguably "surpassed all existing representative governments" of the period by enfranchising "all men, except those of African ancestry, members of regular orders, domestic servants, convicted criminals, and public debtors, without requiring either literacy or property qualifications," it

---

10   Constitución de 1812 [Constitution of 1812], art. 1 (Spain) (emphasis added).

simultaneously defined the term "Spaniard" restrictively enough so that when it came time to allot representatives in the Cortes, the American colonies would still trail the peninsular provinces.

Spain's first constitutional experiment proved short-lived: although the 1812 text provided for a constitutional monarchy and the delegates proclaimed their loyalty to the Spanish king, Ferdinand was not impressed. Upon his return from exile in 1814, he set out to restore the pre-constitutional status quo "as if such things had never happened," repealing the Constitution of 1812, reestablishing his absolutist regime, and unleashing a campaign of persecution against the "liberals" who had been the main force behind a written constitution.[11] But Ferdinand proved incapable of holding onto both his empire and his power. By the next decade, Spain's colonies on the Spanish-American mainland had achieved their independence, reducing Spain's overseas empire to the islands of Cuba and Puerto Rico in the Caribbean, and the Philippines and Guam in the Pacific.

The tumultuous decades that followed saw the adoption and repeal of successive Spanish constitutions. In 1822, proponents of a written constitution secured the reinstatement of the Constitution of 1812. Yet Ferdinand's loss of empire proved more lasting than his loss of power: the second constitutional experiment was even shorter lived than the first, and within a year, the Constitution was again repealed.

The next constitutional period came in 1837, four years after Ferdinand's death, following a series of revolts culminating in a mutiny of the royal guard that forced Queen Regent María Cristina to reinstate the Constitution of 1812.[12] The Constitution of 1837 contained a crucial modification with respect to Spain's remaining Antillean colonies: whereas the 1812 text had declared equality between Spanish provinces on the peninsula and Spanish colonies in the Americas (albeit only in "principle," as noted above), the Constitution of 1837 denied the colonies representation in the Cortes; instead, a provision known as "additional article 2" stated that the "overseas provinces" would be governed by "special laws."[13]

There were at least two reasons for the change. One was a growing sense

---

11 Quoted in Isabel Burdiel, "Myths of Failure, Myths of Success: New Perspectives on Nineteenth-Century Spanish Liberalism," *Journal of Modern History* 70 (1998): 892-912, 901. Burdiel notes that the term "liberal" was first used to describe the proponents of a written constitution during the Cortes de Cádiz. See ibid., 900.

12 Burdiel, "Myths of Failure, Myths of Success," 908.

13 CONSTITUCIÓN DE 1837 [CONSTITUTION OF 1837], additional articles, art. 2 (Spain). See Carlos D'Alzina Guillermety, *Evolución y desarrollo del autonomismo puertorriqueño, siglo XIX* (San Juan: Universidad Politécnica de Puerto Rico, 1995), 36-41.

that a legal regime specific to the colonies would be necessary to maintain order there in light of the large black population, which included slaves and free blacks. Another was that the colonies were geographically distant enough from peninsular Spain that legislation affecting them should be attentive to their distinctive local needs.[14]

Puerto Ricans did not object to the idea of special laws per se: recall that at the Cádiz convention, they had hoped to obtain not only equality with Spanish provinces and inclusion in Spain's constitutional framework but also governmental reforms specific to the island. However, they strenuously objected to the denial of representation. Before they had learned that the new Constitution had deprived them of voting rights, Puerto Ricans had elected delegates to the Cortes on the assumption that the Constitution of 1812 was back in force; when these delegates arrived in Madrid to take their seats, they were barred from the assembly. Their arguments in protest—that the Constitution of 1837 was supposed to reinstate the Constitution of 1812 and that the 1812 text had recognized the principle of equality for the colonies— proved unavailing: they would not regain representation in the Cortes until 1869.[15] They would not see any special laws, either: neither the 1837 provision nor an analogous one in the Constitution of 1845 took effect.[16]

The Constitution of 1869 restored representation in the Cortes for the colonies and simultaneously promised them governmental reforms in a provision with a veiled allusion to the need for a special legal regime: it stated that the Cortes would "reform the current system of government of the overseas provinces, as soon as the delegates from Cuba or Puerto Rico have taken their seats, to extend to the same, *with the modifications deemed necessary*, the rights guaranteed in the Constitution."[17] Using the term that would come to be associated with colonial calls for greater self-government— "autonomy"—one of the delegates to the convention that produced this constitutional text had argued that Spain should implement in Cuba and Puerto Rico "*a particular Constitution, an autonomy of their own*, so that

---

14 D'Alzina Guillermety, *Evolución y desarrollo*, 38-39.

15 Javier Alvarado, *Constitucionalismo y codificación en las provincias de Ultramar: La supervivencia del Antiguo Régimen en la España de XIX* (Madrid: Centro de Estudios Políticos y Constitucionales, 2001), 46; Christopher Schmidt-Nowara, *Empire and Anti-Slavery: Spain, Cuba, and Puerto Rico, 1833-1974* (Pittsburgh: University of Pittsburgh Press, 1999), 15.

16 CONSTITUCIÓN DE 1845 [CONSTITUTION OF 1845], art. 80 (Spain).

17 CONSTITUCIÓN DE 1869 [CONSTITUTION OF 1869], art. 108 (Spain) (emphasis added). The Philippines was treated separately: "The regime under which the Spanish colonies located in the Philippine archipelago shall be governed shall be reformed by law." Ibid., art. 109.

they may govern themselves, and not share with the rest of the country more than the national bond."[18] Nevertheless, as on previous occasions, no reforms were implemented, nor were constitutional rights actually extended to the colonies. And so it was with the Constitution of 1876: it too promised that "[t]he overseas provinces will be governed by special laws."[19] But the special laws were not forthcoming, and the wait continued.

"The Maximum Decentralization Compatible with National Unity"

Although Puerto Rico's struggle for greater self-government spanned the decades from the Napoleonic invasion through the end of the nineteenth century, historians have designated as the "autonomist period" only the final phase of the struggle, beginning with the founding of the Partido Autonomista Puertorriqueño, or Puerto Rican Autonomist Party, in 1887.[20] The party's creation (a rechristening of the Partido Liberal Reformista) took place at a gathering in Ponce on March 7-9, 1887, which came to be seen as an iconic event—the founding moment of the "autonomist period" in Puerto Rican politics. This event, known as the Ponce Assembly, was convened by the leading Puerto Rican liberal of the time, Román Baldorioty de Castro, who for years had been advocating for the party's reorganization into an autonomist party from the pages of the newspaper *La Crónica*, and who himself came to be seen as the founding father of the Puerto Rican autonomist movement.[21]

Baldorioty, who died two years after the Ponce Assembly, had established himself as a preeminent advocate of Puerto Rico's autonomy as early as 1870, when as a delegate to the Cortes he gave a speech calling for the enactment of the special laws promised by the Constitution of 1869.[22] Despite Baldorioty's reputation, however, the Ponce Assembly featured a contest between his vision of autonomy and an alternative vision associated with another leading advocate of autonomy for the colonies, Rafael María de Labra. A native of Cuba, Labra had moved to Spain as a child, eventually becoming a delegate in the Cortes representing Infiesto, Asturias. Both Labra and Baldorioty were

---

18 Quoted in Alvarado, *Constitucionalismo y codificación*, 58 ("una Constitución particular, una autonomía propia, para que se gobiernen por si mismas, y no tengan con el resto del país más lazo que el nacional") (emphasis added).

19 CONSTITUCIÓN DE 1876 [CONSTITUTION OF 1876], art. 89 (Spain).

20 See generally, e.g., D'Alzina Guillermety, *Evolución y desarrollo*; Burgos Malavé, *Génesis y praxis*.

21 On advocacy of autonomy in *La Crónica*, see Burgos Malavé, *Génesis y praxis*, 41; and Lidio Cruz Monclova, *Baldorioty de Castro: Su vida, sus ideas* (San Juan: Instituto de Cultura Puertorriqueña, 1966), 98; but see D'Alzina Guillermety, *Evolución y desarrollo*, 121.

22 Burgos Malavé, *Génesis y praxis*, 37; Cruz Monclova, *Baldorioty*, 28.

republicans: Baldorioty made clear his view that sovereignty resided in the people, not the monarch; Labra, in turn, was active in republican circles in Spain, though he avoided joining any party, including the republican ones. But they had differences of opinion as well, and among the delegates at the Ponce Assembly, it was Labra's version of autonomy, not Baldorioty's, that prevailed.

The principal distinction between Baldorioty's and Labra's proposals concerned legislative power and representation. An admirer of the autonomy then enjoyed by Canada, Australia, and New Zealand under Great Britain, Baldorioty argued that it was "impossible to ignore the superiority of the autonomist system" in these places, and his articles in *La Crónica* repeatedly cited them as models that should guide Spain's colonial reforms.[23] Under Baldorioty's preferred Canadian-style system, the colonies would each have a *cámara insular*, or local legislature, that would exercise legislative power over local matters (although always with the caveat that such control would extend only as far as "the maximum degree compatible with Spanish unity").[24] Autonomy along these lines, wrote Baldorioty, "contains the maximum liberty for the colonies, and is superior to all other systems. Australia and Canada owe their progress to it."[25]

But in Spanish politics, the line between autonomy and separatism was considered a fine one, and the suggestion that the colonies should adopt a foreign model of autonomy came too close to crossing that line. For this reason, Labra distanced himself from the Canadian model. Under Labra's preferred system, legislative power would reside in the national legislature (the Cortes), while each colony would have a *diputación provincial* exercising only administrative power over local matters. Under this form of autonomy, there would be "political identity": that is, both peninsular and overseas provinces would have equal representation in the Cortes.[26]

Labra did allude to the example of Canadian autonomy; however, he did so merely in order to defend the ideal of autonomy against accusations of separatism. As he explained, the Canadian model was useful insofar as it offered evidence that an imperial power might quell separatist agitation by granting its colonies autonomy.[27] However, he took pains to distance himself

23 Burgos Malavé, *Génesis y praxis*, 37. See also Cruz Monclova, *Baldorioty*, 98, 104-5.
24 Cruz Monclova, *Baldorioty*, 105 ("control local . . . *hasta el mayor grado compatible con la unidad española*").
25 Quoted in Cruz Monclova, *Baldorioty*, 105. See also J. C. M. Oglesby, "The Cuban Autonomist Movement's Perception of Canada, 1865-1898: Its Implication," *The Americas* 48 (1992): 445-61.
26 Both rejected pure assimilation—that is, each advocated a measure of administrative and economic autonomy for the colonies. See Cruz Monclova, *Baldorioty*, 122-25.
27 Rafael María de Labra, *La autonomía colonial en España* (1892), xxxv, cited in Oglesby, "The Cuban Autonomist Movement's Perception of Canada," 456.

from the idea that Spain should grant her colonies a system identical to the Canadian one, and contrasted the version he preferred by describing it as an autonomy that was more faithful to his Spanish heritage. As Labra explained in a speech in 1885:

> [W]e do not think that the autonomic regime in Canada is the autonomic regime for our overseas provinces. We have a solution of Spanish vintage, reflecting national tradition, having a proper and clear form, a form outlined in the proposals of the Cuban Autonomist Party [and] sanctioned by the courts of justice . . . ; which means that the arguments in favor of or against [autonomy], based on what happens in Canada, cannot be accepted as a reason to oppose the reforms we propose for Puerto Rico.[28]

In Labra's calls for a solution "of Spanish vintage, reflecting national tradition," we see the precursor of the view that there should be correspondence between political status and ethnic identity: in other words, that there was something that could accurately be described as a specifically "Puerto Rican" form of autonomy and that it was this form of autonomy that Puerto Rico should have.

Before the Ponce Assembly, Baldorioty had made clear that, to him, it mattered more that the party achieve consensus on an autonomist platform than that it adopt all of the elements of his preferred version. The gathered delegates acted accordingly and produced a platform—the Program and Declarations of the Autonomist Party of Puerto Rico, or Ponce platform— that explicitly embraced Labra's version of autonomy, though it contained certain features of Baldorioty's version. The Ponce platform identified as the party's "fundamental principle" the autonomist slogan quoted above: "the maximum decentralization compatible with national unity."[29] Following Labra, it sought "identity" in the "political" sphere, accompanied by "purely internal or local administration."[30]

Despite Baldorioty's willingness to accept the party's consensus, the Ponce meeting produced a splinter group led by Luis Muñoz Rivera. A journalist, writer, poet, and founder of the leading autonomist newspaper, *La Democracia*, who would soon become the island's most popular politician, Muñoz, too, was a supporter of autonomy, but his emphasis was somewhat different: he believed that the overriding goal of autonomists should be to

---

28 D'Alzina Guillermety, *Evolución y desarrollo*, 130 (emphasis added).

29 See *Plan de Ponce para la Reorganización del Partido Liberal de la Provincia y Acta de la Asamblea Constituyente del Partido Autonomista Puertorriqueño* (San Juan: Instituto de Cultura Puertorriqueña, 1991), 74.

30 Ibid., arts. 2, 3, 5.

put an end to the preferences that gave peninsular-born Spaniards a virtual monopoly on governmental power on the island, and to secure power for native-born islanders (creoles, or *criollos*). To this end, universal suffrage was critical; beyond that, however, Muñoz was less interested in questions of substance, such as whether autonomy should involve political decentralization or political identity. The issue, he believed, was quite simply, power: once native islanders were finally in power—in whatever form of government existed—they could then turn their attention to fine questions of precisely what form of autonomy the island should have.

This view had implications for the party's strategy: specifically, Muñoz believed that it was a mistake for Puerto Ricans to form an autonomist political party at all. The reason, he argued, was that the only way for Puerto Rican autonomists actually to achieve anything was for them to have power in the island's government, and the only way for them to achieve power was to form an alliance with a political party in power in Spain. There were only two Spanish parties—the two leading monarchical parties—with any realistic prospect of holding power in the national government. Rather than form an autonomist political party, he argued, Puerto Rican autonomists should join one of Spain's monarchical parties.

The political reality underlying Muñoz's strategy was the *turno de partidos*, or *turno pacífico*, a system that had been in place in Spain since 1874, after the short-lived First Spanish Republic had been displaced and the monarchy restored under Alfonso XII. Designed by the leaders of Spain's two leading monarchical parties, Antonio Cánovas del Castillo of the Partido Liberal Conservador (Liberal Conservative Party) and Práxedes Mateo Sagasta of the Partido Liberal Fusionista (Liberal-Fusionist Party), the goal of the *turno* system was to put an end to the violent coups that had plagued Spain for decades, while keeping the anti-monarchical republican opposition out of power.

According to the *turno* system, one monarchical party would hold power until both parties agreed that it was time to dissolve the government and allow the other party a turn (an event that would be formally precipitated by a vote of no-confidence in the Cortes). At that point, the monarchy would select a new *jefe de gobierno*, or head of government, from the other party and issue a decree dissolving the Cortes, and elections would be held. Although universal suffrage had been formally established in Spain by this time, the elections were fixed and would reliably yield a victory for the party whose turn it was to govern.[31] "Under these circumstances," observes one Spanish

---

31 Luis Sánchez Agesta, *Historia del constitucionalismo español*, 2nd ed. (Madrid: Instituto de Estudios Políticos, 1964), 325-30.

constitutional historian, "the parliamentary system [was] clearly a fiction. But a fiction that worked passably for a quarter century, while Cánovas and Sagasta maintained the nearly unchallenged hegemony of two parties, which accepted the rules of the game as a [matter of] honor."[32]

Given the *turno*, Muñoz argued that the only way forward was for Puerto Rican autonomists to join one of Spain's monarchical parties. Thus, even as the autonomists organized themselves formally into a political party, Muñoz advocated the dissolution of the party and its absorption into one of the two monarchical parties. Of the two options, Muñoz favored Sagasta's Liberal-Fusionist Party, so called due to its practice of doing with other political groupings precisely what Muñoz advocated for the Autonomist Party: "fusing" with them and thereby absorbing them into his own party (for which reason Muñoz's proposed pact also came to be known as "fusion" and his followers as *fusionistas*).

From the perspective of his fellow Puerto Rican autonomists, the problem with Muñoz's strategy was that autonomists had a core, even constitutive, commitment to a republican form of government: to them, the relationship between autonomy and republicanism was substantive, not accidental, and to fuse with a monarchical party would be to abandon the core principles of autonomy. To be sure, they also wanted, as Muñoz did, to see an end to the exclusion of native-born Puerto Ricans from the island's government; but the form of government in which native-born Puerto Ricans would participate once their exclusion ended mattered more to them. Muñoz, in turn, was motivated by what he saw as the fatal flaw in his contemporaries' strategy. To him, Puerto Rican autonomists did not enjoy the luxury of a choice between one form of autonomy or another; they had a choice either to attain power by compromising republican principles or to never attain power at all. A pragmatist, he dismissed the niceties of autonomist theorizing about alternative forms of constitutional republicanism as a naïve failure to reckon with political realities.[33]

A Fleeting Autonomy

As the rift that had emerged at the Ponce Assembly between Muñoz's faction and the rest of the Autonomist Party grew worse, Spain's sovereignty over its remaining colonies grew increasingly tenuous. Cuba's struggle for independence from Spain regained momentum and, finally, in 1895, turned violent one last time. Meanwhile, Puerto Rican autonomists held fast to the

32 Sánchez Agesta, *Historia del constitucionalismo*, 328.
33 Lidio Cruz Monclova, *Luis Muñoz Rivera: Diez años de su vida política* (San Juan: Instituto de Cultura Puertorriqueña, 1959); D'Alzina Guillermety, *Evolución y desarrollo*, 123-26.

hope that reform remained possible. But while peace prevailed in Puerto Rico, the autonomists themselves continued to find consensus elusive. Muñoz remained critical of what seemed to him the counterproductively uncompromising republicanism of the Autonomist Party leaders. Although he still could not convince the party's leadership to embrace his "pragmatic" strategy, his idea had begun to gain traction.[34] Concerned by the possibility that Muñoz might be tempted to form a competing political party, in June 1896 the party's leadership decided to form a five-member commission, the Comisión Autonomista (Autonomist Commission), to make the case for autonomy to politicians in Madrid. They appointed members representing both sides of the disagreement: on the anti-fusionist side, Federico Degetau y González, a lawyer and writer who while living in Madrid had founded the newspaper *La Isla de Puerto Rico* to promote reformist ideas for the island, and José Gómez Brioso, a medical doctor who was then serving as president and political director of the Autonomist Party; and on the pro-fusionist side, Rosendo Matienzo Cintrón, a lawyer who had served as secretary of the Autonomist Party, and Muñoz.[35] The fifth member of the commission was Labra, their strongest ally in Spain, and like Degetau and Gómez Brioso, an opponent of Muñoz's fusionist strategy.

The members of the commission (except for Labra, who was already in Madrid) left Puerto Rico on September 16, 1896, bearing instructions to meet with the leaders of the "democratic peninsular parties" and to "create an alliance with the party that promises ... to develop our platform *in its entirety*," a reference to the platform the party had adopted at the Ponce Assembly.[36] Disagreement over how to interpret these instructions, particularly in light of the divide that already existed over Muñoz's strategy, would soon lead to a schism in the commission. What did the instructions mean by an "alliance"? Did that term include Muñoz's "pact" or "fusion"? It must not, since fusion would mean abandoning at least some aspects of the Ponce platform, not promoting it "in its entirety." And yet, how clear must the promise to promote the entire Ponce platform actually be? Would it be enough for a mainland political party to offer general assurances of a forthcoming autonomy? Or must it be more specific? Without more concrete guarantees, how would an assurance of autonomy amount to anything more than yet another unfulfilled promise of "special laws"? And if the political party willing to form an alliance

---

34 D'Alzina Guillermety, *Evolución y desarrollo*, 176.

35 René Torres Delgado, *Dos filántropos puertorriqueños: Santiago Veve Calzada y Federico Degetau y González* (San Juan: Obra de José Celso Barbosa y Alcalá, 1983); Carmen Muñiz de Barbosa and René Torres Delgado, *José Gómez Brioso: Nada menos que todo un hombre* (San Juan: Obra de José Celso Barbosa, 1982), 11-13.

36 Quoted in Pilar Barbosa de Rosario, *De Baldorioty a Barbosa: Historia del autonomismo puertorriqueño*, 2nd ed. (San Juan: Model Offset Printing, 1974), 324. I have translated *íntegro* as "in its entirety."

were not one of the two monarchical parties in the *turno*—either that of
Cánovas, who was serving as prime minister at that time, or Sagasta, whose
turn would come again—then how credibly could it promise to "develop" the
Ponce platform, as opposed to merely supporting it?

Even before they arrived in Spain, the commissioners harbored
suspicions about one another's intentions. The commissioners opposed to
Muñoz's strategy—Degetau, Labra, and, at first, Gómez Brioso—worried
about what Muñoz would do to pursue his strategy. Muñoz, in turn, worried
about what the others would *not* do because of their reluctance to abandon
their republican principles. "The river is in turmoil," wrote Gómez Brioso
when Muñoz insisted on separating from the group for several days to pay
a private visit to Sagasta.[37] For his part, Muñoz complained to Degetau of
"[o]ur inaction," which, "until now, has been absolute."[38] Degetau meanwhile
worried that Muñoz suffered from an "obsession" with the pact, and that
Matienzo was "blind" under Muñoz's influence.[39] Yet Muñoz and Matienzo
did not see the pursuit of a pact with one of the monarchist parties in the
turno as inconsistent with the party's instructions at all. Even if it were, to
them it was far better than accomplishing nothing.

Such was the state of things when the commissioners began their series
of meetings with the leaders of Spain's political parties. But if any of them
hoped that one or another strategy would emerge out of these meetings as the
obvious path to autonomy, he was in for a disappointment. If anything, their
meetings served as a reminder of the elusiveness of their goals. Even their
initial meeting with Labra himself, whom they had designated their "leader,"
disappointed them: Labra seemed far more interested in Cuba than in Puerto
Rico, and when he finally got around to mentioning the latter, he offered little
more than the observation that Puerto Rico's problems could be resolved as
soon as Cuba's were.[40] "This thing is perfectly sunk," wrote a dejected Gómez
Brioso to his colleagues back home after that meeting. Another politician

37 Pilar Barbosa de Rosario, ed., *Historia del pacto sagastino a través de un epistolario
    inédito: (El pacto produce el desconcierto, 1897-1898)* (Río Piedras: Editorial de la
    Universidad de Puerto Rico, 1981), 26.
38 Luis Muñoz Rivera, letter to Federico Degetau y González, Oct. 12, 1896,
    Colección Ángel Mergal Llera, Papeles Federico Degetau y González [hereinafter
    Degetau Papers], Centro de Estudios Históricos, Universidad de Puerto Rico, 1/
    VIII/9, 1/VII/31.
39 Barbosa de Rosario, *Historia del pacto sagastino*, 114.
40 Ibid., 13-14. On Labra's being chosen the leader of the group, see D'Alzina
    Guillermety's discussion of the commission in D'Alzina Guillermety, *Evolución y
    Desarrollo*, 178. For references to Labra as "el Leader," see, e.g., Federico Degetau
    y González, draft letter to Manuel Fernández Juncos, Dec. 16, 1897, Degetau
    Papers, 2/I/53.

they met with offered similar fare: a solution to Puerto Rico's problems must wait until the pacification of Cuba.[41] Still another, a member of one of the republican political parties, offered the useless advice that they should wait for the return of the republic; given that the First Spanish Republic had lasted only a single year nearly twenty-five years earlier, he must have known that Puerto Rico's autonomists were unlikely to pin their hopes on a second one.[42] Finally, another politician offered the equally unhelpful observation that if peninsular and colonial republicans had formed a single political party in the first place, they would already be in power.[43]

Francisco Pi y Margall made a more positive, and more lasting, impression. The leading Spanish federalist, head of the Partido Republicano Federal (Federal Republican Party), and an admirer of US federalism, Pi had long argued that Spain should adopt a system similar to that of the United States and that the Antillean colonies should be included in it as equal and autonomous Spanish provinces.[44] "A most excellent man," commented Gómez Brioso in a letter describing the meeting.[45] Recalling the meeting later, Muñoz agreed. Everything Pi said was "logic marching in a straight line toward absolute justice," he wrote; "it was the supreme disinterestedness of an apostle who aspired only to satisfy his conscience; it was the light of an extraordinary mind spilling over us and shining with the radiance of dawn."[46] Yet for all their admiration of Pi, the commissioners left that meeting empty-handed as well. The future belonged to America, Pi told them—and as far as Puerto Rico's future was concerned, he was not wrong. But his foresight, and his unimpeachable reasoning, did not translate into a plausible strategy for the autonomists. As Muñoz put it in the conclusion to his account of the meeting, "Puerto Rico needed not a doctrine, but a *fact*."[47]

That left the monarchist parties led by Cánovas and Sagasta. The commissioners met with each of them as well, but not even these meetings

---

41   Barbosa de Rosario, *Historia del pacto sagastino*, 22.

42   Ibid., 38. There would be a Second Republic, but not until 1931.

43   Ibid., 40.

44   See Sylvia Hilton, "Los Estados Unidos como modelo: Los federalistas españoles y el mito americano durante la crisis colonial de 1895-1898," *Ibero-Americana Pragensia* 32 (1998): 11-29. See also Sylvia Hilton, "U.S. Intervention and Monroeism: Spanish Perspectives on the American Role in the Colonial Crisis of 1895-98," in *Whose America: The War of 1898 and the Battles to Define the Nation*, ed. Virginia Bouvier (Westport, CT: Praeger 2001).

45   Barbosa de Rosario, *Historia del pacto sagastino*, 39.

46   Luis Muñoz Rivera, "Apuntes para un libro (1896-1900)," in *Obras completas de Luis Muñoz Rivera*, vol. 3, ed. Luis Muñoz Marín (Madrid: Editorial Puerto Rico, 1925), 27.

47   Ibid.

offered anything concrete enough to command the commissioners' unanimous enthusiasm. Cánovas responded with an emphatic affirmative when the commissioners asked whether a recent law providing for a series of reforms would actually be implemented in Puerto Rico. But when a skeptical Gómez Brioso pushed for specifics by asking about a particular reform of the electoral laws, he could not get a concrete answer out of Cánovas. Instead, as Gómez Brioso recalled with bemusement, Cánovas "scratched his head, made various funny faces and looked at me cross-eyed."[48] Sagasta, on whom Muñoz had pinned his hopes, made promises as well, but they fell far short of a commitment to implement the Ponce platform "in its entirety," as the instructions required. A tussle in that meeting over the precise terms of the offer to form a "pact" ended with Sagasta prevailing over the commissioners by watering down their proposed language, including the very phrase declaring his party's commitment to implement the Ponce platform. Sagasta also insisted that in order to form an alliance with his Liberal-Fusionist Party, the Autonomist Party would have to give up its name. In other words, he confirmed what they already knew (and what those opposed to the pact had feared): fusion meant the dissolution of the Autonomist Party and its absorption into Sagasta's party.[49]

Back in Puerto Rico, autonomists had been growing increasingly impatient. Manuel F. Rossy wrote to Degetau:

> The country is willing to reach a settlement—without giving up its principles—with Sagasta, *if that is what the leadership [of the Autonomist Party], in whom the country has placed its hopes and trust, recommends.* Such a settlement is accepted without enthusiasm and only due to a desire to get out of the current situation, which inspires despair because it is unsustainable, and also because of two red currents flowing from the mountain to the valley: one, the Cuban solution in favor of insurrection, and the other, the possibility of annexation to the United States.[50]

Yet in the same letter, Rossy wondered whether it would make sense instead for the party to split into monarchical and republican factions.[51] Either way, the party leadership remained silent pending the commission's recommendation:

---

48   Barbosa de Rosario, *Historia del pacto sagastino*, 35.
49   For drafts with and without the reference to the 1887 Ponce program, see "Voto Final," Degetau Papers, [7]/V/2. (This document is in box 7, which would appear to be its appropriate placement, but it is misnumbered "Caja 2.") On Sagasta's requirement that the Autonomist Party give up its name, see "Conferencia con Sagasta," Degetau Papers, 7/V/4.
50   Manuel F. Rossy, letter to Federico Degetau y González, Jan. 14, 1897, Degetau Papers, 1/VIII/9. On the fear of imminent insurrection, see also Guillermo León, letter to Federico Degetau y González, Feb. 28, 1897, Degetau Papers, 1/VIII/30.
51   Rossy, letter to Federico Degetau y González, 7.

we must wait, explained Rossy, because "we lack the national facts, just as you [commissioners] lack the regional facts . . . since you left here."[52]

In the end, it was left to Gómez Brioso to break the impasse. Although he had been an opponent of Muñoz's strategy, the commissioners' failure to identify any party other than Sagasta's that might form an alliance with them had left Gómez Brioso increasingly undecided. Despondent at the thought that the party's fate was in his hands, Gómez Brioso expressed his own conundrum in emotional language (as Degetau recalled it):

> It is necessary to resolve this pact thing once and for all. I can't fight with Muñoz any longer. I just want to free the party from this burden. . . . I'm going crazy. My friends have abandoned me. The directors [of the Autonomist Party] don't write. You too have abandoned me. I'll vote for incorporation, I'll vote for anything. . . . And afterwards I'll go throw myself off a bridge.[53]

In a sense, he followed through. When the Autonomist Commission finally decided to vote on Muñoz's proposal that the Puerto Rico Autonomist Party form a pact with a monarchical party, Gómez Brioso switched sides, voting with Muñoz and Matienzo in favor, while Degetau and Labra were left in the minority, voting against the pact. When the commissioners returned to Puerto Rico, and the Autonomist Party held a meeting to vote on the commission's recommendation, Gómez Brioso defended the pact. And when the party membership voted overwhelmingly in favor of it (by a vote of seventy-nine to fifteen)—in the process dissolving the Autonomist Party and fusing it into Sagasta's Liberal-Fusionist Party—Gómez Brioso temporarily retired from active politics.[54]

But he was not the only one to exit. Faced with defeat, a group led by José Celso Barbosa left the meeting as well, with Barbosa famously declaring, "Goodbye, brothers, I'm leaving, but I'm taking the flag of autonomy with me."[55] Declaring themselves defenders of the Ponce platform, Barbosa's group proceeded to form the Partido Autonomista Ortodoxo (Orthodox Autonomist Party) and to describe themselves as the *ortodoxos* or *puros*. *Puros* means "pure": they saw themselves as the standard-bearers of the

---

52   Ibid., 5.

53   Barbosa de Rosario, *Historia del pacto sagastino*, 114 (Degetau quoting Gómez Brioso).

54   Ibid., 188. Barbosa states that Gómez Brioso retired, but he would soon return to an active political life. Bolívar Pagán gives the vote as 79-17, but other sources give it as 79-15. See Bolívar Pagán, *Historia de los partidos políticos puertorriqueños (1898-1956)*, vol. 1 (Barcelona: Bolívar Pagán, 1972), 14; Barbosa de Rosario, *Historia del pacto sagastino*; Rosendo Matienzo Cintrón, letter to Federico Degetau y González, Mar. 12, 1897, Degetau Papers, 1/IX/5.

55   Pagán, *Historia de los partidos*, 15.

"pure" (read republican) version of autonomy.[56] Those who remained with what was now a provincial arm of Sagasta's Liberal-Fusionist Party came to be known as *fusionistas*. The *fusionistas* accused Barbosa and his supporters of being unwilling to accept the will of the majority and political reality. But the *puros* insisted that by entering into an alliance with a monarchist party, the *fusionistas* had betrayed core republican principles and therefore ceased to be autonomists.

The *puros* focused their criticisms on the rationale for fusion: securing power specifically for natives of the island. True republicanism, argued the *puros*, abhors *any* geographic preferences in the distribution of power—including those favoring native-born Puerto Ricans. Hadn't Puerto Rico's autonomists been fighting for decades against geographic preferences in favor of peninsular-born Spaniards and their conservative political party on the island, the Partido Incondicional Español (Unconditional Spanish Party)? As an article in the *puro* newspaper *El País* described, the goal of autonomy was supposed to be to ensure "that the colony govern itself by way of men of confidence, it matters little that they be *incondicionales*; if they accept responsibility for their actions, and the penal sanction of the laws reaches them, let them govern."[57] In other words, autonomists should not be striving for a monopoly on power for native-born Puerto Ricans; they should be striving for a republican form of government, under which no one would be excluded from power based on place of birth and where those who did end up in power would be subject to the rule of law.

The *puros* were motivated not only by their understanding of autonomist principles but also by their concerns over Muñoz's personal ambitions. Brokering a pact with Sagasta would certainly increase Muñoz's own power. But if it involved dissolution of the party, what else would it accomplish? "Muñoz insists that the essential thing is *power*," observed Degetau in his diary; "for these reasons, [other] laws and reforms are not important to him."[58] Elsewhere, he wrote, "All [Muñoz] can see is the rise to power."[59] Degetau worried that Muñoz's vision for Puerto Rico did not extend beyond Muñoz's own rise to political prominence. Privately, he wrote:

> Muñoz says that he is willing to ask for and accept autonomy from whomever will give it to him. Muñoz uses the term autonomy in a special sense, for he then adds, in response to an observation of mine,

---

56   D'Alzina Guillermety, *Evolución y desarrollo*, 187; Pagán, *Historia de los partidos*, vol. 1, 15.

57   *El País*, Aug. 26, 1897. Another article argued that the rights of the citizen should not be affected "by the coincidence of the region in which one has been born." *El País*, Aug. 28, 1897.

58   Degetau's diary, Degetau Papers, 7/V/unnumbered, 56.

59   Ibid., 61.

that what matters is power: in return for this he accepts anything, and elaborating on this view it turns out that he accepts Carlism here and a military dictatorship there, all in "exchange for" a general who will obey his orders. . . . In a word, an absolute lack of orientation and therefore of political sense. I do not think he himself knows what he wants, in terms of ideas and for the country. . . . Muñoz is buried in the idea of making a pact. He wastes his time combating my republicanism.[60]

Acknowledging that Muñoz defended his strategy as the most effective way to promote the island's welfare, Degetau wondered, "But in what does [the island's] welfare consist? In Muñoz's replacing [the leader of the Partido Incondicional] Don Pablo Ubarri?"[61]

The rift between *puros* and *fusionistas* did not heal, but what occurred soon after the creation of the pact reduced their disagreements to largely inconsequential bickering. After decades in which the tireless efforts of Puerto Rico's autonomists had yielded little more than short-lived variations on the status quo and unfulfilled promises of "special laws" in successive Spanish constitutions, events suddenly unfolded at a dizzying pace. On August 8, 1897, an Italian anarchist's bullet killed Prime Minister Cánovas. On October 2, Sagasta took power, consistent with the *turno*. Days later—and faced with the reality of Spain's increasingly tenuous grip on Cuba as the fighting there wore on—Sagasta announced that he would finally grant autonomy to the Antillean colonies. Less than two months later, he fulfilled his promise with a "charter of autonomy" for each one of these colonies: one for Cuba and one for Puerto Rico.[62]

During the brief interim between Sagasta's announcement and the arrival of the charters in Puerto Rico, before anyone knew precisely what the autonomy that had been granted looked like in its particulars, the debate between *fusionistas* and *puros* raged on. But now that autonomy was about to become a reality, the *puros* reconsidered their support for the Ponce platform— the more moderate alternative that had won the day at the Ponce Assembly— deciding instead to embrace the more robust Canadian-style autonomy that Baldorioty had originally espoused. Defending their change in position, they explained that it was due to the change in circumstances: as an article in *El País* put it, with autonomy now actually poised to become government policy, the modest Ponce platform had been rendered "deficient."[63] Now, "everything's different," and they should demand more.[64]

Ironically, it was at this moment that Muñoz finally decided to throw his

60 Ibid., 47-49.
61 Ibid., 50.
62 Carta Autonómica de 1897 [Charter of Autonomy of 1897] (Spain).
63 *El País*, Oct. 19, 1897.
64 Ibid.

support behind one of the two versions of autonomy that had competed at the Ponce Assembly: he chose the Ponce platform embodying Labra's proposals, even as the *puros* were abandoning it in favor of Baldorioty's Canadian-style proposal. Muñoz now distinguished the *fusionistas* from the *puros* by associating the former with support for the Ponce platform, and he defended the Ponce platform itself with an argument reminiscent of Labra's advocacy of autonomy "of Spanish vintage, reflecting national tradition." As Muñoz explained, were they to be offered a choice between the "creed of Ponce or the regime of Canada," the *fusionistas* would choose the former, because it was *lo nuestro*—that is, "what is ours." He declared, "[W]e are Spaniards, not Englishmen."[65]

The *puros* responded by yet again challenging the idea that any given form of autonomy, in substance, should be considered more or less authentically "Spanish": "Canada's autonomic regime is not British, nor will the regime established in the Antilles be Spanish, because autonomy is a system derived from science, without racial lineage," argued an article in *El País*.[66] Another article took issue with Muñoz for his view that "*we are not Canadian autonomists, but Puerto Rican autonomists*." As the article observed:

> [T]his makes no sense: we are Spanish Autonomists; and because being Spanish is inherent in us, any kind of autonomy that is conceded to us cannot alter that condition; if they grant us a regime identical to that of Canada's, . . . will we suffer some detriment of our essential natural quality, that of being Spaniards?[67]

Neither side convinced the other.

When the charters of autonomy finally arrived in Spain's Antillean colonies, they exceeded everyone's expectations, granting both Puerto Rico and Cuba a robust form of autonomy, with a local legislature and representation in the Cortes. Upon realizing that the charter gave them more than they had asked for, Muñoz revised his earlier comments about Puerto Rico's need for "Spanish" autonomy, claiming in a speech on the new charter that he had made the argument against Canadian-style autonomy merely in order to deflect the *incondicionales'* accusations of disloyalty. The *puros*, in turn, claimed that the charter granted a form of autonomy along the lines of what they had advocated all along.[68]

---

65 Quoted in *El País*, Oct. 20, 1897.
66 *El País*, Oct. 29, 1897.
67 *El País*, Nov. 3, 1897.
68 See Astrid Cubano Iguina, "Los debates del autonomismo y la Carta Autonómica en Puerto Rico a fines del siglo XIX," in *Centenario de la Carta Autonómica de Puerto Rico (1897-1997)*, ed. Juan E. Hernández Cruz (San Germán: Universidad Interamericana, 1998); Luis Muñoz Rivera, "Discurso pronunciado en Ponce al

Yet even as the two autonomist factions scrambled to take credit for the charter, events were about to overtake them once more. On February 9, 1898, a provisional autonomist cabinet consisting of a fragile alliance of autonomist leaders from both the *fusionista* and the *puro* factions took office.[69] Elections for the *cámara insular* (the local legislature) were held, and its opening session was scheduled for April 25, 1898. And then, on April 25, the United States intervened in Cuba's fight for independence by declaring war on Spain. The opening session of the *cámara* was rescheduled for July 17, 1898, and took place on that date. One week later, US forces invaded Puerto Rico, and Puerto Rico's fledgling autonomist government ceased to be.

Imperial Constitutionalism and US Sovereignty

Thus it was that Puerto Rico's autonomists found themselves confronting the question whether Puerto Rico should become a state of the Union. And the answer came easily. Within a year, each faction had formed a new political party—Barbosa became the head of the Partido Republicano and Muñoz the head of the Partido Federal—and both parties had adopted platforms embracing the island's annexation by the United States. The Republican Party "accept[ed] Puerto Rico's territorial annexation into the States of the Federal Union with enthusiasm"; the Federal Party "accept[ed] and applaud[ed] the fact of annexation, consummated following the war, considering that Puerto Rico will be a prosperous and happy country in the shadow of the American flag and under the shelter of federal institutions."[70] Both platforms explicitly called for Puerto Rico's accession to the status of a territory of the United States, followed by its admission into statehood in the Union on an equal footing with the other states.[71]

All of this brings us back to the question posed at the opening of this chapter: what accounts for this immediate and unqualified switch in allegiance? At one moment, the autonomists were proclaiming their loyalty to the mother country; at the next, they were heartily greeting their foreign conqueror. Today, it gives us pause. But the challenge is to understand it rather than to dismiss it as the rash act of a colonial elite that lost its mind or its pride. What at first glance looks like a startling willingness to cast aside an entire heritage

---

decretar Sagasta la autonomía para Puerto Rico el 28 de noviembre de 1897," in *Obras completas de Luis Muñoz Rivera*, vol. 1, ed. Luis Muñoz Marín (Madrid: Editorial Puerto Rico, 1925), 231.

69 Burgos Malavé, *Génesis y praxis*, 172-74.

70 Pagán, *Historia de los partidos*, 35 (Republican Party platform, art. 2), 49 (Federal Party platform, art. 2).

71 Ibid., 35-36 (Republican Party platform, art. 4), 50 (Federal Party platform, arts. 4, 5).

essentially overnight, replacing it with an alien form of government, looks very different when considered in light of the nineteenth-century history of Puerto Rican efforts to achieve autonomy—and, in particular, the state of the debate concerning the relationship between autonomy and ethnicity as it stood when the United States invaded.

As we have seen, in the period immediately preceding the island's annexation by the United States, the argument for a specifically "Spanish" or "Puerto Rican" autonomy had finally given way, as the reality sank in that Puerto Rico had been granted an autonomy more "radical" than even Baldorioty's Canadian-style proposals. Muñoz, who had argued that Puerto Ricans should have an autonomy for "Spaniards, not Englishmen"—embodying *lo nuestro*—had quickly distanced himself from that view once he learned what was actually in the charter and how much it resembled the autonomy that "Englishmen" enjoyed. On the eve of annexation, in short, it was the *puro* view of the relationship between autonomy and ethnicity that held sway: as they had argued, "because being Spanish is inherent in us, any kind of autonomy that is conceded to us cannot alter that condition." The idea that a "foreign" form of autonomy could not deprive Puerto Ricans of their ethnic identity not only was fresh in the minds of the autonomists but had been recently and vocally embraced by all of them when they found themselves subject to US sovereignty.

Annexation gave Puerto Rican autonomists cause for celebration not because they had inexplicably jettisoned their constitutional vision in order to substitute it with an imported novelty but because it meant that statehood in the Union was on the horizon (or so they expected) and, therefore, that Puerto Rico's prospects for the implementation of a regime of genuine, robust, and lasting autonomy were better than ever. Far from a departure from their ethnic heritage, statehood was perfectly consistent with it: the autonomists' embrace of statehood was firmly rooted in autonomist principles. In language reminiscent of the autonomists' longstanding call for "the maximum decentralization compatible with national unity," the Federal Party platform declared its goal as the "intelligent and honest administration of local interests" combined with an "absolute identity with the United States."[72] Explicitly associating autonomy with US federalism, the Republican Party confirmed its adherence to "the principles of the [US] Federal Constitution *and the regime of local autonomy derived from it*."[73]

American federalism, recall, had been the system that Spanish federalist Pi y Margall had defended as the best form of autonomy—for Spaniards, too. When the Autonomist Commission met with Pi on its trip to Madrid in 1896, the commissioners had found Pi's arguments compelling. Even Muñoz had

---

72   Ibid., 49-50 (Federal Party platform, art. 3).
73   Ibid., 36 (Republican Party platform, art. 5) (emphasis added).

described them, as we saw above, as "logic marching in a straight line toward absolute justice." The fatal flaw in Pi's arguments, according to Muñoz, had not been his ideas; the flaw had been that "Puerto Rico needed not a doctrine, but a *fact*." Now that Puerto Rico had been annexed by the United States, it appeared the doctrine was about to become a fact.[74]

Until it didn't. In 1900, Congress enacted legislation creating a government for Puerto Rico,[75] which departed from the United States' traditional practices with respect to newly annexed territory in a number of ways and subjected Puerto Rico to a status subordinate even to that of previous territories: most significantly, Congress had declined to extend the US Constitution by statute to Puerto Rico, as it had done in all prior territories, and instead of granting US citizenship to the island's inhabitants, it declared native-born Puerto Ricans "citizens of Porto Rico," a nebulous and undefined status that seemed to amount to little more than an embellished form of statelessness. On top of all that, the act dispensed with the free trade that had been the norm between US territories and states, imposing duties on certain goods traded between Puerto Rico and the rest of the United States. Challenged in court, these duties became the basis for the litigation that produced the Insular Cases of 1901. The Supreme Court upheld the duties, reasoning that Puerto Rico had not been "incorporated" into the United States and that it was "foreign to the United States in a domestic sense." Signaling that only incorporated territories were on a path to statehood, whereas the fate of unincorporated territories remained uncertain, the court dealt a fatal blow to the autonomists' consensus in support of Puerto Rico's admission into statehood.

To the autonomists—who had patiently advocated autonomy for decades while Spain repeatedly enacted and repealed unfulfilled promises of reform, had tasted the fruit of victory in the form of the 1897 Charter of Autonomy just before the US invasion replaced it with a military occupation, and had seen the prospect of statehood in the Union dangled before them only to be abruptly snatched away—these developments were devastating. The rejection of Puerto Rican statehood by the United States led to the demise of Puerto Rico's autonomist constitutionalism as it stood at the end of the nineteenth century. The autonomists had come to embrace the idea that whatever form of autonomy the island achieved need not threaten its people's ethnic heritage. It was a hard-won consensus, and it informed the conviction with which

---

74   As noted in the introduction and discussed below, the autonomists were in for a serious disappointment. Pi beat them to it: upon witnessing the United States' imperialistic approach to the war of 1898 and the annexation of Spain's former colonies, Pi soured on the United States and became a critic of what he saw as its betrayal of its own principles. See Hilton, "U.S. Intervention and Monroeism."

75   Organic Act of 1900 (Foraker Act), ch. 191, 31 Stat. 77 (1900) (codified as amended in scattered sections of 48 U.S.C. (2013)).

Puerto Rican autonomists met the United States: that American federalism could accommodate ethnic diversity to encompass a state of Puerto Rico—a diversity far broader than it turned out Americans were actually willing to accept.

The effect was to strip the autonomists not only of their hopes but also of their ideas. Faced with rejection, the autonomists abandoned their constitutional vision, as each faction retreated into its own version of a more narrowly nationalistic stance on autonomy. Barbosa and his followers would continue to pursue statehood, but in a more assimilationist vein: they became the party of Americanization. Muñoz retreated, returning yet again to the view that what Puerto Rico needed was not a foreign imposition but *lo nuestro*—an authentically Puerto Rican status. These hardened nationalistic views displaced the more robustly pluralist constitutionalism that had prevailed among Puerto Rico's autonomists at the end of the nineteenth century, when they had embraced the idea that Puerto Rico could become a state of the Union without ceasing to be Puerto Rican. The autonomists, who easily embraced the idea of Puerto Rican statehood, had been "postnational" before their time. But the United States wasn't ready. Apparently, it still isn't.

CHAPTER TWO

The Insular Cases

What Is There to Reconsider?

Efrén Rivera Ramos

I would like to congratulate and thank the Legal History and Human Rights Programs of Harvard Law School for hosting the conference that led to the publication of this volume. As we all know, the *Harvard Law Review* played a prominent part in the discussion generated by the US acquisition of foreign territory at the end of the nineteenth century.[1] The arguments posed in those seminal articles not only found their way into the multiple opinions of Supreme Court justices in the so-called Insular Cases. They also began to contribute to the gloss that would eventually be cast onto those complex legal texts. It is fitting, then, for Harvard Law School to engage in the reconsideration of the issues involved in those cases as we enter another century still grappling with the conundrums generated by territorial governance.

---

1 See, e.g., Carman F. Randolph, "Constitutional Aspects of Annexation," *Harvard Law Review* 12 (1898): 291-315; Simeon E. Baldwin, "The Constitutional Questions Incident to the Acquisition and Government by the United States of Island Territory," *Harvard Law Review* 12 (1899): 393-416; C. C. Langdell, "The Status of Our New Territories," *Harvard Law Review* 12 (1899): 365-92; James Bradley Thayer, "Our New Possessions," *Harvard Law Review* 12 (1899): 464-85; Abbott Lawrence Lowell, "The Status of Our New Possessions: A Third View," *Harvard Law Review* 13 (1899): 155-76.

Most critiques of the Insular Cases[2] lead to the conclusion that those early twentieth-century decisions should be abandoned either because they perpetrated a great injustice against the peoples of the territories at the time of their adoption or because they no longer hold water in light of current political values. As we embark on the project of "reconsidering the Insular Cases," it is worthwhile to pose several basic questions regarding this notion. For example: What is there to reconsider? And for what purpose?

At least two possibilities come to mind.

One possibility is to mine the cases to try to generate a new understanding of what the different majorities in the Insular Cases meant or intended to mean with their decisions. Of course, doctrinal clarification is always useful. But there are several challenges involved. As all canonical texts—in fact, as all durable and effective canonical texts—the opinions in the Insular Cases are full of ambiguities, contradictions, and paradoxes. Different interpreters (myself included) could find—and have found—eloquent citations in those opinions to sustain the most diverse interpretations of what the justices decided. Those divergent citations can be found in the majority, concurrent, and dissenting opinions; in the different opinions of the same justice or group of justices; and even within single opinions themselves. There is also the question whether we want to discern what the justices intended to do or what they actually did. Moreover, the question always arises as to whose voices we wish to interrogate and with what weight.

Another possibility is to evaluate the cases and their aftermath from the perspective of twenty-first-century values and political and jurisprudential understandings. Here the following questions arise: If, as expected, we find

---

2   Although there is some discussion as to which cases should be included within the general category of the Insular Cases, for the sake of this chapter, I consider that the label should be applied to at least the following twenty-three decisions of the US Supreme Court: *De Lima v. Bidwell*, 182 U.S. 1 (1901); *Goetze v. United States*, 182 U.S. 221 (1901); *Grossman v. United States*, 182 U.S. 221 (1901); *Dooley v. United States*, 182 U.S. 222 (1901); *Armstrong v. United States*, 182 U.S. 243 (1901); *Downes v. Bidwell*, 182 U.S. 244 (1901); *Huus v. N.Y. & Porto Rico S.S. Co.*, 182 U.S. 392 (1901); *Dooley v. United States (Dooley II)*, 183 U.S. 151 (1901); *Fourteen Diamond Rings v. United States*, 183 U.S. 176 (1901); *Hawaii v. Mankichi*, 190 U.S. 197 (1903); *Gonzáles v. Williams*, 192 U.S. 1 (1904); *Kepner v. United States*, 195 U.S. 100 (1904); *Dorr v. United States*, 195 U.S. 138 (1904); *Mendozana v. United States*, 195 U.S. 158 (1904); *Rassmussen v. United States*, 197 U.S. 516 (1905); *Trono v. United States*, 199 U.S. 521 (1905); *Grafton v. United States*, 206 U.S. 333 (1907); *Kent v. Porto Rico*, 207 U.S. 113 (1907); *New York ex rel. Kopel v. Bingham*, 211 U.S. 468 (1909); *Dowdell v. United States*, 221 U.S. 325 (1911); *Ochoa v. Hernández*, 230 U.S. 139 (1913); *Ocampo v. United States*, 234 U.S. 91 (1914); and *Balzac v. Porto Rico*, 258 U.S. 298 (1922).

that the cases are not compatible with current political values, what should the normative conclusion be? Should the cases be simply discarded? *Can* they be simply discarded, given the constitutional text and the history that accompanies their interpretative gloss? What do we mean when we say that the Insular Cases should be repealed?

In the first part of this chapter, I will limit myself to raising several additional queries that flow from those basic questions, without pretending to give answers. In the second part, I will briefly address other considerations.

For the sake of argument, let us say that the Insular Cases and their further judicial elaborations stand for, at least, the following thirteen propositions:

1. The United States has an inherent sovereign right to acquire foreign territory.[3]

2. As a corollary to that right, the US government has the power to govern the territory so acquired.[4]

3. The territory clause of the US Constitution grants Congress plenary power to govern US territories.[5]

4. There is a distinction to be made between something called incorporated territory and something else called unincorporated territory.[6]

5. Incorporated territory is to be considered an integral part of the United States, while unincorporated territory is only appurtenant to, but not a part of, the United States.[7]

6. Not all provisions of the US Constitution apply in the territories. Further, there may be some provisions (for example, the right to a jury trial) that apply in incorporated territories but not in unincorporated territories.[8] Determining which constitutional provisions apply in the territories is up to the US Supreme Court.[9]

---

3   Downes v. Bidwell, 182 U.S. 244 (1901).
4   Ibid.; De Lima v. Bidwell, 182 U.S. 1 (1901); Dorr v. United States, 195 U.S. 138 (1904).
5   De Lima v. Bidwell, 182 U.S. 1 (1901); Downes v. Bidwell, 182 U.S. 244 (1901).
6   Downes v. Bidwell, 182 U.S. 244 (1901) (White, J., concurring); Dorr v. United States, 195 U.S. 138 (1904).
7   Downes v. Bidwell, 182 U.S. 244 (1901) (White, J., concurring); Dorr v. United States, 195 U.S. 138 (1904).
8   Hawaii v. Mankichi, 190 U.S. 197 (1903); Dorr v. United States, 195 U.S. 138 (1904); Balzac v. Porto Rico, 258 U.S. 298 (1922).
9   Downes v. Bidwell, 182 U.S. 244 (1901); Hawaii v. Mankichi, 190 U.S. 197 (1903); Dorr v. United States, 195 U.S. 138 (1904); Balzac v. Porto Rico, 258 U.S. 298 (1922).

7. Congress may decide, in accordance with its plenary powers, to extend all federal laws to the territories under US jurisdiction. It may also decide that some laws will apply and others will not.[10]

8. Political rights of full participation in the governance of the United States, including representation in the US Congress and the election of federal officials, have been granted only to residents of the states, not to residents of the territories.

9. Regarding unincorporated territory (for argument's sake, I will not include incorporated territory here), Congress can dispose of the territory as it sees fit. This includes providing for diverse forms of self-government (without relinquishing Congress's ultimate authority under the territory clause), incorporating the territory into the US political community, admitting it as a state, or getting rid of the territory by granting it independence or ceding it to another country. Congress has the power to do all those things. However, under the Constitution, it is not obligated to do any of them.

10. The decision to incorporate an unincorporated territory belongs exclusively to Congress.[11]

11. The mere extension of US citizenship to a territory's residents does not have the effect of incorporating that territory.[12]

12. Puerto Rico is to be considered an unincorporated territory of the United States.[13]

13. Arguably for different reasons, the uniformity clause, the export clause, and the right to a trial by jury in local courts do not apply in Puerto Rico. Other clauses of the Constitution may not apply, but that is up to the US Supreme Court to decide.[14]

---

10 See, e.g., Califano v. Torres, 435 U.S. 1 (1978) (Congress can constitutionally exclude Puerto Rico from the applicability of the Supplemental Security Income program, which provides aid to qualified aged, blind, and disabled persons in the United States); Harris v. Rosario, 446 U.S. 651 (1980) (Congress can determine that Puerto Rico will receive less financial assistance than the states to provide aid to families with needy dependent children).
11 Balzac v. Porto Rico, 258 U.S. 298 (1922).
12 Ibid.
13 Ibid.
14 Downes v. Bidwell, 182 U.S. 244 (1901); Dooley v. United States (Dooley II), 183 U.S. 151 (1901); Balzac v. Porto Rico, 258 U.S. 298 (1922).

Here are, then, thirteen propositions that the Insular Cases can reasonably be said to stand for. There may be more, at different levels of generality.

Which of these thirteen propositions would have to be repealed for the Constitution to be brought in line with current political values and aspirations? Which of them need to be abolished in order to surmount the acute criticism to which the cases have been subjected over the course of more than a century? Which of them are susceptible to abrogation, given the text of the Constitution and its interpretative history? Which of them can be cast aside without causing a substantial change in the US political system as we know it? And which of them would the US Supreme Court actually be willing to supersede?

Space does not allow me to examine each of the thirteen propositions under the lens of those inquiries. Suffice it to say that they entail different levels of complexity. Predictably, the probabilities of their repeal or modification by the US Supreme Court will also differ. For example, is it conceivable that the court will decide that the United States does not have an inherent sovereign right to acquire foreign territory? Or that it lacks the power to govern territory so acquired? Will the court be willing to affirm that the power Congress enjoys over the territories under the territory clause of the US Constitution[15] is less than plenary? Will it have the judicial appetite to declare that Congress cannot dispose of a given territory's political condition as it sees fit, including providing for diverse forms of self-government, incorporating the territory into the US political community, admitting it as a state, or getting rid of the territory by granting it independence or ceding it to another country?

Moreover, the implications of the repeal of each of the thirteen propositions listed above are not commensurate. For instance, it would be one thing for the Supreme Court to decide that jury trials should be available in local courts in the unincorporated territory of Puerto Rico, thus repealing one aspect of *Balzac v. Porto Rico*;[16] but it would be quite another to conclude that Puerto Rico must be regarded as incorporated territory, thus departing from one aspect of *Downes v. Bidwell*[17] and one aspect of the rationale in *Balzac*.[18] Deciding that the right to a jury trial in criminal cases should extend to Puerto Rico as a matter of US constitutional law—for such a guarantee is fundamental to the American scheme of justice[19]—would not require altering Puerto Rico's status as unincorporated territory, just as deciding that the First Amendment extends to Puerto Rico did not in any way modify Puerto

---

15 U.S. CONST., art. IV, § 3, cl. 2 ("The Congress shall have Power to dispose of and make all needful Rules and Regulations respecting the Territory or other Property belonging to the United States.").

16 Balzac v. Porto Rico, 258 U.S. 298 (1922).

17 Downes v. Bidwell, 182 U.S. 244 (1901).

18 Balzac v. Porto Rico, 258 U.S. 298 (1922).

19 See, e.g., Duncan v. Louisiana, 391 U.S. 145 (1968).

Rico's political status.[20] On the other hand, deciding that Puerto Rico has become incorporated territory would have larger constitutional and political implications. But even if the court were to arrive at both conclusions, these would still remain within the discursive framework produced by the Insular Cases, leaving intact some of the other basic propositions those cases stand for.

A more substantial departure would be to abolish altogether the distinction between incorporated and unincorporated territory, introduced in Justice Edward White's concurring opinion in *Downes*[21] and accepted by a majority of the court in *Dorr v. United States*.[22] A still more radical stance would be for the court to proclaim that the territory clause should not apply at all to the territories acquired in 1898 and thereafter, returning to the kind of argument adopted by the majority in *Dred Scott v. Sanford*.[23] In such an eventuality, the Supreme Court would have to ground the US government's power to govern the existing territories on other provisions of the Constitution. Possible candidates would be the nation's inherent sovereign powers, presidential and congressional war powers, and powers relating to foreign affairs. But this could hardly be regarded a significant gain from the perspective of the territories, given the extensive scope of those powers as they have been interpreted by the US Supreme Court and as they have been historically asserted by Congress and the executive branch.

Even those results would not have the same implications as those emanating from a determination by the court that the residents of the present territories should have full participatory rights in federal decision making, or from a ruling that the US Congress may not keep the residents of unincorporated territory in a permanent condition of political subordination and is therefore obligated to provide for a democratic resolution of the territory's political status—which means either admitting the territory as a state or granting it its independence. These are propositions with hugely different consequences than those attached to some of the others mentioned above.

At this stage of the game, then, what should be the level, depth, and scope of the claim that the Insular Cases should be abandoned? And what are the possibilities of that claim in the case of each one of the thirteen propositions mentioned and their attendant consequences? I am content with leaving these questions on the table.

---

20 See, e.g., Posadas de P.R. Associates v. Tourism Co. of P.R., 478 U.S. 328 (1986).

21 Downes v. Bidwell, 182 U.S. 244 (1901) (White, J., concurring).

22 Dorr v. United States, 195 U.S. 138 (1904).

23 Dred Scott v. Sandford, 60 U.S. 393 (1856) (the territory clause of the US Constitution was originally meant to apply only to the Northwest Territory and not to territory subsequently acquired by the United States).

Moving Forward

In this section, I will briefly discuss what I consider the long-term sociohistorical and political effects of the Insular Cases and their sequel. I will then conclude with a comment on the possibilities for addressing the main concerns of the people of the current territories, who have endured more than one hundred years under the shadow of those decisions. I am assuming that in the case of Puerto Rico, the central question is what can be done to do away with Puerto Rico's colonial relationship with the United States. In the other territorial possessions, there may be other ways of formulating their principal claims.

Let me begin by stating that I agree with my colleague Christina Duffy Ponsa that the Insular Cases did not have the effect of creating an extra-constitutional zone in the unincorporated territories.[24] On the contrary, the decisions were intended to provide a constitutional basis for US rule over those lands. They legitimized, via constitutional argument, the possibility of an indefinite condition of political subordination. In that sense, the Insular Cases put the US Constitution at the service of colonialism.

I have argued before, and still believe, that one of the main results of the positions that prevailed in the Insular Cases was to give Congress very wide latitude in dealing with the new possessions.[25] The need for that flexibility was premised on the perception among most of the justices—shared by legislators, military and executive officers, scholars, sectors of the press, and others—that those recently acquired possessions posed new challenges and should somehow be treated differently from previous acquisitions. There is ample language in the opinions to support this contention. Justice Joseph McKenna referred to this "need" for flexibility in his dissent in *De Lima v. Bidwell*;[26] Justice Henry Billings Brown explicitly stated that "a false step at this time might be fatal to the development of . . . the American Empire."[27] Writing for the majority in *Dorr*, Justice William Day underlined that the framers of the Treaty of Paris[28] intended to give Congress "a free hand" in dealing with the newly acquired possessions.[29] And in *Balzac*, Chief Justice William Howard Taft expressed that the real issue of the Insular Cases had been the extent of

---

24 See Christina Duffy Burnett, "*Untied* States: American Expansion and Territorial Deannexation," *University of Chicago Law Review* 72 (2005): 797-879.

25 Efrén Rivera Ramos, *The Legal Construction of Identity: The Judicial and Social Legacy of American Colonialism in Puerto Rico* (Washington, DC: American Psychological Association, 2001), 138-9.

26 De Lima v. Bidwell, 182 U.S. 1, 218-20 (1901) (McKenna, J., dissenting).

27 Downes v. Bidwell, 182 U.S. 244, 286 (1901).

28 Treaty of Peace between the United States of America and the Kingdom of Spain, U.S.-Spain, Dec. 10, 1898, 30 Stat. 1754.

29 Dorr v. United States, 195 U.S. 138, 143 (1904).

Congress's power to deal with these "new conditions and requirements."[30]

The Insular Cases represented both a continuation of and a break from the past. The continuity included resorting to concepts such as the long-existing plenary power doctrine and creating a symbolic space to be inhabited by peripheral populations, similar to the spaces that had been designed for African Americans, Native Americans, new immigrants, and women. The break involved the message that neither Congress nor the Supreme Court should feel excessively constrained by previous decisions or doctrines, even those that had been developed for the governance of former territories. In a sense, the court was constructing for itself and for Congress a relatively clean slate upon which to write the future of the new possessions. This was one of the principal symbolic effects of the doctrine of incorporation.

In the longer term, the Insular Cases have had the following social, political, and ideological effects.[31]

First, they created a discursive universe that included categories, concepts, approaches, justifications, and understandings that have controlled, even to this day, the nation's and the territories' ways of thinking, analyzing, and imagining solutions. All of us have become inhabitants of the conceptual territory carved out by the justices in those decisions.

Second, the Insular Cases constituted a new legal and political subject: the resident of an unincorporated territory. This new social agent would be endowed with entitlements and obligations. Residents of these territories would be capable of making claims, willing, and acting, but they also would be submitted to the full political authority of Congress. That authority was considered legitimate by virtue of the United States' inherent powers as a sovereign nation and by the textual foundation provided by the territory clause of the US Constitution.

Third, like all salient legal events, the cases constructed a context for future action. Most relevant actors in the territorial drama have proceeded under the assumption that the claims, counterclaims, congressional legislation, executive determinations, and even processes aimed at addressing the territories' colonial condition have to be formulated, designed, and executed under the fundamental premises adopted by the Insular Cases and their progeny. This is a very powerful constraining effect.

But the justices in those cases did something else. They produced an understanding akin to a political question doctrine to be applied in the context

---

30 Balzac v. Porto Rico, 258 U.S. 298, 312 (1922).
31 For more detailed discussions of the points succinctly made below, see Rivera Ramos, *The Legal Construction of Identity*, 121-42; and Efrén Rivera Ramos, "Puerto Rico's Political Status: The Long-Term Effects of American Expansionist Discourse," in *The Louisiana Purchase and American Expansion, 1803-1898*, ed. Sanford Levinson and Bartholomew Sparrow (Lanham, MD: Rowman and Littlefield, 2005).

of the territories. Chief Justice Taft vigorously consolidated this viewpoint in *Balzac*. According to this conception, there is a distinction to be made between constitutional and political claims. Constitutional claims—such as those pertaining to certain fundamental rights (due process, freedom of expression, and the like)—are for the Supreme Court to decide. But political claims—for example, those relating to participation rights or to the definition of the territories' political condition—are for Congress, or for the people of the United States, to determine. In that determination, Congress has paramount power, except for the limitations imposed by the Constitution itself, as interpreted by the Supreme Court. Historical evidence shows that, in this respect, the court has always acted in accordance with congressional policy.

It is in this terrain—and not necessarily in the judicial sphere—that we find the possibilities for moving forward with a resolution of the condition of the territories. Of course, these possibilities confront enormous difficulties. The US Congress has more than five hundred members. Puerto Rico and the other territories are not even on the radar of most of them. Moreover, extracting a consensus on the future of the territories in that complex, partisan, and highly divisive body has proven to be a veritable challenge.[32] Yet this seems to be the most viable route to accomplish the goal of bringing the relationship between the United States and its territories in line with current notions of self-determination, democracy, and human rights.

Congress, however, needs prodding. The pressure must come from the peoples of the territories themselves, from sympathetic sectors of the American people, from the international community, and perhaps even from the White House.

---

32 For an analysis of some of the difficulties encountered whenever efforts have been made to move the process of self-determination for Puerto Rico forward in the US Congress, see, e.g., Rivera Ramos, *The Legal Construction of Identity*, 57-59, 128-29, 223-25.

CHAPTER THREE

The Centennial of *Ocampo v. United States*

Lessons from the Insular Cases

Bartholomew H. Sparrow

On May 25, 1914, Justice Mahlon Pitney ruled for a unanimous Supreme Court in *Ocampo v. United States*[1] that a resident of the Philippines was not entitled to a preliminary finding of probable cause before his arrest and trial. Justice Pitney's opinion for a unanimous court relied on the precedents of *Hawaii v. Mankichi*,[2] *Dorr v. United States*,[3] and *Dowdell v. United States*[4]— the first two cases being among the most prominent of the thirty-five Insular Cases.[5] In a series of US Supreme Court decisions between 1901 and 1922, now collectively known as the Insular Cases, the Supreme Court established that residents of US territories are not entitled to the same constitutional protections as citizens of the mainland United States; some provisions of the Constitution apply to the territories, whereas others—including certain civil liberties protections—do not.[6] *Ocampo v. United States* thus represented a continuation of the court's restriction of civil liberties protections in the US island territories per its rulings in the other Insular Cases.

---

1 Ocampo v. United States, 234 U.S. 91 (1914).
2 Hawaii v. Mankichi, 190 U.S. 197 (1903).
3 Dorr v. United States, 195 U.S. 138 (1904).
4 Dowdell v. United States, 221 U.S. 325 (1911).
5 See Bartholomew H. Sparrow, *The* Insular Cases *and the Emergence of American Empire* (Lawrence: University Press of Kansas, 2006).
6 Ibid.

The centennial of Justice Pitney's unanimous ruling in *Ocampo* prompts three reflections on the Insular Cases.

First, despite the constitutional and political significance of *Ocampo* and the other Insular Cases for the territories of the United States, the cases are almost entirely absent from political discourse within the fifty states. The cases are rarely covered in print or by the broadcast media. Seldom do politicians refer to them in their remarks on the House or Senate floors or in proposed legislation, campaign advertisements, political debates, or campaign stump speeches. Public opinion polls do not ask about them. Casebooks on US constitutional law infrequently discuss the Insular Cases, thus discouraging students from learning about these important cases. All of these silences relegate the Insular Cases to near obscurity.

A second lesson of *Ocampo* and the Insular Cases is that just as *Ocampo* followed the first ten Insular Cases of 1901 in being almost lost to history, so, too, has the more recent history of the Insular Cases escaped public scrutiny. Although there has been a flow of cases in recent decades challenging the Insular Cases, especially with respect to political representation in the territories and the rights of the criminally accused, this litigation has been largely unsuccessful. The result is that the federal courts have continued to deny equal constitutional protections to the US citizens (and, for American Samoa, the US nationals) residing in the United States' island territories.

A third lesson of *Ocampo* and the other Insular Cases concerns the relationship between law and the United States' political and strategic aims. The United States acquired both Puerto Rico and the Philippines for geostrategic purposes, and consistent with this objective the Supreme Court in *Ocampo* deferred to the US government's plenary authority over its unincorporated territories. This same logic prevailed with respect to the other territories annexed by the United States following the 1898 Spanish-American War. Indeed, the US government still systematically discriminates politically against those US citizens who reside in Puerto Rico, the US Virgin Islands, Guam, and the Northern Mariana Islands, as well as the US nationals of American Samoa, on the basis of geography—read strategic interests—notwithstanding the end of de jure discrimination on the basis of race, religion, sex, and other ascriptive characteristics.

This chapter considers each of these three lessons. It reviews the legacy of the Insular Cases—a legacy that is in evidence more in the lower federal courts than in the Supreme Court. It investigates the coverage and attention given to the Insular Cases in politics and legal education (as reflected in the content of constitutional law casebooks). And it considers the logic behind the establishment of the US government's plenary power over the property and territory of the United States, per the territory clause.[7]

---

7   U.S. CONST., art. IV, § 3, cl. 2 ("The Congress shall have Power to dispose of and

The Insular Cases as Palimpsests

Despite the significance of the Insular Cases and the fact that they continue to be upheld by the courts, the decisions remain almost invisible in US national politics.

In the last quarter century, only five Supreme Court cases cite at least one of the Insular Cases, with the 2008 decision in *Boumediene v. Bush*[8] being the most recent. In *Boumediene*, Justice Anthony Kennedy, writing for the 5-4 majority, acknowledged that the "century old [incorporation] doctrine informs our analysis in the present matter" with respect to the plaintiff's right of habeas corpus.[9] Justice Kennedy reasoned that the rulings of the Insular Cases, in conjunction with those in *Johnson v. Eisentrager*[10] and *Reid v. Covert*,[11] revealed that "questions of extraterritoriality turn on objective factors and practical concerns, not formalism." He held that the US government's powers are not "absolute and unlimited" when the government acts outside its borders, though they are still subject to constitutional restrictions.

Yet the citation of the Insular Cases by the majority in *Boumediene* may well be the exception that proves the rule. The case would surely have been decided differently had it been heard in 2002 or 2003—and as Laurence Tribe and Joshua Matz point out, the ruling in *Boumediene* has been whittled away at in the years since.[12] Indeed, Justice Antonin Scalia denied the applicability of the Insular Cases in his dissent. As Scalia contended, "None of the Insular Cases stands for the proposition that aliens located outside U.S. sovereign territory have constitutional rights"—a point, he argued, that the Supreme Court had made abundantly clear in an earlier case involving aliens during the United States' postwar occupation of Nazi Germany.[13]

The major US news media have likewise barely mentioned the Insular Cases over the past twenty-five years, whether in print, on radio, or on television. As revealed by a combined search of the LexisNexis and Factiva databases, the most frequent mentions of the Insular Cases, whether in whole or in part, occurred in *Hispanically Speaking News*, an online newspaper; Pacnews, the Pacific News Agency Service; the *Virgin Islands Daily News*; and official US government sources. There were even fewer mentions in the mainstream commercial media, with the *Boston Globe* mentioning the Insular Cases three times, the Associated Press twice, the *New York Times*

---

make all needful Rules and Regulations respecting the Territory or other Property belonging to the United States.").

8   Boumediene v. Bush, 553 U.S. 723 (2008).
9   Ibid., 765.
10   Johnson v. Eisentrager, 339 U.S. 763 (1950).
11   Reid v. Covert, 354 U.S. 1 (1957).
12   Laurence Tribe and Joshua Matz, *Uncertain Justice: The Roberts Court and the Constitution* (New York: Henry Holt, 2014), 196-202.
13   Boumediene v. Bush, 553 U.S. 723, 839-42 (2008) (Scalia, J., dissenting).

once, National Public Radio once, CNN Wire once, the New York-based *Daily News* once, and the Cedar Rapids *Gazette* once.[14]

Nor do politicians talk much about the Insular Cases. This is true despite interest in the Puerto Rican debt crisis in late 2013, the Puerto Rican presidential primaries of 2008 (among Democrats) and 2012 (among Republicans), and referenda on Puerto Rican statehood in the 1990s. Moreover, of the thousands of proposed bills, House reports, statements by House and Senate members, and congressional resolutions of the past twenty-five years, the Insular Cases—whether the term itself or any of the principal cases—were mentioned in only twenty-two of them.[15] Nor do any of the major public opinion polls (those sponsored by media companies or by academically oriented nonprofit organizations) ask respondents about the status of the territories or about the Insular Cases. (The one exception to this omission in opinion polling pertains to referenda regarding Puerto Rico's political status and potential statehood.[16])

Even students of US constitutional law do not learn about the cases. Of fifteen of the most popular constitutional law casebooks, only three mention

---

14 Ray Suarez, "Talk of the Nation," NPR, Apr. 23, 1998; James A. Miller, "Books: Two New Looks at the Consequences of an Expansive Foreign Policy, Both at Home and Abroad American Ambitions," *Boston Globe*, Feb. 2, 2003; Martin F. Noonan, "Op Ed: Where Is Mr. Dooley When We Need Him," *Boston Globe*, Nov. 30, 2000; Editorial, "The Court and Mr. Dooley," *Boston Globe*, Mar. 2, 1990; Jim Day, "Judge Hears Argument in Lawsuit Calling U.S. Virgin Islands' Status Unconstitutional," Associated Press, Mar. 21, 2002; "A Package of News Briefs from the Caribbean," Associated Press, Mar. 21, 2002; Juan González, "Puerto Rico Demands Prez Ballot," *Daily News*, Oct. 10, 2000; Neil Weare, "Citizenship is a Birthright in U.S. Territories," CNN Wire, Feb. 19, 2014; Adam Liptak, "A Hint of New Life to a McCain Birth Issue," *New York Times*, July 11, 2008; Erin Jordan, "Disgruntled Iowans Form Own Governments," *Gazette*, Aug. 4, 2012.

15 The results were obtained using www.congress.gov (formerly www.thomas.gov), an online archive of congressional behavior.

16 The Washington Post/Kaiser Family Foundation/Harvard University Survey Project asked one question on a June 1999 survey, Gallup asked one question each in March 1998 and February 1991, the ABC News/Washington Post Poll asked one question each in October 1993 and November 1993, the Time-CNN-Yankelovich Clancy Shulman Poll asked one question in October 1992, and the NBC/Wall Street Journal Poll asked a question in September 1990. See http://www.ropercenter.uconn.edu. These results were obtained on the Roper Center's website using the search terms "Insular Cases" or "Incorporation Doctrine" or "Puerto Rico," or "Northern Marianas," with "lived" or "born" excluded (which eliminated questions about change of residence and cultural comparisons). A search using the names of the other US territories and any of the names of the individual Insular Cases did not yield any other poll questions being asked over the past twenty-five years.

Downes v. Bidwell,[17] *Dorr v. United States,*[18] *Balzac v. Porto Rico,*[19] or the "Insular Cases" as a group. Only one—*Processes of Constitutional Decision-Making*, by Paul Brest, Sanford Levinson, Jack M. Balkin, Reva B. Siegel, and Akhil Reed Amar—mentions the Insular Cases in some detail (it even refers to *Ocampo*) and discusses the territory clause and US territorial sovereignty.[20] The absence of a mention of the Insular Cases, whether in whole or in part, in the other twelve textbooks indicates that teaching the Insular Cases, the incorporation doctrine, and the territory clause is a low priority in most law schools and undergraduate constitutional law classes.

In short, the fact that the US government continues to discriminate politically against the US citizens and US nationals of the island territories, and that it does so under the authority of the incorporation doctrine, remains an essentially unknown fact among the electorate of the fifty states. Nor do policy makers or other opinion leaders enlighten the electorate—or most law school students—of this fact.

The Judicial Legacy of the Insular Cases

The decision in *Ocampo v. United States* is consistent with numerous US Supreme Court precedents, many decided well before the Insular Cases, that established Congress's legal authority over the inhabitants of areas annexed by the US government. The plenary power of the US government applied to Creoles, Cajuns, French, Spanish, and free blacks with the Louisiana Purchase; to the Spanish, Indians, and Anglo-Americans with the acquisition of West Florida and then East Florida; to a handful of British and white Americans in the Oregon Territory; and to Mexicans and Spanish descendants in the Mexican Cession and then the Gadsden Purchase.[21] The United States' legal dominion or sovereignty similarly prevailed over the nonnative inhabitants of Alaska and residents of Hawaii, and to the peoples of Puerto Rico, the Philippines, and Guam following the Spanish-American War, just as it did

---

17 Downes v. Bidwell, 182 U.S. 244 (1901).
18 Dorr v. United States, 195 U.S. 138 (1904).
19 Balzac v. Porto Rico, 258 U.S. 298 (1922).
20 See Paul Brest, Sanford Levinson, Jack M. Balkin, Reva Siegal, and Akhil Reed Amar, *Processes of Constitutional Decision-Making: Cases and Materials*, 5th ed. (New York: Aspen Publishers, 2006), 386-98, 870; Jerome A. Barron, C. Thomas Dienes, Wayne McCormack, and Martin H. Reddish, *Constitutional Law: Principles and Policy*, 7th ed. (Los Angeles: LexisNexis, 2012), 419; Daniel A. Farber, William N. Eskridge, Jr., and Philip Frickey, *Constitutional Law: Themes for the Constitution's Third Century*, 4th ed. (Eagan, MN: West, 2009), 131.
21 Sarah H. Cleveland, "Powers Inherent in Sovereignty: Indians, Aliens, Territories, and the Nineteenth Century Origins of Plenary Power over Foreign Affairs," *Texas Law Review* 81 (2002): 1-284.

with the peoples living in the United States' other, later insular possessions—the persons affected by the Insular Cases.

Recent cases in the territorial and federal courts involving the citizens of the US territories confirm as much.

The courts have upheld Congress's authority over the territories pursuant to the commerce clause and, by extension, the uniformity clause and the preference clause. Congress may set the rules of commerce between the states and the unincorporated territories, with broad discretion pursuant to its taxing powers, consistent with the holding in *Downes v. Bidwell*.[22] "Despite the fact that the United States mainland and the Virgin Islands share the same sovereign, the United States can nevertheless establish a border between 'incorporated' and an 'unincorporated' territory, which would have the characteristics of an international border."[23]

There are significant consequences of this special treatment of the territories. To cite one example, as the Supreme Court held in *Balzac v. Porto Rico*,[24] the Sixth Amendment's right to a jury trial does not apply to territorial citizens. In 2003, the Territorial Court of the Virgin Islands affirmed that US citizens residing in the territories were not entitled to trial by jury: "U.S. citizens and other inhabitants of a U.S. territory do not have the same constitutional guarantees as U.S. citizens and other inhabitants of the fifty states. This is because of the 'Territorial Incorporation' doctrine devised by the Supreme Court in the Insular Cases."[25] As the court ruled:

> This doctrine acknowledges that under Article IV section 3 of the U.S. Constitution, Congress is given power to legislate concerning the U.S. territories. . . . If a territory is not "incorporated" into the United States, then Congress is given plenary power to determine what rights are applicable to that territory limited only by the Constitution's "general prohibitions" protecting the fundamental rights of all citizens. See *Dorr v. United States*, 195 U.S. 138, 142 (1904).[26]

Following the US Supreme Court's ruling in *Balzac*, "the *constitutional* right of a jury trial in criminal prosecutions is deemed only a remedial right, so Congress is not required to extend it to the Territory of the U.S. Virgin Islands."[27]

The Tenth Amendment's guarantee that powers not enumerated in the

---

22 Thomson Multimedia Inc. v. United States, 219 F. Supp. 2d 1322 (Ct. Int'l Trade 2002); Virgin Islands v. David, 45 V.I. 100 (Territorial Ct. V.I. 2002).
23 Virgin Islands v. David, 45 V.I. 100, 109-10 (Territorial Ct. V.I. 2002).
24 Balzac v. Porto Rico, 258 U.S. 298 (1922).
25 Virgin Islands v. Boynes, 45 V.I. 195 (Territorial Ct. V.I. 2003).
26 Ibid., 198-99.
27 Ibid., 200.

Constitution "are reserved to the States respectively, or to the People"[28] has similarly not been extended to the US citizens residing in the territories, despite the fact that these persons would seem to be entitled to the Constitution's reserved powers as "people" of the United States. In *Granville-Smith v. Granville-Smith,*[29] the US Supreme Court overturned a Virgin Islands divorce law, and in 1977 the courts invalidated the Guam legislature's establishment of its own supreme court on the grounds that Guam needed the express authority of the US Congress to do so.[30] Both decisions run contrary to the Tenth Amendment.

Voting rights are also implicated by the incorporation doctrine. As the United States District Court for the District of the Virgin Islands held in a ruling denying Virgin Island citizens the right to vote in US presidential and congressional elections, "locality" (citing Chief Justice William Howard Taft's ruling in *Balzac*) was "determinative of the application of the Constitution . . . and not the status of the people who live in it."[31] The ruling in the Virgin Islands case followed Chief Justice William Rehnquist's opinion in *United States v. Verdugo-Urquidez,*[32] in which Rehnquist cited *Balzac, Dorr, Mankichi, Downes,* and other Insular Cases to argue that not every provision of the US Constitution applies to all places over which the United States has sovereignty.[33]

Consequently, the Insular Cases can hardly be described as "dead letters, as constitutional aberrations," as Eric Posner writes in the *New Republic.* For the citizens of the island territories, and those in Puerto Rico and Guam especially (see below), the Insular Cases and incorporation doctrine are by no means "meaningless."[34] On the contrary, they are very much alive; it is just that they receive scant attention.

Even so, the Supreme Court's ruling in *Boumediene* and several lower court decisions disclose cracks in the edifice of the incorporation doctrine. As the majority held in *Boumediene,* the conjunction of the Insular Cases

---

28   U.S. CONST., amend. X.
29   Granville-Smith v. Granville-Smith, 349 U.S. 1 (1955).
30   Guam v. Olsen, 431 U.S. 195 (1977).
31   Ballentine v. United States, No. 1999-130, 2006 WL 3298270, at 12-13 (D.V.I. 2006).
32   United States v. Verdugo Urquidez, 494 U.S. 259 (1990).
33   The incorporation doctrine established in the Insular Cases is supported by other court rulings. In *United States v. Lara,* for instance—a case concerning the sovereign power of Indian tribes to prosecute nontribe Indians—Justice Stephen Breyer ruled that in the instances of Hawaii, the Northern Marianas, Puerto Rico, and the Philippines, Congress was able to exercise its power "to modify the degree of autonomy enjoyed by a dependent sovereign that is not a State." United States v. Lara, 541 U.S. 193, 203 (2004). Congress was therefore constitutionally permitted to legislate on the authority of Indian tribes to prosecute nonmember Indians. Ibid., 210.
34   Eric A. Posner, "Books and Arts: The Limits of Limits," *New Republic,* May 5, 2010.

rulings and those in *Eisentrager* and *Reid* revealed that "questions of extraterritoriality turn on objective factors and practical concerns, not formalism."[35] Justice Kennedy and the majority stated that the United States' powers are not "absolute and unlimited" when the United States acts outside its borders but rather subject to constitutional restrictions.[36] The implication of the majority's opinion was that the suspension clause of Article I, Section 9 posed a high bar to the US government's denial of habeas corpus. Short of attaining that standard, habeas corpus was a "right of first importance" for Justice Kennedy[37]—in other words, a "fundamental right" that applied to persons under US sovereignty (in contrast to the right to a jury trial, the right to vote in US federal elections, being subject to uniform tariffs, and the right to indictment by grand jury in cases of felony, among others).[38]

In other recent cases, lower court judges have rebelled against the incorporation doctrine, only to be reversed on appeal. In *United States v. Pollard*,[39] the United States District Court for the District of the Virgin Islands ruled that the permanent immigration departure checkpoint set up at the Saint Thomas airport violated the defendant's (a black woman's) civil rights under the protections of the Fourteenth, Fifth, and Fourth Amendments of the Constitution.[40] The court highlighted the "racist doctrine" judicially created for the United States' "unincorporated" territories, and specifically cited twenty-three of the Insular Cases, from *De Lima v. Bidwell* through *Balzac v. Porto Rico*.[41] It noted the "racism and cultural superiority that permeated these thoroughly ossified cases [the Insular Cases] that embody the intrinsically racist imperialism of a previous era of United States colonial expansion."[42] The court concluded that the "mandatory stop of each traveler at Departure Control is a 'seizure' for Fourth Amendment purposes" and that "the persons within the Virgin Islands are fully protected by the fundamental rights set forth in the Fourth Amendment."[43] The Third Circuit reversed.[44]

In addition, at least two US judges have voiced strong criticisms of the Insular Cases. Judge Juan R. Torruella of the United States Court of Appeals has repeatedly expressed fundamental philosophical differences with the precedent of the Insular Cases and the Supreme Court's subsequent rulings.[45]

---

35 Boumediene v. Bush, 553 U.S. 723, 764 (2008).
36 Ibid., 765.
37 Ibid., 798.
38 Dorr v. United States, 195 U.S. 138, 148 (1904).
39 United States v. Pollard, 209 F. Supp. 2d 525 (D.V.I. 2002).
40 Ibid., 538, 549-50, 558.
41 Ibid., 539-40 n.17.
42 Ibid., 540-41.
43 Ibid., 549.
44 United States v. Pollard, 326 F.3d 397 (3d Cir. 2003).
45 Igartúa de la Rosa v. United States, 229 F.3d 80, 86 n.7, 87 n.14, 88-89 (1st Cir.

Similarly, Judge Anne Thompson wrote in *Ballentine v. United States* that "this court regrets the enduring 'vitality' of the Insular Cases[,] which ... articulate the Constitution's limits on the government's ability to intrude in the lives of its citizens, depending on the physical location of those citizens."[46]

Locality as Security

The geography of the US federal government—the aggregate area of the states and the citizens therein—continues to dictate judicial decision making. "It is locality," as Chief Justice Taft proclaimed in his lead opinion in *Balzac*, "that is determinative of the application of the Constitution, in such matters as judicial procedure, and not the status of the people who live in it."[47] And because of the "difficulties [presented by the] incorporation of the Philippines and Porto Rico," Taft wrote for a unanimous Supreme Court, the facts of geography determined the constitutional status of Puerto Ricans.[48] He continued:

> [T]he Porto Rican cannot insist upon the right of trial by jury, except as his own representatives in his legislature shall confer it on him. The citizen of the United States living in Porto Rico can not there enjoy a right of trial by jury under the Federal Constitution, any more than the Porto Rican.[49]

As Taft argued:

> It is well settled that these provisions for jury trial in criminal and civil cases apply to the territories of the United States. . . . But it is just as clearly settled that they do *not* apply to territory belonging to the United States which has *not been incorporated* into the Union.[50]

Puerto Ricans, Taft explained, were "trained to a complete judicial system which knows no juries, living in compact and ancient communities, with definitely formed customs and political conceptions."[51] They were therefore unsuited to sit on juries or be judged by a jury of their peers. Puerto Rico was one of several "distant ocean communities of a different origin and language from those of our continental people," he pointed out.[52] Alaska "was

---

2000) (Torruella, C.J., concurring). See also Juan R. Torruella, *The Supreme Court and Puerto Rico: The Doctrine of Separate and Unequal* (Río Piedras: Editorial de la Universidad de Puerto Rico, 1985).

46   Ballentine v. United States, No. 1999-130, 2006 WL 3298270, at 12 (D.V.I. 2006).
47   Balzac v. Porto Rico, 258 U.S. 298 (1922).
48   Ibid., 309.
49   Ibid.
50   Ibid., 305-6 (internal citations omitted; emphasis added).
51   Ibid., 310.
52   Ibid., 311.

a very different case," Taft held, because it "was an enormous territory, very sparsely settled, and offering opportunity for immigration and settlement by American citizens."[53] The basis for Taft's ruling was Justice William Day's lead opinion in *Dorr v. United States*[54]:

> If the right to trial by jury were a fundamental right which goes wherever the jurisdiction of the United States extends, or if Congress, in framing laws for outlying territory belonging to the United States was obliged to establish that system by affirmative legislation, it would follow that, no matter what the needs or capacities of the people, trial by jury, and in no other way, must be forthwith established, although the result may be to work injustice and provoke disturbance rather than to aid the orderly administration of justice. . . . Again, if the United States shall acquire by treaty the cession of territory having an established system of jurisprudence, where jury trials are unknown, but a method of fair and orderly trial prevails under an acceptable and long-established code, the preference of the people must be disregarded, their established customs ignored and they themselves coerced to accept, in advance of incorporation into the United States, a system of trial unknown to them and unsuited to their needs. We do not think it was intended, in giving power to Congress to make regulations for the territories, to hamper its exercise with this condition.[55]

According to Justice Day, joined by Chief Justice Melville Fuller, Justice Edward White, and Justice Oliver Wendell Holmes, the US government could discriminate against persons under the sovereignty of the United States according to their place of residence. The Constitution might apply to the new island territories, but the territory clause bestowed on Congress the right to decide which provisions regarding political rights and governmental processes would be extended.

But the reason why the United States needed to acquire these territories despite "the needs or capacities of the people" residing on the islands was because of the United States' larger geopolitical ambitions. The US government first extended its plenary authority over its possessions and territories of continental North America—thirty-three of the separate states were at one point territories—and then extended it overseas. This is a history of the geographic expansion of the United States—that is, one of the growth and then arrest of territorial expansion, where Congress and the Supreme Court have been ever sensitive to the United States' security concerns.[56]

---

53   Ibid., 309.
54   Dorr v. United States, 195 U.S. 138 (1904).
55   Balzac v. Porto Rico, 258 U.S. 298, 309-10 (1922) (quoting Dorr v. United States, 195 U.S. 138, 148 (1904)).
56   Fred Anderson and Andrew Cayton, *The Dominion of War: Empire and Liberty*

Throughout the history of American expansion, strategic interests were paramount, if not always the sole determinant of the country's geographic expansion. Could Americans settle beyond the Appalachian Mountains and lessen the threat from the Spanish, English, and foreign-allied Indians?—a question resolved by the terms of the 1783 Treaty of Paris[57] in which Britain ceded the trans-Appalachian West to the United States. Could the United States control New Orleans and thus gain access to the mouth of the Mississippi River and the movement of goods and persons into the continent's interior?—a question resolved by the Louisiana Purchase of 1803,[58] whereby France sold the western half of the Mississippi River valley to the United States. Could the United States secure its southeastern coast and control trade routes to the West Indies?—an issue settled by the acquisition of West and East Florida in 1811 and 1818, respectively.

Could the United States gain control of the Columbia River and secure its northern border with British Canada?—a question resolved with the annexation of what is now the Pacific Northwest of Washington, Oregon, Idaho, and portions of Montana in the British Cession of 1846.[59] Could the United States secure the Pacific coast and therefore the breadth of the North American continent?—a question resolved by the Mexican-American War and the subsequent 1848 Treaty of Guadalupe Hidalgo,[60] which gave the United States ownership of California, New Mexico, and most of what is now the southwestern United States. Could the United States secure a southern route for a transcontinental railroad?—a question answered with the 1853 Gadsden Purchase.[61] Could the United States remove Russia from North America?—a question resolved in 1867 by the US government's purchase of Alaska.[62]

In 1898, President McKinley and prominent Republicans in his administration and Congress took the United States overseas. With the US government's plans in the 1890s for an isthmian canal, with a larger navy

---

in North America, 1500-2000 (New York: Penguin, 2005); Walter LaFeber, *The Cambridge History of American Foreign Relations: Volume II; The American Search for Opportunity 1865-1913* (New York: Cambridge University Press, 1993); Sparrow, *The* Insular Cases *and the Emergence of American Empire*, 212-51.

57   Definitive Treaty of Peace between the United States of America and His Britannic Majesty, U.S.-Gr. Brit., Sept. 3, 1783, 8 Stat. 80.

58   Louisiana Purchase Agreement, U.S.-Fr., Apr. 30, 1803, 8 Stat. 200.

59   Treaty Establishing the Boundary in the Territory on the Northwest Coast of America Lying Westward of the Rocky Mountains, U.S.-Gr. Brit., June 15, 1846, 9 Stat. 869.

60   Treaty of Peace, Friendship, Limits, and Settlement with the Republic of Mexico, U.S.-Mex., Feb. 2, 1848, 9 Stat. 922.

61   Gadsden Purchase, U.S.-Mex., Dec. 30, 1853, 10 Stat. 1031.

62   Convention Ceding Alaska, U.S.-Russ., Mar. 30, 1867, 15 Stat. 539.

under construction, and with the growth of trade and foreign investment—growth interrupted by and subsequently seen as ever-more necessary after the Depression of 1893—the United States needed naval bases in the Pacific and Caribbean. As Secretary of State James G. Blaine wrote to President Harrison in 1890, "There are only three places that are of value enough to be taken, one is Hawaii and the others are Cuba and Puerto Rico."[63] Control of the Mona Passage, which ran between the Dominican Republic to the west and Puerto Rico to the east, was one of the few ways to approach the Caribbean from the North Atlantic and was thus of critical importance for the McKinley administration's plans for an isthmian canal. As Navy Secretary John Davis Long wrote to Secretary of State John Hay on December 21, 1900, the US Navy was looking at the Cuban ports of Guantánamo and Cienfuegos, as well as sites in Puerto Rico.[64] Alfred Thayer Mahan noted that

> the pre-eminent intrinsic advantages of Cuba [can be obtained] . . . only if naval supremacy in the West Indian waters could be asserted. Assuming the latter condition, Porto Rico, with the fortified port of San Juan, 1,000 miles from Havana and 5,300 miles from Cadiz [the Spanish seaport], was also a strategic point of importance.[65]

The Philippines, for their part, were considered a gateway to China. It was also thought that the islands could provide sites for naval bases, deprive Spain of naval stations, and supply the US domestic market with hemp and unrefined sugar (the Philippines was the third-largest exporter of sugar to the United States). Guam, 3,000 miles west of Hawaii and 6,000 miles west of California, was the southernmost and largest island of the Northern Mariana Islands and had an excellent harbor. Given Guam's value as a harbor and coaling station in the Western Pacific, the newly formed Naval War Board recommended, on May 9, 1898, that the United States seize Guam as "a strategic point between Honolulu and Manila."[66]

The United States quickly defeated Spanish forces in Cuba, Puerto Rico, and the Philippines in the Spanish-American War, and the McKinley administration's negotiators proceeded to add Puerto Rico, the Philippines,

---

63 Quoted in Sparrow, *The* Insular Cases *and the Emergence of American Empire*, 67.
64 Ibid.
65 Quoted in ibid., 66.
66 Quoted in ibid., 67. Hawaii, meanwhile, had been used by the US Navy as a coaling and watering station since 1875, and the end of fighting in the war against Spain allowed the Republican-controlled Congress to pass the Newlands Resolution to annex Hawaii—fueled by the momentum for expansion following the United States' victory. Hawaii had good harbors, of course, an Anglo ruling class, and extensive ongoing trade (especially in sugar) with the states.

and Guam to the terms of the 1898 Treaty of Paris.[67] Earlier, on July 7, 1898, only three days after the end of hostilities, the United States had annexed Hawaii as a territory. Later, in August 1899, the United States established a naval station on Guam.

US naval strategists wanted to acquire American Samoa because of Pago Pago's value as a port and Tutuila's value as a base and refueling station (the navy had leased the Pago Pago harbor on Tutuila since 1872). In 1894, Navy Assistant Secretary Theodore Roosevelt called for the United States to expand into the Pacific and to establish a naval station in the eastern Samoan islands (2,200 miles southwest of Hawaii). The United States then annexed the eastern Samoan Islands in 1899, in the Southern Hemisphere, through a tripartite agreement with Great Britain and Germany.[68] The US Navy used Pago Pago as a base until 1951.

The Virgin Islands were likewise desired for their use as naval bases and coaling stations, since their harbors, Saint Thomas especially, were among the best in the Caribbean. Too, the Virgin Islands lay close to the Anegada Passage, the third of the three "navigable breaks in the northern barrier enclosing the Caribbean Sea," as observed by the strategist W. V. Judson.[69] One of the planks of the 1896 Republican platform even called for the United States to take over the Virgin Islands. Although the islands remained in the hands of Denmark, the United States bought them in 1917 out of fear that they might fall into the hands of Germany or another hostile power. The Navy Department proceeded to administer the US Virgin Islands until 1931, just as it did Guam until 1950 and Samoa until 1952, at which times the Department of the Interior took over responsibility.

The United States' new Caribbean and Pacific territories allowed it to dominate the West Indies and the Gulf of Mexico, station its military closer to Central and South America, control access to the Panama Canal from the North Atlantic (thereby facilitating inter-ocean and bicoastal trade and giving the US Navy more flexibility in its ship deployment), protect trans-Pacific trade routes, and establish naval bases closer to China and other countries in the Far East. During World War II, the US Pacific territories served as key military outposts against Japan. They provided sites from which to survey enemy action, station personnel and supplies, and launch attacks. If the Philippines, Hawaii, Guam, Alaska, Midway, and Wake Island—the latter two being unoccupied (and unincorporated) US possessions—were manifestly

---

67 Treaty of Peace between the United States of America and the Kingdom of Spain, U.S.-Spain, Dec. 10, 1898, 30 Stat. 1754.

68 Convention between the United States, Germany, and Great Britain to Adjust Amicably the Questions between the Three Governments in respect to the Samoan Group of Islands, Dec. 2, 1899, 31 Stat. 1878.

69 Sparrow, *The* Insular Cases *and the Emergence of Empire*, 232.

vulnerable to Japanese aggression, they also served as needed buffers for states in the West Coast and as places from which to attack Japan.[70]

After World War II and during the Cold War, the United States' island territories enabled the War and Navy Departments—after 1949, the Department of Defense—to control the Pacific up to and often inside the Soviet Union's territorial waters throughout the "short twentieth century" of 1917 to 1989. Those same territories allowed the United States to control the South China and Philippine Seas in the late twentieth century and early 2000s.

The United States' acquisition of the Northern Marianas in 1975 would seem to be a puzzle: Why would the United States add the Chamorros and other residents of the Northern Mariana Islands and allow them to become US citizens in the process, given their cultural differences, much lower standards of living, and remoteness from the North American continent?

The reasons for the island residents' endorsement of US annexation in an island-wide referendum is straightforward: the economically fragile Northern Marianas wanted a political union with the United States because the islands would receive financial subsidies and economic support from US government programs; the protections of US law enforcement and the US legal system; military defense; and potential economic growth from enhanced tourism, investment, and trade opportunities.

The reason why the Ford administration and the US Congress agreed to annex the islands is similarly straightforward and can be found in the records of deliberations from the mid-1970s on annexing the islands, especially in article VIII of the Covenant to Establish a Commonwealth of the Northern Mariana Islands in Political Union with the United States of America.[71] The US Department of Defense wanted to be able to lease area on the islands for airstrips, proving grounds, and other purposes, and the terms of article VIII allowed the department to secure long-term leases on 17,800 acres on two islands for establishing military installations.[72] As Deputy National Security Advisor Brent Scowcroft noted in an internal National Security Council study, the US government's primary objectives were the "denial of the area for use by third parties; US control over the foreign and defense affairs of the Mariana Islands; and the right to establish military bases on those islands."[73]

---

70 The *Enola Gay* flew from the Northern Marianas, then under US possession, when it bombed Hiroshima and Nagasaki in August 1945, just as did the B-29 firebombing of Tokyo in early 1945.

71 Covenant to Establish a Commonwealth of the Northern Mariana Islands in Political Union with the United States of America, art. VIII, Pub. L. No. 94-241, 90 Stat. 263 (1976).

72 Howard P. Willens and Deanne C. Siemer, *An Honorable Accord: The Covenant between the Northern Mariana Islands and the United States* (Honolulu: University of Hawaii Press, 2002).

73 Brent Scowcroft, "Negotiating Instructions on the Future Status of the Marianas

"There are a number of reasons for our regarding these islands of 'strategic importance,'" the Interagency Group for Micronesian Status Negotiations reported.

> Among these are their location, proximity to Guam, Hawaii and important trade routes; the many uncertainties confronting our continued tenure and operating rights in areas closer to the mainland of Asia, especially the Philippines; the future need for training and logistical facilities in the area; the potential risks or threats which would arise from the presence of the military forces of unfriendly powers on one or several of these islands; and the need to meet contingencies in East Asia or the Indian Ocean.[74]

Assistant Secretary of Defense Robert Ellsworth likewise later testified before the Senate Armed Services Committee that the United States had "broad national interests" in the Northern Marianas. Not only did the United States have "a specific responsibility for the defense of Hawaii, Midway, Johnston, Wake, and Guam islands against unlawful or hostile actions," Ellsworth remarked, but it also had responsibility for air traffic control, rescue operations, and the protection of the sea lanes "in that ocean area between Hawaii and the Marianas."[75] It was important that Defense Department personnel "live in a supportive environment," Admiral William Crowe added, and the Northern Marianas had long sought to associate themselves with the United States rather than reunite with Guam, become independent, or remain part of the Trust Territory of the Pacific Islands.[76] Senator Gary Hart (D-Colorado), the foremost congressional opponent of the covenant, viewed the strategic rationale as the principal reason why the US government sought sovereignty over the Northern Marianas.[77]

Despite the US government's strategic interest in the Northern Marianas, the United States has not seen fit to build any military installations on the

---

District of TTPI," memorandum to the chairman of the Under Secretaries Committee, May 9, 1973, folder "Marianas (Working File) (5)," box 36, National Security Council, East Asia files, Ford Presidential Library. See also Franklin Haydn Williams, letter to Gerald Ford, Dec. 31, 1974, folder "7500270 Micronesian Status Negotiations," box 12, press files of the National Security Council, Ford Presidential Library.

74 Interagency Group for Micronesian Status Negotiations, "II. U.S. Interests, Requirements and Negotiating Objectives," 2, "Review of U.S. Policy Toward the Future Political Status of Micronesia," n.d., folder "7602540 – Political Status of Micronesia (1)," box 38, President's NSC Logged Documents (1973), 1974-1977, Ford Presidential Library.

75 Quoted in Willens and Siemer, *An Honorable Accord*, 321.

76 Ibid., 322.

77 Ibid., 293-94.

islands thus far and has not even used the islands or their waters as proving grounds. Furthermore, in 2003, the US Navy stopped using the Puerto Rican island of Vieques as a proving ground and, in 2004, closed down the Roosevelt Roads Naval Station. It would thus seem that the strategic reasons behind the annexation of the Northern Mariana Islands, as well as the McKinley administration's desire to annex Puerto Rico and the US Virgin Islands, no longer apply.

Guam holds the key. The presence of the US military has dominated Guam's economy and society, with the US Air Force and Navy bases and other facilities occupying more than one-third (39%) of Guam's land area.[78] US military personnel currently total about 6,000, not counting dependents.[79] As one scholar of US military bases finds, Guam has "the highest ratio of US military spending and military hardware," the highest proportion of land takings, and the worst environmental record of any US military base.[80] Furthermore, the Department of Defense plans to relocate 5,000 marines with the III Marine Expeditionary Force from Okinawa to Guam;[81] inclusive of support personnel and dependents, this would provide for thousands of additional persons on Guam. In addition, the Pacific Air Forces has planned to base a global strike force at Andersen Air Force Base, which will result in several additional thousands of military personnel, contract workers, and civilians living on the island.[82] By themselves, these developments will increase the island's overall population by 25%.

Even though this increased military presence—over 10,000 US military personnel and approximately 15,000 dependents, support personnel, and contract workers—will exert tremendous effects on property values, rental prices, and the demand for resources, goods, and services, Guam has virtually no voice in the matter. With only one nonvoting delegate in the US House of Representatives, the people of Guam exert no effective oversight over the Defense Department's plans to expand the Marines or Air Force presence on the island. Conversely, those same US citizens have no voice in a hypothetical decision to withdraw forces, with the resulting economic collapse that would follow—just as the citizens on Guam had no say in April 1975 when the US military temporarily relocated tens of thousands

---

78   Catherine Lutz, "US Military Bases on Guam in Global Perspective," *Asia-Pacific Journal*, July 26, 2010.

79   Shirley A. Kan, "Guam: U.S. Defense Deployments," *Congressional Research Service*, Oct. 28, 2014, 1.

80   Lutz, "US Military Bases on Guam in Global Perspective."

81   Kan, "Guam," 6.

82   *Territories of Guam, American Samoa, the Commonwealth of the Northern Mariana Islands, and the U.S. Virgin Islands: Hearing before the Committee on Energy and Natural Resources, United States Senate*, 109th Cong. 24 (2006); Kan, "Guam," 2-3.

of Vietnamese refugees to the island following the evacuation of Saigon and fall of South Vietnam.

In short, the United States' history of annexation—whether of its continental or insular possessions—has not been benign.[83] The United States did not acquire its new empire in a fit of absent-mindedness or "blindly, unintentionally, accidentally and really in spite of ourselves," in the words of Henry Luce, the founder and publisher of *Time* magazine.[84] Neither did the United States achieve its empire through "the sheer genius" of Americans and "not because we chose to go into the politics of the world," as Woodrow Wilson said.[85] Nor was it the case, as the historian David McCullough asserted in a PBS documentary on Theodore Roosevelt, that "America, like it or not, would have to play a large part in the world."[86] Rather, the United States annexed the overseas territories for strategic reasons, as well as on political and economic grounds, in accordance with the policies of US presidents, cabinet secretaries, Republican and Democratic party leaders, military officials, and other political and strategic experts.[87]

And this was an "empire." The new areas annexed by the United States were all "imperial" annexations in the sense that the occupation and control of geographical areas and their inhabitants were accomplished without residents' expressed consent (with the partial exception of the Northern Mariana Islands).[88]

---

83 See Donald Meinig, *The Shaping of America: A Geographical Perspective on 500 Years of History; Volume 2: Continental America, 1800-1867* (New Haven: Yale University Press, 1993); Donald Meinig, *The Shaping of America: A Geographical Perspective on 500 Years of History; Volume 3: Transcontinental America, 1850-1915* (New Haven: Yale University Press, 1998); Walter Nugent, *Habits of Empire: A History of American Expansionism* (New York: Vintage, 2008).

84 Henry R. Luce, "The American Century," *Life*, Feb. 12, 1941, 61-65.

85 Woodrow Wilson, "Des Moines, Iowa, Peace Treaty," in *Addresses Delivered by President Woodrow Wilson on His Western Tour, September 4 to 25, 1919* (Washington, DC: Government Printing Office, 1919), 62.

86 Quoted in Matthew Frye Jacobson, *Barbarian Virtues: The United States Encounters Foreign Peoples at Home and Abroad, 1876-1917* (New York: Hill and Wang, 2000), 264.

87 Sparrow, *The* Insular Cases *and the Emergence of American Empire*, 58-69, 218-20.

88 Ibid., 8, 119. The Marianas Political Status Commission succeeded in attaching the residents of the fourteen islands to the United States by holding a plebiscite consisting of a simple yes-or-no vote. It is a "partial exception" because the Northern Marianas, under the initiative of the commission and with the incentive of US economic benefits, hived off from Micronesia without the approval of the other Trust Territories of the Pacific Islands or the United Nations (under whose auspices the United States served as trustee). See Ediberto Román, *The Other American Colonies: An International and Constitutional Law Examination of the*

One of the premises of the Insular Cases was that the 1898 Treaty of Paris applied to Puerto Rico and the Philippines equally. As Senator Orville Platt said in reference to the legal status of these two territories, "It is the first step that counts; it is the establishment of a precedent that gives trouble."[89] Whereas almost all Americans were willing to annex Puerto Rico following the Spanish-American War, almost none wanted to annex the Philippines. Yet there was no way to distinguish between them under the terms of either the Treaty of Paris or the US Constitution. The same would seem to apply here: to overrule the Insular Cases would endanger the US government's plenary control over Puerto Rico, Guam, and the other territories. In the words of one legal scholar in reference to the majority's decision in *Downes v. Bidwell*, "an empire had to be constitutionally possible."[90] The same logic applied for Martin Ocampo and Teodoro M. Kalaw, the two plaintiffs in *Ocampo v. United States*.

The implication of the US Supreme Court's rulings and those of the federal courts is one of judicial deference to Congress's and the executive's plenary authority under the territory clause—as with the refusal of the Supreme Court to grant certiorari to *Igartúa v. United States* in 2012. The Supreme Court has refused to extend equal constitutional protections to the US citizens in its unincorporated territories and, as a result, has left standing Justice White's incorporation doctrine as articulated in *Downes* and manifest in *Ocampo* and other Insular Cases.

Conclusion

In his dissent in *Downes*, Chief Justice Fuller described the court majority as establishing that the United States could acquire "an organized and settled province of another sovereignty" and "keep it, like a disembodied shade, in an intermediate state of ambiguous existence for an indefinite period ... absolutely subject to the will of Congress, *irrespective of constitutional provisions*."[91] Justice John Marshall Harlan, in his separate dissent, noted that the *Downes* majority was making the Constitution internally inconsistent: "Congress has no existence and can exercise no authority outside of the Constitution. Still less is it true that Congress can deal with new territories just as other nations have done or may do with their new territories."[92]

United States' Nineteenth and Twentieth Century Island Conquests (Durham, NC: Carolina Academic Press, 2006), 249-52.
89   Quoted in Sparrow, *The* Insular Cases *and the Emergence of American Empire*, 77.
90   Linda Przbyszewski, *The Republic According to John Marshall Harlan* (Chapel Hill: University of North Carolina Press, 1999), 140.
91   Downes v. Bidwell, 182 U.S. 244, 372 (Fuller, C.J., dissenting) (emphasis added).
92   Ibid., 380 (Harlan, J., dissenting).

Yet in this second decade of the new millennium, this discrimination on the basis of physical geography seems greatly outdated. In an era when the United States has deeply eroded, if not eliminated, de jure discrimination on the basis of race, ethnicity, gender, and religion, spatial discrimination persists for those US citizens who reside in the territories.

This record of political discrimination stands in stark contrast to the political status of other formerly marginalized peoples. African Americans have been granted full de jure equality in the United States, notwithstanding the US Supreme Court's long record of withholding civil rights per its decisions in *United States v. Reese,*[93] *United States v. Cruikshank,*[94] the *Civil Rights Cases,*[95] *Plessy v. Ferguson,*[96] and *Williams v. Mississippi.*[97]

American Indians have achieved full constitutional and legal protection as US citizens, notwithstanding the Supreme Court's long history of rulings against aboriginal Americans, such as the *Cherokee Tobacco Case,*[98] *United States v. Kagama,*[99] and *Lone Wolf v. Hitchcock.*[100]

Chinese Americans and other Asian Americans have achieved political equality, notwithstanding the decisions in the *Chinese Exclusion Case,*[101] *Fong Yue Ting v. United States,*[102] and other cases. Chinese immigration is now handled in the same way as immigration from other countries—in other words, a reflection of quotas, kinship, and other considerations. Even residents of Washington, DC, who lived under a territorial government between 1871 and 1874, have been guaranteed full rights under the Constitution and, with the Twenty-Third Amendment of 1961, have three votes in the Electoral College (although no voting representation in the House of Representatives or Senate).

Women, too, have been made equals under the law. This is not to deny that women in the United States, similar to other formerly marginalized populations, live and work in a political world in which their lives as women no doubt regularly and significantly impinge on the fullness of their existence as members of American political society. It is to point out, however, that the ascriptive qualities that formerly limited citizenship in the United States have been remedied in constitutional and (most) statutory law. The same cannot be said of the continuing discrimination against US citizens on the basis of geography.

---

93   United States v. Reese, 92 U.S. 214 (1876).
94   United States v. Cruikshank, 92 U.S. 542 (1876).
95   Civil Rights Cases, 109 U.S. 3 (1883).
96   Plessy v. Ferguson, 163 U.S. 537 (1896).
97   Williams v. Mississippi, 170 U.S. 213 (1898).
98   Cherokee Tobacco, 78 U.S. 616 (1870).
99   United States v. Kagama, 118 U.S. 375 (1886).
100 Lone Wolf v. Hitchcock, 187 U.S. 553 (1903).
101 Chae Chan Ping v. United States, 130 U.S. 581 (1889).
102 Fong Yue Ting v. United States, 149 U.S. 698 (1893).

Such differentiation and discrimination may be an aspect of what Levinson identifies as the multicultural exception: frequent decisions by the Supreme Court and lower courts to protect diversity and exception in the American polity.[103] Many of the persons residing in the United States' unincorporated territories see themselves as members of separate societies and are deeply ambivalent about relinquishing their distinct identities. In contrast, most US citizens residing in the states identify much more with the United States as a whole rather than with their state of residence. Accordingly, Congress, the Department of Interior, and US courts have often acted to uphold the distinct characters of the US territories (especially the Northern Marianas and American Samoa).

Yet this argument hardly seems sufficient. The protection of cultural and ethnic difference need not necessarily imply political hierarchy and promulgate inferior status.

Nor can the present condition be justified or explained away by saying that it is a "political question,"[104] as Judge Torruella wrote in his concurrence in the First Circuit Court's decision in *Igartúa de la Rosa v. United States*—no more so than can the persistence of judicial passivity in opposition to long-standing precedents on behalf of other powerless groups be explained away. The powerless groups are caught "in an untenable Catch-22," in the words of Judge Torruella.[105] Although he cited *Brown v. Board of Education*[106] and *Carolene Products*[107] as the pathbreaking cases in point,[108] he could have equally mentioned *Hammer v. Dagenhart*[109] or *Hernández v. Texas*.[110]

Congress's control over areas beyond its electorate, beyond the residents of the fifty states and the area of the United States as it is typically understood— but not beyond the areas occupied by US citizens and American nationals, and therefore distinct from most interpretations of "extraterritoriality"—remains a peculiar and little-understood authority.

The incorporation doctrine may be seen as exerting a Mobius-like effect, consistent with Justice Harlan's dissent in *Downes*. Harlan argued that the majority, by rejecting the argument that the Constitution applied *ex proprio vigore* to the United States' new territories, was determining that

103 Sanford Levinson, "Why the Canon Should Be Expanded to Include the Insular Cases and the Saga of American Expansionism," *Constitutional Commentary* 17 (2000): 241-66.
104 Igartúa de la Rosa v. United States, 229 F.3d 80, 88 (1st Cir. 2000) (Torruella, C.J., concurring).
105 Ibid., 89 (Torruella, C.J., concurring).
106 Brown v. Bd. of Educ., 347 U.S. 483 (1954).
107 United States v. Carolene Products Co., 304 U.S. 144 (1938).
108 Igartúa de la Rosa v. United States, 229 F.3d 80, 89 (1st Cir. 2000).
109 Hammer v. Dagenhart, 247 U.S. 251 (1918).
110 Hernández v. Texas, 347 U.S. 475 (1954).

"Congress may, by action taken outside of the Constitution, engraft upon our republican institutions a colonial system such as it exists under monarchical governments."[111] In other words, the Supreme Court's interpretation of the territory clause allows the Constitution to contradict itself—recursive in terms of logic—since one of the Constitution's own clauses has the capability of negating the Constitution's other provisions, depending on how Congress and the executive decide to apply that single territory clause.

Instead, the Supreme Court and the other federal courts have declined to revisit *Ocampo* and the other Insular Cases. They have thereby essentially left the incorporation doctrine, and the spatial discrimination that necessarily accompanies it, intact.

---

111 Downes v. Bidwell, 182 U.S. 244, 380 (1901) (Harlan, J., dissenting).

CHAPTER FOUR

The Insular Cases

A Declaration of Their Bankruptcy and My Harvard Pronouncement

Juan R. Torruella[*]

Today, I speak on the subject of the Insular Cases,[1] and how they impact, negatively in my opinion, the relationship of this nation with the nearly four million of its citizens who reside in Puerto Rico, within the confines of the time allotted to me this afternoon. I will do my best to discuss what in my view is an unconstitutional condition that has been in place for 116 years. I must preface these remarks by pointing out that I am, of course, expressing my own

---

[*] This chapter was delivered as the keynote address at Harvard Law School's "Reconsidering the Insular Cases" conference on February 19, 2014.

[1] See Huus v. N.Y. & Porto Rico S.S. Co., 182 U.S. 392 (1901) (holding that a vessel engaged in trade between Puerto Rico and New York was engaged in coastal trade and not foreign trade); Downes v. Bidwell, 182 U.S. 244 (1901) (holding that Puerto Rico did not become a part of the United States within the meaning of Article I, Section 8 of the Constitution); Armstrong v. United States, 182 U.S. 243 (1901) (invalidating tariffs imposed on goods exported from the United States to Puerto Rico after ratification of the treaty between the United States and Spain); Dooley v. United States, 182 U.S. 222 (1901) (holding that the right of the president to exact duties on imports into the United States from Puerto Rico ceased after the ratification of the peace treaty between the United States and Spain); Goetze v. United States, 182 U.S. 221 (1901) (holding that Puerto Rico and Hawaii were not foreign countries within the meaning of US tariff laws); De Lima v. Bidwell, 182 U.S. 1 (1901) (holding that Puerto Rico, once acquired by the United States through cession from Spain, was not a "foreign country" within the meaning of the tariff laws).

opinions, for which no one else can or should be held accountable. I do not feel inhibited in expressing them publicly because, with a few exceptions that will become apparent before I finish, almost everything that I will say today has previously been stated by me officially, and thus publicly.[2] Somewhat related to this caveat, and also for reasons that will become apparent later during the course of my comments, I should commence by stating that I was born a US citizen in Puerto Rico, which is my home and where I have my residence and domicile.

With those preliminary matters resolved, I will get directly to the subject at hand. In a nutshell, the Insular Cases represent classic *Plessy v. Ferguson*[3] legal doctrine and thought that should be eradicated from present-day constitutional reasoning. The Insular Cases were flawed when decided because they (i) directly clashed with our Constitution, (ii) were disobedient to controlling constitutional jurisprudence in place at the time, and (iii) contravened, without exception, every single historical precedent and practice of territorial expansion since our beginning as a nation, starting with the lands subject to the Northwest Ordinance of 1789,[4] through our final continental expansion in 1848 as a result of the war with Mexico.[5] There is, of course, an additional, powerful reason why the Insular Cases should be disavowed by the Supreme Court; and that is because the principles that they promote run contrary to the express provisions of international treaties entered into by the United States, including but not limited to the International Covenant on Civil and Political Rights (ICCPR), which has been the law of the land since its ratification by the Senate on June 8, 1992.[6] Lastly, but perhaps most

---

2   See, e.g., Igartúa de la Rosa v. United States, 417 F.3d 145, 158-84 (1st Cir. 2005) (Torruella, J., dissenting).

3   Plessy v. Ferguson, 163 U.S. 537 (1896).

4   An Act to Provide for the Government of the Territory of the United States North-West of the River Ohio, ch. 8, 1 Stat. 50 (1789); Arnold H. Leibowitz, *Defining Status: A Comprehensive Analysis of United States Territorial Relations* (Dordrecht: Martinus Nijhoff, 1989), 6. Leibowitz writes: "The Northwest Ordinance not only set forth the pattern of territorial development which exists even today but also stated the underlying principle of territorial evolution in U.S. law and tradition: that the goal of all territorial acquisition eventually was to be Statehood." The lands covered by the Northwest Ordinance were acquired as a result of the Treaty of Paris, ending the war for independence. Great Britain ceded its claims to all lands west of the Appalachian Mountains as far west as the Mississippi River, north to Canada, and south to Florida. See Definitive Treaty of Peace between the United States of America and His Britannic Majesty, U.S.-Gr. Brit., Sept. 3, 1783, 8 Stat. 80.

5   Treaty of Peace, Friendship, Limits, and Settlement with the Republic of Mexico, U.S.-Mex., Feb. 2, 1848, 9 Stat. 922.

6   International Covenant on Civil and Political Rights, G.A. Res. 2200A (XXI), U.N. GAOR, 21st Sess., Supp. No. 16, at 52, U.N. Doc. A/6316 (Dec. 16, 1966), 999

significantly even in today's cynical world, the Insular Cases should be soundly rejected because they represent the thinking of a morally bankrupt era in our history that goes against the most basic precept for which this nation stands: *the equality before the law of all its citizens.*

It is appropriate that we gather today to reconsider the Insular Cases here at Harvard, for it was here, and to a lesser extent at Yale, that we find the intellectual origins of both the Insular Cases and the discriminatory rules they purposely promoted to keep the several million residents of Puerto Rico—who in 1917 became American citizens—in an inferior colonial status. These policies did not come about by chance or accident, for as Rubin Frances Weston convincingly states in his book, *Racism in U.S. Imperialism*:

> Those who advocated overseas expansion faced this dilemma: What kind of relationship would the new peoples have to the body politic? Was it to be the relationship of the Reconstruction period, an attempt at political equality for dissimilar races, or was it to be the Southern "counterrevolutionary" point of view which denied the basic American constitutional rights to people of color? The actions of the federal government during the imperial period and the relegation of the Negro to a status of second-class citizenship indicated that the Southern point of view would prevail. The racism which caused the relegation of the Negro to a status of inferiority was to be applied to the overseas possessions of the United States.[7]

There is ample evidence to support Weston's account. To give you just a smattering, let me quote Simeon Baldwin, at the time a Yale law professor. Baldwin's article "The Constitutional Questions Incident to the Acquisition and Government by the United States of Island Territory" was published in the *Harvard Law Review* in 1899. In that article, he made his views on the rights of Puerto Ricans very clear. According to Baldwin, "[It would be unwise] to give . . . the ignorant and lawless brigands that infest Puerto Rico . . . the benefit[s] of [the Constitution]."[8]

Actually, at the time the eminent professor from Yale made this derogatory statement about the "ignorant and lawless brigands that infest Puerto Rico," nearly 400 years had passed since the founding of Puerto Rico's capital city, San Juan, in 1509. This means that Puerto Rico's capital city predates the pilgrims landing here in Massachusetts by over one

---

U.N.T.S. 171, *entered into force* Mar. 23, 1976 [hereinafter ICCPR].

7   Rubin Francis Weston, *Racism in U.S. Imperialism: The Influence of Racial Assumptions on American Foreign Policy, 1893-1946* (Columbia: University of South Carolina Press, 1972), 15.

8   Simeon E. Baldwin, "The Constitutional Questions Incident to the Acquisition and Government by the United States of Island Territory," *Harvard Law Review* 12 (1899): 393-416, 415.

hundred years. And when US troops landed in Puerto Rico in 1898—the year before Professor Baldwin characterized Puerto Ricans as ignorant and lawless—Puerto Ricans were already full-fledged Spanish citizens with the same voting rights as other Spanish subjects, including representation in the Spanish Parliament, where Puerto Rico was entitled to fifteen delegates and five senators. Notably, these are rights that we have yet to achieve after 116 years of US sovereignty.

Articles like Professor Baldwin's, including those by Harvard's own professors Christopher Langdell,[9] Abbott Lowell,[10] and James Thayer,[11] provided the academic ammunition for what eventually became the Insular Cases doctrine. This doctrine, concocted out of thin air, created two kinds of territories: first, incorporated territories, which as it turned out, were all those acquired prior to the Spanish-American War and included Hawaii and Alaska, and second, unincorporated ones, all of which happened to have been annexed after the Spanish-American War, and which included Puerto Rico, the Philippines, Guam, and later, the US Virgin Islands (purchased from Denmark in 1917). It is thus apparent that the Insular Cases doctrine—which held that the Constitution did not apply in full force to the unincorporated territories and instead extended only a certain subset of rights deemed fundamental by the Supreme Court—was tailor-made to fit squarely into the racist views that, as I have described, were prevalent in US society at the time, particularly in the circles of power.

Importantly, under the Insular Cases doctrine, Congress was bestowed with "plenary power" to govern both kinds of territories pursuant to the so-called territory clause of the Constitution.[12] Thereafter, in a corollary to the Insular Cases, the Supreme Court ruled in 1922 in *Balzac v. Porto Rico*[13] that not even the 1917 grant of US citizenship to the inhabitants of Puerto Rico changed their constitutional rights as long as they remained residents of Puerto Rico. According to Chief Justice William Howard Taft, who authored *Balzac*, locality, not their individual status as citizens, was what determined which constitutional rights were bestowed upon individuals.[14] In the case of Puerto Ricans, all that the grant of citizenship meant—according to Taft—was

9   C. C. Langdell, "The Status of Our New Territories," *Harvard Law Review* 12 (1899): 365-92.

10   Abbott Lawrence Lowell, "The Status of Our New Possessions: A Third View," *Harvard Law Review* 13 (1899): 155-76.

11   James Bradley Thayer, "Our New Possessions," *Harvard Law Review* 12 (1899): 464-85.

12   U.S. Const., art. IV, § 3, cl. 2 ("The Congress shall have Power to dispose of and make all needful Rules and Regulations respecting the Territory or other Property belonging to the United States.").

13   Balzac v. Porto Rico, 258 U.S. 298 (1922).

14   See ibid., 309.

that they could travel to the mainland and there, upon establishing residency, exercise the full rights of other US citizens.

Of course, Taft's unfortunate views on the rights of Puerto Ricans are not particularly surprising when one considers his troubled history with the US territories prior to his taking the bench. By way of background, Taft had been governor of the Philippines in the middle of its three-year insurrection, during which time the United States lost more troops than in the entire Spanish-American War.[15] He had also been president of the United States when the federal government had a run-in with the Puerto Rico legislature over judicial appointments. As a result of that conflict, sometimes referred to as the "Puerto Rican Appropriation Crisis of 1909,"[16] the Puerto Rico legislature refused to approve the budget, as was its right under the Foraker Act that governed Puerto Rico.[17] Then-President Taft responded by going before Congress to say that Puerto Ricans had been given more power than was good for them.[18]

It came as little surprise, then, when the court in *Balzac* ultimately concluded that the right to trial by jury was not a fundamental right applicable to the citizens who resided in Puerto Rico.[19] In so ruling, the court totally bypassed its holdings in *Hawaii v. Mankichi*[20] and *Rassmussen v. United States*,[21] in which it had ruled that the granting of US citizenship to the inhabitants of Hawaii and Alaska, respectively, upon acquisition of these territories indicated a desire to incorporate these territories into the United States, so the full application of the Constitution to their inhabitants was required, including the right to trial by jury.

Now, I realize that my calling the United States a "colonial" nation is repugnant to most Americans, and thus, when I proceed to make this claim, I do so with some hesitation. As Americans, we do not consider ourselves to

---

15 With regard to the Philippines, the "Philippine-American War lasted three years and resulted in the death of over 4,200 American and over 20,000 Filipino combatants." US Department of State, Office of the Historian, "Milestones: 1899-1913," accessed Oct. 29, 2014, http://history.state.gov/milestones/1899-1913/war. And with regard to the Spanish-American War, "From combat, 345 American officers and men died; from disease, 2,565." Donald H. Dyal, *Historical Dictionary of the Spanish-American War* (Westport, CT: Greenwood Press, 1996), 97.
16 Truman Clark, "President Taft and the Puerto Rican Appropriation Crisis of 1909," *Americas* 26 (1969): 152-70, 152, quoted in Juan R. Torruella, "Ruling America's Colonies: The Insular Cases," *Yale Law and Policy Review* 32 (2013): 57-95, 76.
17 See Organic Act of 1900 (Foraker Act), ch. 191, 31 Stat. 77 (1900) (repealed 1917).
18 William Howard Taft, "Message to Congress (May 10, 1909)," in *The Collected Works of William Howard Taft*, vol. 3, ed. David Burton (Athens: Ohio University Press, 2002), 96.
19 See Balzac v. Porto Rico, 258 U.S. 298, 309-11 (1922).
20 Hawaii v. Mankichi, 190 U.S. 197 (1903).
21 Rassmussen v. United States, 197 U.S. 516 (1905).

be within this anachronistic category. I thus apologize if my statement causes a modicum of discomfort. But do you think that the reality of this fact of life is any less repugnant to those of us who find ourselves in the degrading status of second-class citizens, merely because we reside *as citizens* of the United States in a piece of land that, although belonging to the United States and owing allegiance thereto, has been declared by judicial fiat to be an unequal part of this nation? How do you think this status sits with me who, although sitting on the second-highest federal court of the nation, often deciding issues of national importance, am denied the right to vote for those who occupy the national offices that decide my destiny and pass the laws that I enforce and that permeate every facet of my daily life? Leaving aside all the legal niceties that we are discussing today, does that make any sense to you? It certainly does not to me.

Let me digress a moment and explain why Puerto Rico's relationship to the United States is a colonial one, regardless of the label we may use—and there have been many—including "territory"; "unincorporated territory"; my favorite, "the state of eternal inequality"; or, as Chief Justice Melville Fuller described it in his masterful dissent in *Downes v. Bidwell*, "a disembodied shade."[22] Our official English title, the Commonwealth of Puerto Rico, is translated as *estado libre asociado*, or "free associated state," a legal oxymoron, with emphasis on the moron, if ever I have heard one. No matter the label used, I will explain why the relationship between Puerto Rico and the United States is a colonial one and why the resolution of this conundrum that is Puerto Rico's colonial condition is of prime relevance to the invalidation of the Insular Cases and all that emanates from them.

UNESCO's *Dictionary of Social Sciences* defines "colony" as "a territory, subordinate in various ways—political, cultural, or economic—to a more developed country. Supreme legislative power and much of the administration rest[s] with the controlling country, which [is] usually of a different ethnic group from the colony."[23] This definition fits the United States–Puerto Rico relationship like a glove. And while I will focus only on the issue of political subordination today, it should be readily apparent that the economic subordination of Puerto Rico to US interests is equally overwhelming.

As I have stated, the US citizens who reside in Puerto Rico have no vote for national offices, nor do they have any voting members of Congress in either house. The office of resident commissioner, our single so-called representative in Congress, has no vote before that body in the enactment of legislation.[24] The office is, constitutionally speaking, a sad commentary on a

---

22   Downes v. Bidwell, 182 U.S. 244, 372 (Fuller, C.J., dissenting).
23   Julius Gould and William Kolb, eds., *A Dictionary of the Social Sciences* (New York: Free Press, 1964), 102. This source is sanctioned by UNESCO.
24   See U.S. General Accounting Office, *Report to the Chairman, Committee on*

nation that prides itself on being the bastion of democracy; in polite terms, the office is "politically impaired." Were Puerto Ricans treated equally and in the same manner as the rest of the nation, with our present population, we would have a larger congressional delegation than more than half of the states, and that is a principal reason why Congress keeps us in our present colonial condition.

I will never forget the meeting that I had several years ago with Senator John Chafee of Rhode Island when I was the chief judge of the First Circuit, and met with him on matters related to our court building in Old San Juan. At the time, there was pending in Congress one of the interminable Puerto Rico status proposals. The senator asked me for my views on what the ultimate status should be. I expressed my well-known personal views, to which he retorted:

> I don't know. I come from one of the original thirteen colonies. We have two Senators and one Congressman. If Puerto Rico becomes a state, you'll have two Senators also, and seven or eight Congressmen, and they'll probably all be democrats! I don't know if I can go for that.

But this problem is not confined to Congress; the federal bureaucracy in Puerto Rico follows suit. It is appointed, controlled, and led from afar, in a place where we have no political clout and where we who are without electoral significance must go hat in hand asking for charity. We are at their mercy. "Plenary power" is how the courts have described Congress's power over us under the Insular Cases,[25] which again, in this era where false labeling is commonplace, means "practically unfettered colonial power." Regarding political subordination, can there be any question that Puerto Rico and the US citizens who reside therein are totally subordinated politically to the United States?

Particularly irritating, to say the least, but illustrative, are two fairly recent cases that rely on the Insular Cases as the legal basis for upholding the unequal treatment of Puerto Ricans. In the first case, *Califano v. Torres*,[26] a woman living in Connecticut qualified to receive Supplemental Security Income, or SSI, as this program is cryptically labeled.[27] SSI is a Social Security program that grants benefits to qualified aged, blind, and disabled persons. After qualifying for SSI, the woman found her benefits withdrawn when she moved from Connecticut to Puerto Rico because the Social Security

---

Resources, House of Representatives: U.S. Insular Areas; Application of the U.S. Constitution (Washington, DC: General Accounting Office, 1997), 26-28.

25 Downes v. Bidwell, 182 U.S. 244, 268 (1901).
26 Califano v. Torres, 435 U.S. 1 (1978).
27 42 U.S.C. § 1381.

statute granted SSI benefits only to residents of the "United States,"[28] whose definition included only the states of the Union. The court, in approving the unequal treatment as authorized by the Insular Cases, gave three grounds to justify its holding: First, Puerto Rican residents did not "contribute to the public treasury," a statement that should be irrelevant considering that the US residents of Puerto Rico fully contribute to the Social Security system.[29] Second, the court ruled that the cost of giving SSI benefits to qualified aged, blind, and disabled citizens residing in Puerto Rico would be great—estimated at $300 million per year.[30] While I have my doubts, even if we accept the court's math, the cost of equality is a factor that is not usually determinative when correcting a constitutional violation.[31] And most disturbing of all, the court's third point, related to its second, was that "inclusion of [Puerto Rico residents in] the SSI program might seriously disrupt the Puerto Rican economy."[32] This is an outrageous reason for denying needy citizens benefits that are provided nationwide, an argument that is best answered by quoting Justice Thurgood Marshall's riposte in *Harris v. Rosario*,[33] a similar case involving the Aid to Families with Dependent Children program, in which he said:

> This rationale [that giving larger economic relief to the needy would disrupt the Puerto Rican economy] has troubling overtones. It suggests that programs designed to help the poor should be less fully applied in those areas where the need may be the greatest, simply because otherwise the relative poverty of the recipients compared to other persons in the same geographic area will somehow be upset. Similarly, reliance on the fear of disrupting the Puerto Rican economy implies that Congress intended to preserve or even strengthen the comparative economic position of the States vis-à-vis Puerto Rico.[34]

Setting aside for a moment the subject of where the Insular Cases have gotten us today, I would like to briefly turn now to the question of how we got here. The historical context in which these decisions were crafted speaks volumes as to how they came about, but in the interest of brevity, I will touch only upon some buzz words descriptive of the most important subject headings in this regard. First on the list is Manifest Destiny, the mantra of Darwinian imperialism that promoted American territorial expansion under

28   42 U.S.C. § 1382c(E) (1970 ed., Supp. V).
29   Califano v. Torres, 435 U.S. 1, 5 n.7 (1978).
30   See ibid.
31   See Rozecki v. Gaughan, 459 F.2d 6, 8 (1st Cir. 1972) ("Humane considerations and constitutional requirements are not, in this day, to be measured or limited by dollar considerations." (quoting Jackson v. Bishop, 404 F.2d 571, 580 (8th Cir. 1968))).
32   Califano v. Torres, 435 U.S. 1, 5 n.7 (1978).
33   Harris v. Rosario, 446 U.S. 651, 655-56 (1980) (Marshall, J., dissenting).
34   Ibid.

a mixed bag of geopolitical theory, religious righteousness, and economic entrepreneurship. The concept of Manifest Destiny was at its peak in public opinion and governmental circles before and during the time the Insular Cases were decided, as evidenced by Chief Justice John Marshall's references to the "American Empire."[35] Second, the Civil War had just ended, and the nation wanted to focus its attention away from that horrendous fratricidal conflict. Third, *Plessy v. Ferguson*, decided in 1896 by almost the same court as the one that ruled on the Insular Cases, provided the immediate backdrop and a legal basis for the disparate racial treatment of persons under the jurisdiction of the United States. Fourth, it was argued—although in my opinion not in a constitutionally significant way—that the newly conquered territories were different from those previously acquired in that they were noncontiguous to the mainland United States, separated by large expanses of oceans, and home to different races, languages, religions, and cultures than those found in the continental United States.

I should point out that, in fact, these cases were decided by a bare 5-4 plurality, in which the opinions of the dissenting justices received the largest number of unanimous votes. The shaky grounds of this plurality led President Theodore Roosevelt in 1902, at the retirement of Justice Horace Gray, a member of the plurality, to ask Massachusetts Senator Henry Cabot Lodge to inquire from Oliver Wendell Holmes, Jr., then being considered for appointment to substitute Justice Gray, about his views on the outcomes of these cases. It was only after the senator assured the president that Holmes agreed with their outcome that President Roosevelt appointed him to the court.[36]

With this brief sketch of the pertinent historical background in mind, we come to the constitutional and legal failings of the Insular Cases, what I would label their original sin or *ab initio* infirmity. We commence with the language of the treaty by which the United States acquired Puerto Rico—that is, article IX of the Treaty of Paris, which states that "the civil rights and political status of the native inhabitants of the territories . . . ceded to the United States shall be determined by the Congress."[37]

This is clearly in direct contravention to the Constitution—the source from which civil and political rights and status emanate, *not* Congress—a failing that was vehemently pointed out by Justice John Marshall Harlan in his dissent in the key Insular Case of *Downes v. Bidwell*[38] and has been equally emphasized by Justice Anthony Kennedy in the recent Guantánamo case of

35 See, e.g., Loughborough v. Blake, 18 U.S. 317, 319 (1820) ("Does this term designate the whole, or any particular portion of the American empire?").

36 See G. Edward White, *Justice Oliver Wendell Holmes: Law and the Inner Self* (New York: Oxford University Press, 1993), 234-37.

37 Treaty of Peace between the United States of America and the Kingdom of Spain, U.S.-Spain, art. IX, Dec. 10, 1898, 30 Stat. 1754.

38 Downes v. Bidwell, 182 U.S. 244, 380 (1901) (Harlan, J., dissenting).

Boumediene v. Bush.[39] Concluding that a treaty cannot trump the Constitution does not require the IQ of a rocket scientist. This very point was summed up by Justice Harlan in *Downes* when he stated:

> The idea that this country may acquire territories anywhere upon the earth, by conquest or treaty, and hold them as mere colonies or provinces,—the people inhabiting them to enjoy only such rights as Congress chooses to accord them,—is wholly inconsistent with the spirit and genius, as well as with the words of the Constitution.[40]

To this, Justice Kennedy cogently added in *Boumediene*: "The Constitution grants Congress and the President the power to acquire, dispose of, and govern territory, not the power to decide when and where its terms apply."[41]

The further fact is that there is nothing in the text *or* legislative history (e.g., the *Federalist Papers*) of the Constitution in which the word "colony" is even mentioned,[42] much less in which colonies or colonial government are made a part of our governmental structure. This is not surprising considering that after our long, cruel, and exhausting war to break our own colonial chains, the idea that we would turn around and consider establishing that same method of government as a component of our new nation would have been hypocritical to say the least.

Moreover, that the so-called territory clause—on which the Insular Cases court relied as the source of power allowing Congress to create an

---

39   Boumediene v. Bush, 553 U.S. 723, 727 (2008).
40   Downes v. Bidwell, 182 U.S. 244, 380 (1901) (Harlan, J., dissenting).
41   Boumediene v. Bush, 553 U.S. 723, 765 (2008).
42   In the interest of accuracy, I must acknowledge that Federalist No. 52 does contain the word "colony," used in the following context: "Virginia was the colony which stood first in resisting the parliamentary usurpations of Great Britain." More pertinently, the *Federalist Papers* do address the existence of "colonies," but only in terms of how preexisting colonies might be admitted as states; nothing in the text suggests that the United States might possess colonies and retain them as such. In Federalist No. 43, when discussing the powers conferred by the Constitution, James Madison noted the following:

> In the articles of Confederation, no provision is found on this important subject [of the admission of new states]. Canada was to be admitted of right, on her joining in the measures of the United States; and the other colonies, by which were evidently meant the other British colonies, at the discretion of nine States. The eventual establishment of new States seems to have been overlooked by the compilers of that instrument. We have seen the inconvenience of this omission, and the assumption of power into which Congress have been led by it. With great propriety, therefore, has the new system supplied the defect.

American colonial empire—did not in fact or law grant such power had been clearly established by the Supreme Court in two cases decided before the Insular Cases. In the first of these, *Loughborough v. Blake*,[43] the Supreme Court decided the same issue that came before it in the leading Insular Case, *Downes v. Bidwell*—namely, whether the Constitution applied in a territory. In *Loughborough*, which dealt with the District of Columbia, Chief Justice Marshall in clear and unflinching language stated that the term "United States," when used in the Constitution, included both the states and territories, and that "[t]he District of Columbia, or territory west of the Missouri, is not less within the United States, than Maryland or Pennsylvania," and thus the Constitution applied in the territories as well.[44]

The applicability of the Constitution in a territory came up again thirty-six years after *Loughborough* in *Dred Scott v. Sandford*,[45] this time in relation to the due process clause of the Fifth Amendment. Although the *Scott* case is discredited for other reasons, and rightly so, it nevertheless established two important constitutional principles related to the subject of today's discussion. The first principle is that the United States lacks constitutional authority to have colonies or to hold territory in a colonial condition. As Chief Justice Roger B. Taney stated:

> There is certainly no power given by the Constitution to the Federal Government to establish or maintain colonies bordering on the United States or at a distance, to be ruled and governed at its own pleasure; nor to enlarge its territorial limits in any way, except by the admission of new States. . . . [N]o power is given to acquire a Territory to be held and governed [in a] permanently [colonial] character.[46]

The second principle established by *Scott* relates to the reach of the territory clause, which as you are aware by now is the alleged source for the exercise of plenary power (i.e., colonial power) by Congress over Puerto Rico. The *Scott* court had this to say about the territory clause:

> [T]he plaintiff has laid much stress upon that article in the Constitution which confers on Congress the power "to dispose of and make all needful rules and regulations respecting the territory or other property belonging to the United States;" but, in the judgment of the court, that provision . . . was intended to be confined, to the territory which at [the] time [of its independence from Great Britain] belonged to, or was claimed by, the United States . . . and can have no influence upon a territory afterwards acquired from a foreign Government. It was a

---

43   Loughborough v. Blake, 18 U.S. 317 (1820).
44   Ibid., 319.
45   Dred Scott v. Sandford, 60 U.S. 393 (1856).
46   Ibid., 446.

special provision for a known and particular territory, and to meet a
present emergency, and nothing more.[47]

Although there are clearly many problems with the Insular Cases
that warrant discussion, one point that is often overlooked is the fact that
these cases have been applied in a selectively discriminatory manner by the
court, even in relatively modern times. A prime example of this is the case
of *Reid v. Covert*[48] and its companion case of *Kinsella v. Krueger*,[49] involving
the murder convictions of two accompanying wives of servicemen, tried
by courts-martial in England and Japan, respectively, pursuant to the then
prevalent code of military justice. The convictions by these military tribunals
were overturned by the Supreme Court for failure to afford the accused the
constitutional benefits of indictment by a grand jury and trial before a petit
jury of twelve of their peers. Notably, the court refused to apply the Insular
Cases or *Balzac* doctrines. In rejecting the claim by the government that the
convictions should stand under the Insular Cases, Justice Felix Frankfurter, in
a separately filed opinion, stated that this doctrine "represent[ed], historically
and juridically, an episode of the dead past about as unrelated to the world
of today as the one-hoss shay to the latest jet plane."[50] The powerful plurality
opinion of Justice Hugo Black followed suit, observing that the Insular Cases
had been decided "at the turn of the century" and that "neither the cases nor
their reasoning should be given any further expansion."[51]

Unfortunately, although *Reid* gave hope for an early demise of the
Insular Cases, that expectation has come to naught as the later court has
continued to breathe life into these cases in a manner that perpetuates the
unequal treatment of Puerto Ricans.[52]

Continuing on to the subject of treaties relevant to the topic at hand,
I turn to the ICCPR, by which the United States undertook "to respect and
to ensure to all individuals within its territory and subject to its jurisdiction
the [right to vote], without distinction of any kind,"[53] and agreed "to take the
necessary steps, in accordance with its constitutional processes and with the

---

47 Ibid., 432.
48 Reid v. Covert, 351 U.S. 487 (1956), on reh'g, 354 U.S. 1 (1957).
49 Kinsella v. Krueger, 351 U.S. 470 (1956), on reh'g, 354 U.S. 1 (1957).
50 Ibid., 482 (Frankfurter, J., reserving judgment).
51 Reid v. Covert, 354 U.S. 1, 14 (1957).
52 See, e.g., Harris v. Rosario, 446 U.S. 651, 651-52 (1980) (per curiam) ("Congress,
    which is empowered under the Territory Clause of the Constitution, U.S. Const.,
    art. IV, § 3, cl. 2, to 'make all needful Rules and Regulations respecting the Territory
    ... belonging to the United States,' may treat Puerto Rico differently from States so
    long as there is a rational basis for its actions.").
53 ICCPR, art. 2(1).

provisions of the present Covenant, to adopt such laws or other measures as may be necessary to give effect to [that right]."[54]

The executive branch, however, has vigorously opposed the enforcement of these treaty rights, a position with which the courts have repeatedly sided,[55] holding that this treaty is not self-executing and thus does not create private causes of action. This outcome clearly ignores the fact that the treaty establishes the United States' affirmative obligation "[t]o ensure that any person whose rights or freedoms [as recognized in the ICCPR] are violated shall have an effective remedy,"[56] to provide that such person "shall have [his or her] right determined by a competent judicial . . . authorit[y]," and to "develop the possibilities of judicial remed[ies]."[57] Unfortunately, the courts of the United States have refused to enforce this treaty domestically. But these outcomes notwithstanding, this treaty is still the law of the land, even if the courts refuse to allow individuals to enforce these rights.

At the time of the ICCPR's ratification by the Senate, the US Department of State made the affirmative representation that "existing US law generally complies with the ICCPR"[58] and that "[i]n general, the substantive provisions of the [ICCPR] are consistent with the letter and spirit of the United States Constitution and laws, both state and federal."[59] This diplomatic doublespeak, not to call it by its true name, is sadly in keeping with the now more than one-hundred-year history of the three branches of government turning a blind eye to the ongoing inequities to which the people of Puerto Rico have been and continue to be subjected.

In sum, I believe that the following principles emanate from what I have discussed, establishing the constitutional infirmity of the Insular Cases and requiring their rejection: (i) first, article IX of the Treaty of Paris, delegating to Congress the power to determine the constitutional rights of the inhabitants of Puerto Rico, contravenes the Constitution because the Constitution is the source and instrument that establishes such rights, and no treaty can grant Congress the power to abridge them; (ii) second, pursuant to article IX of the Treaty of Paris, and relying on a faulty interpretation of the territory clause of the Constitution, Congress has established a colonial relationship between the United States and Puerto Rico; (iii) third, the Constitution does not authorize the United States to acquire or hold territory in a colonial relationship; (iv) fourth, the territory clause cannot be the basis for exercising "plenary

---

54 Ibid., art. 2(2).
55 See Igartúa de la Rosa v. United States, 417 F.3d 145 (1st Cir. 2005) (en banc).
56 See ICCPR, art. 2(3)(a).
57 Ibid., art. 2(3)(b).
58 S. Exec. Rep. No. 102-23, at 19 (1992).
59 Ibid., 10.

powers" over Puerto Rico because such powers amount to the establishment of a colonial relationship in that, at a minimum, the United States exercises supreme legislative power over Puerto Rico while depriving its inhabitants of all national suffrage rights with regard to Congress and the national executive branch; (v) fifth, the actions of the United States regarding the rights of its citizens who reside in Puerto Rico contravene all incidences and historical practices and precedents regarding all other territories acquired by the United States prior to 1898; (vi) sixth, the intellectual origins of the Insular Cases are patently discriminatory and morally reprehensible; and (vii) seventh, the United States' ongoing perpetuation of Insular Cases–sanctioned policies violates international human rights principles and treaties entered into by the United States, which are the law of the land by virtue of the supremacy clause of the Constitution.

Although this completes my official presentation regarding the Insular Cases, I am compelled to add a brief postscript, which I have pompously labeled "my Harvard pronouncement."

In 1964, Justice Black stated the case more eloquently than I possibly could when he said:

> No right is more precious in a free country than that of having a voice in the election of those who make the laws under which, as good citizens, we must live. Other rights, even the most basic, are illusory if the right to vote is undermined.[60]

Given that the US citizens of Puerto Rico have no political power and that the courts have turned their backs on Puerto Ricans' rights as citizens, we have to wonder what comes next. The people of Puerto Rico may soon have no alternative but to look for other peaceful avenues of obtaining relief from these enduring inequities. This is particularly the case given that in a recent referendum, a majority of the Puerto Ricans who voted rejected the continuation of our present colonial status. It is now an unassailable fact that what we have in the United States–Puerto Rico relationship is government without the consent or participation of the governed. I cannot imagine a more egregious civil rights violation, particularly in a country that touts itself as the bastion of democracy throughout the world. This is a situation that cannot, and should not, be further tolerated.

Although there is pending before Congress possible legislation to break this Gordian knot, unfortunately, judging by history and considering what we have seen in recent times, one would have to be optimistic beyond reality to expect that anything significant will emerge in the foreseeable future.

---

60   Wesberry v. Sanders, 376 U.S. 1, 17 (1964).

Given the prospect of the continuation of our interminable status quo, Puerto Ricans may reasonably come to believe that the time has come to take some more noticeable action than in the past, because there exists, and has existed, a major civil rights issue that has been lingering for more than one hundred years and does not seem to get resolved by the exercise of only patience and good manners. One step that the US citizens of Puerto Rico may consider is gradually engaging in time-honored civil rights actions, of which there are many successful examples. One that comes to mind, because economics—that is, hitting the pocketbook—seems to bring about results, is the use of economic boycotts to attract attention to ongoing civil rights violations. This is a mode of protest that has been used successfully to correct civil rights violations, starting with the Boston Tea Party, to Mahatma Gandhi's march to the sea and boycott to protest the salt tax by the British in India, to the bus boycott in Montgomery to protest segregation and Rosa Parks's treatment, to the California grape boycott, etc., etc.

Note carefully, this is not a call for drastic action but rather a call for recognition of the simple fact that Puerto Rico's consumers represent one of the most important markets for US products, constituting the largest per capita importers of US goods in the world.[61] Puerto Rico also produces $35 billion in annual retail sales alone,[62] mostly of US goods. Additionally, some of the US-owned companies conducting business in Puerto Rico are among the most successful in the entire nation, against which concerted economic action would quickly attract attention. When we add to the almost four million consumers in Puerto Rico the equal number of Puerto Ricans residing throughout other parts of the United States, we can begin to imagine the potential impact that such concerted actions would provide. And of course, we ought not forget the larger Latino constituency, which is now the largest minority in the United States and which could be sympathetic to correcting the inequalities to which the US citizens of Puerto Rico are being subjected, merely because they reside in Puerto Rico. There are, of course, others who may be sympathetic to the plight of the US citizens residing in Puerto Rico because of their own experiences with inequality, so the number of possible actors is truly impressive.

Lack of political clout can perhaps be substituted by economic impact, which in many cases is equally or even more effective. I believe economic

---

61   Juan González, *Harvest of Empire: A History of Latinos in America* (New York: Penguin, 2000), 85. See also World Business Organization, *Americas Review 2003-2004: Economic and Business Report* (London: Kogan Page, 2003), 281-82.

62   See "Puerto Rico Remains a Retail Mecca," *Caribbean Business*, accessed Oct. 29, 2014, http://www.caribbeanbusinesspr.com/cbdirectory/cb_retail.php?cat_id=13.

pressure is a logical avenue to consider, because if experience teaches us anything, it is that when there is a just cause that citizens can sympathize with, combined with national attention and economic concerns, the chances of ultimate success increase exponentially. Thus, because the judiciary and legislature continue to turn a blind eye to the present injustice, we should not be surprised if Puerto Ricans seek a more sympathetic, and powerful, audience.

Mine is but an idea that I place in the public forum. How these civil rights actions might be carried out, if at all, is beyond my expertise or power. But the suggested ideas bear consideration by those in a position to effect change.

There is now in circulation a postage stamp that has as its logo "equality forever." Unfortunately, we as a nation have yet to catch up to the postal department.

CHAPTER FIVE

From Conquest to Consent

Puerto Rico and the Prospect of Genuine Free Association

Chimène I. Keitner*

Introduction

The United States, like all countries, is both a geopolitical unit and an idea used to organize human activity. The term "United States" denotes a territorial, political, and legal construct whose boundaries are contextual, contingent, and at times contested. At the turn of the twentieth century, debates about the boundaries of the United States and its citizenry manifested themselves in litigation over issues from tariffs to the right to a jury trial in acquired territories. The judicial resolution of these disputes, known as the Insular Cases, helped build the doctrinal edifice for American economic imperialism. Their legacy continues to shape the relationship between the United States and its "insular areas."[1]

The Insular Cases illustrate how the boundaries of the "United States" could shift depending on the context. For example, Justice Henry Billings

---

* Thanks are due to Maggi Qerimi and Igor Voloshin for research assistance and to Gerald L. Neuman and Tomiko Brown-Nagin for convening the conference "Reconsidering the Insular Cases."

1 The US Department of the Interior uses this term to refer to "[a] jurisdiction that is neither a part of one of the several States nor a Federal district." US Department of the Interior, Office of Insular Affairs, "Definitions of Insular Area Political Organizations," accessed Oct. 29, 2014, http://www.doi.gov/oia/islands/politicatypes.cfm.

Brown reasoned in *Downes v. Bidwell* that the expansive definition of the term
"United States" in a consular convention with France was not decisive for its
meaning in the Constitution because, "in dealing with foreign sovereignties,
the term 'United States' has a broader meaning than when used in the
Constitution, and includes all territories subject to the jurisdiction of the
Federal government, wherever located."[2] Parsing different meanings of the term
"United States" enabled Justice Brown to conclude that "there may be territories
subject to the jurisdiction of the United States, which are not *of* the United
States."[3] This distinction facilitated the judicial creation of what Christina Duffy
Ponsa and Burke Marshall have called a "liminal category of territories subject
to U.S. sovereignty."[4] Puerto Rico belongs to this "liminal category."[5]

The reasonings of the Insular Cases are rooted in what might be called a
"conquest paradigm" of territorial governance, under which conquest remains
a lawful means of acquiring territory. Moreover, "acquired territory, in the
absence of agreement to the contrary, will bear such relation to the acquiring
government as may by it be determined."[6] Consistent with this paradigm,
the 1898 Treaty of Paris ending the war with Spain provided that "[t]he civil
rights and political status of the native inhabitants of the [formerly Spanish]

---

2   Downes v. Bidwell, 182 U.S. 244, 263 (1901).
3   Ibid., 278.
4   Christina Duffy Burnett (Ponsa) and Burke Marshall, "Between the Foreign
     and the Domestic: The Doctrine of Territorial Incorporation, Invented and
     Reinvented," in *Foreign in a Domestic Sense: Puerto Rico, American Expansion,
     and the Constitution*, ed. Christina Duffy Burnett and Burke Marshall (Durham,
     NC: Duke University Press, 2001), 16.
5   The remaining US territories include three polities currently on the United
     Nations' list of non-self-governing territories (the US Virgin Islands, American
     Samoa, and Guam) and two polities no longer on the list (the Commonwealth
     of Puerto Rico and the Commonwealth of the Northern Mariana Islands). See
     United Nations, "The United Nations and Decolonization: Non-Self-Governing
     Territories," accessed Oct. 29, 2014, http://www.un.org/en/decolonization/
     nonselfgovterritories.shtml. Three other polities that formed part of the Trust
     Territory of the Pacific Islands (the Republic of the Marshall Islands, the Federated
     States of Micronesia, and the Republic of Palau) are now United Nations member
     states and have compacts of "free association" with the United States. See
     US Department of the Interior, "Insular Areas of the United States and Freely
     Associated States," accessed Oct. 29, 2014, http://www.doi.gov/library/internet/
     insular.cfm.
6   Downes v. Bidwell, 182 U.S. 244, 306 (1901) (White, J., concurring). Not all turn-of-
     the-century observers agreed that the conquest paradigm prevented the inhabitants
     of acquired territories from enjoying equal rights under the US Constitution
     without further congressional action. See, e.g., Edward B. Whitney, "The Porto Rico
     Tariffs of 1899 and 1900," *Yale Law Journal* 9 (1900): 297-321, 321.

territories . . . shall be determined by the [US] Congress."[7] By the mid-twentieth century, the conquest paradigm had been replaced by a "consent paradigm," as detailed below. In 1900, however, the prevailing view denied the inhabitants of the United States' new acquisitions equal membership in the US political community, based on the territory clause of the US Constitution.[8] The subordination entailed by this approach has shaped the relationship between the United States and its current and former territories.

More than a century after the Treaty of Paris, the conquest paradigm continues to cast a long shadow. This is reflected in the work of the President's Task Force on Puerto Rico's Status.[9] In its 2011 report, the task force indicated that

> [t]he policy of the Federal executive branch has long been that Puerto Rico's status should be decided by the people of Puerto Rico. . . . Nevertheless, if a change of status is chosen by the people of the [*sic*] Puerto Rico, such a choice must be implemented through legislation enacted by Congress and signed by the President.[10]

The task force's emphasis on choice, which is consistent with the consent paradigm, is tempered by its emphasis on the need for congressional approval, which is a legacy of the conquest model.

Even if the consent model were implemented fully, there does not seem to be a clear consensus within Puerto Rico about the island's optimal political status. In 1998 and again in 2012, Puerto Ricans rejected the status quo and its attendant economic dysfunction—without, however, agreeing on a better alternative.[11] At the time of writing, Congress had allocated $2.5

---

7   Treaty of Peace between the United States of America and the Kingdom of Spain, U.S.-Spain, art. IX, Dec. 10, 1898, 30 Stat. 1754.

8   U.S. CONST., art. IV, § 3, cl. 2 ("The Congress shall have Power to dispose of and make all needful Rules and Regulations respecting the Territory or other Property belonging to the United States."). Kal Raustiala recounts, "On January 11, 1900, the *New York Times* ran this headline, seemingly stripped from the pages of today's satirical newspaper *The Onion*: 'Status of New Possessions: House Committee Named to Ascertain If They Are in Fact Parts of the United States.'" Kal Raustiala, *Does the Constitution Follow the Flag? The Evolution of Territoriality in American Law* (New York: Oxford University Press, 2009), 80.

9   President Clinton created this task force in 2000. See President's Task Force on Puerto Rico's Status, *Report by the President's Task Force on Puerto Rico's Status* (Washington, DC: White House, 2011), 15.

10 Ibid., 18.

11 "Elections in Puerto Rico: November 6, 2012 Political Status Plebiscite Canvass; Islandwide Totals," accessed Oct. 29, 2014, http://electionspuertorico.org/2012/plebiscite.vote.php; "Elections in Puerto Rico: 1998 Status Plebiscite Vote Summary," accessed Oct. 29, 2014, http://electionspuertorico.org/1998/summary.html.

million for a plebiscite on Puerto Rico's status and tasked the State Elections Commission with proposing voter education materials and a plebiscite ballot "not incompatible with the Constitution and laws and policies of the United States."[12] The recurring status question might be thought of in the following manner: What is the best way to ensure the material and psychic well-being of the island's 3.6 million residents while also taking into account the interests of the more than 4.8 million members of the Puerto Rican diaspora living in the United States?[13]

This chapter canvasses the international legal aspects of the status question. It traces the movement in international law from the conquest paradigm to the consent paradigm, which makes Puerto Rico's status an ongoing subject of inclusive international concern.[14] It highlights the disjunction between postcolonial aspirations and the reality of Puerto Rico's status as a "commonwealth" that is nevertheless still a US territory, and concludes by suggesting possible elements of a genuine free association agreement between Puerto Rico and the United States that would remove Puerto Rico from the purview of the territory clause.

From Conquest to Consent

At the turn of the twentieth century, Justice Edward White's influential concurrence in *Downes v. Bidwell* cited the conquest paradigm as a "general principle" of international law:

---

12 See "Explanatory Statement Submitted by Mr. Rogers of Kentucky, Chairman of the House Committee on Appropriations Regarding the House Amendment to the Senate Amendment on H.R. 3547, Consolidated Appropriations Act, 2014," Jan. 15, 2014, http://www.puertoricoreport.com/wp-content/uploads/2014/01/1-15-14-Joint-Explanatory-Statement-for-Final-Bill.pdf, 8. See also Pedro R. Pierluisi, letter to Angel Gonzalez Roman, Jorge Davila Torres, Eder Ortiz, and Juan Dalmau Ramirez, May 8, 2014, https://pierluisi.house.gov/sites/pierluisi .house.gov/files/5.8.14%20Rep.%20Pierluisi%20Letter%20to%20the%20 State%20Elections%20Commission%20of%20Puerto%20Rico.pdf.

13 Central Intelligence Agency, "Central America and the Caribbean: Puerto Rico," accessed Oct. 29, 2014, https://www.cia.gov/library/publications/the-world-factbook/ geos/rq.html; Juan C. Garcia-Ellin, "Demographic Transitions: Settlement and Distribution of the Puerto Rican Population in the United States," July 2013, http://www .academia.edu/4298905/Demographic_Transitions_Settlement_and_Distribution_of_ the_Puerto_Rican_Population_in_the_United_States.

14 As W. Michael Reisman and I wrote in 2003, even a formal free association arrangement would warrant continued monitoring, since "[a] pattern characterized by the continuing subordination of one community is a constant invocation of international scrutiny." See Chimène I. Keitner and W. Michael Reisman, "Free Association: The United States Experience," *Texas International Law Journal* 39 (2003): 1-63, 5.

> It may not be doubted that by the general principles of the law of nations every government which is sovereign within its sphere of action possesses as an inherent attribute the power to acquire territory by discovery, by agreement or treaty, and by conquest. It cannot also be gainsaid that, as a general rule, wherever a government acquires territory as a result of any of the modes above stated, the relation of the territory to the new government is to be determined by the acquiring power in the absence of stipulations upon the subject.[15]

The conquest paradigm thus entailed both the power to acquire territory by conquest and the ability to dictate the status of territory so acquired. In support of the United States' prerogative, Justice White cited Henry Wagner Halleck's treatise on international law[16] and the Declaration of Independence, which proclaimed that the United States could "do all other Acts and Things which Independent States may of right do."[17] Denying the United States the authority to determine Puerto Rico's status would be, in Justice White's words, "to say that the United States is helpless in the family of nations, and does not possess that authority which has at all times been treated as an incident of the right to acquire."[18] In a world divided into independent states and colonial possessions, a hallmark of independence was the ability to acquire and dispose of territories. In this respect, Justice White's concurrence in *Downes* was as much about the status of the United States as it was about the status of Puerto Rico.

Determining the status of acquired territory also meant dictating the fate of its inhabitants. Justice White posited that "the conception upon which the Constitution proceeds is that no territory, as a general rule, should be acquired unless the territory may reasonably be expected to be worthy of statehood";[19] however, "the determination of when such blessing is to be bestowed is wholly a political question"[20] within the discretion of the US Congress. At the time

---

15   Downes v. Bidwell, 182 U.S. 244, 300 (1901) (White, J., concurring).
16   Henry Wager Halleck, *Halleck's International Law, Or, Rules Regulating the Intercourse of States in Peace and War* (New York: D. Van Nostrand, 1861), 126, quoted in Downes v. Bidwell, 182 U.S. 244, 300-301 (1901) (White, J., concurring).
17   THE DECLARATION OF INDEPENDENCE (U.S. 1776), quoted in in Downes v. Bidwell, 182 U.S. 244, 302 (1901) (White, J., concurring).
18   Downes v. Bidwell, 182 U.S. 244, 306 (1901) (White, J., concurring). This idea of "powers which are absolutely inherent in and essential to national existence" (ibid., 311) was used to justify a variety of constitutional moves during this period. See Sarah H. Cleveland, "Powers Inherent in Sovereignty: Indians, Aliens, Territories, and the Nineteenth Century Origins of Plenary Powers over Foreign Affairs," *Texas Law Review* 81 (2002): 1-284.
19   Downes v. Bidwell, 182 U.S. 244, 312 (1901) (White, J., concurring).
20   Ibid.

of the Insular Cases, congressional discretion over statehood meant that the potentially "savage" inhabitants of newly acquired territories and their future children would not become "immediately upon annexation, citizens of the United States . . . entitled to all the rights, privileges and immunities of citizens."[21] Treating statehood as a "blessing" to be "bestowed" by Congress meant that Congress controlled—and could prevent—the extension of a crucial form of membership in the US political community.

In the US federal model, statehood remains the key to meaningful representation at the national level. Gerald L. Neuman has noted that the "fundamental republican defect" of the Constitution is that it "restricts national representation to the states while giving the national organs governing power over the territories."[22] This defect was not cured by granting US citizenship to Puerto Ricans in 1917 because Puerto Rico was not given electoral votes for the US president or voting representation in the US Congress.[23] The unilateral nature of the conferral of citizenship constituted an exercise of the United States' prerogatives under the conquest paradigm, in the form of the Jones Act.

President Wilson signed the Jones Act into law on March 2, 1917.[24] Ten months later, he delivered his Fourteen Points speech, in which he referred to the idea of popular consent as one factor in redrawing postwar boundaries.[25] Over the following decades, the consent paradigm replaced the conquest paradigm, in theory if not always in practice. Members of the international community became increasingly proactive in identifying and condemning colonial arrangements. Although "the United States [long] claimed that

---

21 Ibid., 279 (majority opinion).
22 Gerald L. Neuman, "Constitutionalism and Individual Rights in the Territories," in Burnett and Marshall, *Foreign in a Domestic Sense*, 196-97.
23 See Efrén Rivera Ramos, *The Legal Construction of Identity: The Judicial and Social Legacy of American Colonialism in Puerto Rico* (Washington, DC: American Psychological Association, 2001), 146. US citizenship has been held not to entail a right to vote in US presidential elections. See Igartúa-De La Rosa v. United States, 417 F.3d 145 (1st Cir. 2005).
24 Jones Act, Pub. L. No. 64-368, 39 Stat. 951 (1917) (codified at 48 U.S.C. §§ 731 et seq. (2013)).
25 Point five provided for
    [a] free, open-minded, and absolutely impartial adjustment of all colonial claims, based upon a strict observance of the principle that in determining all such questions of sovereignty the interests of the populations concerned must have equal weight with the equitable claims of the government whose title is to be determined.
    Yale Law School, "President Woodrow Wilson's Fourteen Points," Jan. 8, 1918, http://avalon.law.yale.edu/20th_century/wilson14.asp.

Puerto Rico was a domestic affair, off-limits to the world community,"[26] the rise of the consent paradigm brought international attention to the question of Puerto Rico's status.

The yearning for communal control over one's political destiny has a long pedigree. In 1776, the "united States of America" declared their entitlement to a "separate and equal station" under "the Laws of Nature," in response to their disenfranchisement and the extension by the British Parliament of an "unwarrantable jurisdiction" over them.[27] Almost two centuries later, in 1945, the United Nations (UN) Charter proclaimed the purpose of "develop[ing] friendly relations among nations based on respect for the principle of equal rights and self-determination of peoples."[28] UN General Assembly Resolution 1514 (XV) on the Granting of Independence to Colonial Countries and Peoples and subsequent resolutions further enshrined the principle that "[a]ll peoples have the right of self-determination; by virtue of that right they freely determine their political status and freely pursue their economic, social and cultural development."[29] The two international covenants on human rights gave pride of place to self-determination by reprising this language in a common article 1,[30] reflecting and cementing the centrality of consent.

Article 73 of the UN Charter indicated that the inhabitants of all non-self-governing territories should attain "a full measure of self-government," and it imposed a reporting requirement for administering powers to promote this goal.[31] Also in 1945, the UN listed Puerto Rico among the non-self-

---

26 José Julián Álvarez González, "Law, Language, and Statehood: The Role of English in the Great State of Puerto Rico," in Burnett and Marshall, *Foreign in a Domestic Sense*, 292.

27 THE DECLARATION OF INDEPENDENCE (U.S. 1776).

28 United Nations Charter, art. 1(2). See also ibid., art. 55 (promoting "the creation of conditions of stability and well-being which are necessary for peaceful and friendly relations among nations based on respect for the principle of equal rights and self-determination of peoples").

29 G.A. Res. 1514 (XV), U.N. GAOR, 15th Sess., Supp. No. 16, at 66, U.N. Doc. A/4684 (Dec. 14, 1960); G.A. Res. 2621 (XXV), U.N. GAOR, 25th Sess., Supp. No. 28, at 1, U.N. Doc. A/8028 (Oct. 12, 1970); G.A. Res. 2878 (XXVI), U.N. GAOR, 26th Sess., Supp. No. 29, at 16, U.N. Doc. A/8429 (Dec. 20, 1971).

30 International Covenant on Civil and Political Rights, art. 1, G.A. Res. 2200A (XXI), U.N. GAOR, 21st Sess., Supp. No. 16, at 52, U.N. Doc. A/6316 (Dec. 16, 1966), 999 U.N.T.S. 171, *entered into force* Mar. 23, 1976; International Covenant on Economic, Social and Cultural Rights, art. 1, G.A. Res. 2200A (XXI), U.N. GAOR, 21st Sess., Supp. No. 16, at 49, U.N. Doc. A/6316 (Dec. 16, 1966), 993 U.N.T.S. 3, *entered into force* Jan. 3, 1976.

31 United Nations Charter, art. 73.

governing territories administered by the United States, along with Alaska, Hawaii, the Panama Canal Zone, and the Trust Territory of the Pacific Islands.[32] Adherents of the consent paradigm disagreed about whether consent to an unequal relationship could make the relationship lawful.

General Assembly Resolution 1541 (XV), adopted the day after Resolution 1514 (XV), specified that the obligation to transmit information under article 73 of the UN Charter continues until "a territory and its peoples attain a full measure of self-government."[33] Many still view Puerto Rico as a territory that has not yet attained "a full measure of self-government."[34] However, by the time Resolution 1541 (XV) was enacted in 1960, Puerto Rico had already been removed from the UN's list of non-self-governing territories, as described below. The ambiguity of Puerto Rico's political status at the time of delisting in 1952 made many observers uneasy. Roger Clark has suggested that given the UN General Assembly's decreasing tolerance for various forms of neocolonialism, "[i]t is extremely doubtful that a case similar to the Puerto Rican one would be resolved in the same manner today."[35]

From Compact to Commonwealth

Following World War II, the US Congress took steps toward greater local self-government for the people of Puerto Rico. In 1947, Congress passed Public Law 362, which provided for an elective governor.[36] At the same time, Puerto

---

32 See United Nations, "The United Nations and Decolonization."

33 G.A. Res. 1541 (XV), annex, princ. II, U.N. GAOR, 15th Sess., Supp. No. 16, at 29, U.N. Doc. A/4684 (Dec. 15, 1960).

34 See, e.g., Special Committee on the Situation with regard to the Implementation of the Declaration on the Granting of Independence to Colonial Countries and Peoples, Decision of the Special Committee of 18 June 2012 concerning Puerto Rico, para. 1, U.N. Doc. A/AC.109/2013/L.6 (2013) (reaffirming "the inalienable right of the people of Puerto Rico to self-determination and independence in conformity with General Assembly Resolution 1514 (XV)"); Special Committee on the Situation with regard to the Implementation of the Declaration on the Granting of Independence to Colonial Countries and Peoples, Special Committee Decision of 18 June 2012 concerning Puerto Rico: Report Prepared by the Rapporteur of the Special Committee, Bashar Ja'afari (Syrian Arab Republic), para. 68, U.N. Doc. A/AC.109/2013/L.13 (2013).

35 Roger S. Clark, "Self-Determination and Free Association: Should the United States Terminate the Pacific Islands Trust?," Harvard International Law Journal 21 (1980): 1-86, 46.

36 Act of Aug. 5, 1947 (Elective Governor Act), Pub. L. No. 80-362, 61 Stat. 770. For

Rico's resident commissioner Antonio Fernós Isern expressed the desire for "a new and bilateral organic pact which could be amended only through mutual consent rather than unilaterally."[37] Fernós Isern and Puerto Rico's newly elected governor Luis Muñoz Marín interpreted their Popular Democratic Party's success in the island's 1948 elections as "a direct mandate from the people in support of the compact idea."[38] However, the unilateral nature of authority under the territory clause meant that the mutuality of the compact metaphor would remain more illusory than real.

Puerto Rico's ensuing constitutional developments reflect the attempt to implement the consent paradigm within the constraints of the conquest paradigm enshrined in the territory clause. To this end, in 1950, Congress adopted Public Law 600 "in the nature of a compact so that the people of Puerto Rico may organize a government pursuant to a constitution of their own adoption."[39] Public Law 600 emphasized "the principle of government by consent";[40] the House Committee on Public Lands indicated that the law would "fulfill in a most exemplary fashion our obligations with respect to Puerto Rico under chapter XI [article 73] of the charter of the United Nations, relating to the administration of non-self-governing territories."[41] However, the committee also stated that Public Law 600 would not "change Puerto Rico's fundamental political, social, and economic relationship to the United States" or "in any way preclude a future determination by the Congress of Puerto Rico's ultimate political status."[42] Because Congress would always have the last word on Puerto Rico's status, the legacy of conquest circumscribed the principle of consent both structurally and symbolically.

The emphasis on consent in Public Law 600 responded directly to the decolonization provisions of the UN Charter. The US approach equated consent to territorial status with the achievement of self-government. For example, the then assistant secretary of state Jack McFall wrote that the

---

a brief summary of these legislative developments, see Keitner and Reisman, "Free Association," 21-27.

37   Antonio Fernós Isern, *The Significance of Reform* (Washington, DC: Office of Puerto Rico, 1948), 9, quoted in David M. Helfeld, "Congressional Intent and Attitude toward Public Law 600 and the Constitution of the Commonwealth of Puerto Rico," *Revista Jurídica de la Universidad de Puerto Rico* 21 (1952): 255-320, 260.

38   Helfeld, "Congressional Intent and Attitude toward Public Law 600," 260-61.

39   Act of July 3, 1950, Pub. L. No. 81-600, § 1, 64 Stat. 319, 319 (codified at 48 U.S.C. §§ 731 et seq. (2013)).

40   Ibid.

41   H.R. Rep. No. 81-2275, at 2 (1950).

42   Ibid., 3.

legislation would have the important effect of securing "the formal consent of the Puerto Ricans ... to their present relationship to the United States."[43] In his view, this would "be in keeping with the democratic principles of the United States and with our obligations under the Charter of the United Nations to take due account of the political aspirations of the people in our Territories and to develop self-government in them."[44] Enabling the people of Puerto Rico to organize their own constitutional government, he added, "would have great value as a symbol of the basic freedom enjoyed by Puerto Rico, within the larger framework of the United States of America."[45] The Senate Committee on Interior and Insular Affairs' report on the proposed legislation that became Public Law 600 likewise indicated that the act was "designed to complete the full measure of local self-government in the island by enabling the 2¼ million American citizens there to express their will and to create their own territorial government," thereby "giv[ing] further concrete expression to our fundamental principles of government of, by, and for the people."[46] The report cited the obligation to develop self-government contained in article 73 of the UN Charter and expressed the view that the United States' charter obligations toward Puerto Rico had "already ... been fulfilled to an extent that is almost without parallel."[47]

Notwithstanding the emphasis on consent and the idea of a "compact," Public Law 600 did not remove Puerto Rico from the purview of the territory clause under prevailing interpretations of domestic constitutional law. Proponents Fernós Isern and Muñoz Marín may have overestimated the extent to which the "compact" language would actually modify the relationship between Puerto Rico and the United States.[48] As César Ayala and Rafael Bernabe recount in their history of Puerto Rico:

> Muñoz Marín and Antonio Fernós sought to finesse the U.S. Congress into relinquishing its plenary power over Puerto Rico while avoiding any confrontation with any sector of the Washington establishment.

---

43   Jack McFall, letter to Joseph O'Mahoney, Apr. 24, 1950, reprinted in H.R. REP. NO. 81-2275, at 9 (1950).

44   Ibid.

45   Ibid.

46   S. Rep. No. 81-1779, at 2 (1950).

47   Ibid.

48   Some went further and alleged that the governor had intentionally "misrepresented the political meaning of the compact and the political status of Puerto Rico under the new constitution" in his campaign speeches and publications. See Helfeld, "Congressional Intent and Attitude toward Public Law 600," 279. In particular, Representative Vito Marcantonio "severely attacked the Popular Democratic Party and accused the Governor and Resident Commissioner of misleading the people by making campaign promises of one kind in Puerto Rico and dissimilar statements before the Committees of Congress." Ibid., 268-69.

They thus sought to minimize the reach of the proposed reforms in the hope of making them palatable to the Department of the Interior functionaries and the congressmen opposed to any weakening of U.S. claims over Puerto Rico. Meanwhile, they privately hoped that the courts would eventually certify that as a result of the new arrangement, Puerto Rico was no longer a territory of the United States. The U.S. State Department . . . looked favorably upon legislation that would allow the United States to argue Puerto Rico was no longer a colony while not reducing its ultimate rights over the island.[49]

Ayala and Bernabe continue:

> The State Department was far more successful than the PDP [Popular Democratic Party] leaders in furthering its agenda. While the former was, at least until the late 1960s, able to present the [*estado libre asociado*] internationally as a noncolonial status, the PDP's unwillingness to demand a clear definition of the new relation ensured its ambiguous, limited and static nature.[50]

This ambiguity persists and has generated frustration and contrasting views on the best outcome for Puerto Rico's self-determination process.

The ambiguity of Puerto Rico's status also has a linguistic dimension, as the term "commonwealth" is used to describe Puerto Rico in English, while the term *estado libre asociado* is used in Spanish. The English version of the Puerto Rican Constitution, which was adopted in 1952 following a constitutional convention presided over by Fernós Isern, proclaims that "[w]e, the people of Puerto Rico . . . do ordain and establish this Constitution for the commonwealth which, in the exercise of our natural rights, we now create within our union with the United States of America."[51] The Spanish preamble to the Puerto Rican Constitution refers to the establishment of a "Constitución para el Estado Libre Asociado que en el ejercicio de nuestro derecho natural ahora creamos dentro de nuestra unión con los Estados Unidos de América."[52] The use of the Spanish term *estado libre asociado* did not have the meaning or legal effect of the status of free

---

49 César J. Ayala and Rafael Bernabe, *Puerto Rico in the American Century: A History Since 1898* (Chapel Hill: University of North Carolina Press, 2009), 163.

50 Ibid.

51 CONST. OF THE COMMONWEALTH OF PUERTO RICO, pmbl. (1952) (P.R.). In 1951, 76.5% of those voting approved Public Law 600 (with a 65% voter turnout rate). Following the constitutional convention, 81.9% of those voting supported adoption of the Puerto Rican Constitution (with a 59% voter turnout rate). See Keitner and Reisman, "Free Association," 22.

52 CONSTITUCIÓN DEL ESTADO LIBRE DE PUERTO RICO [CONST. OF THE COMMONWEALTH OF PUERTO RICO], preámbulo [pmbl.] (1952) (P.R.).

association under international law, even though it conveyed the impression of a union based on mutual consent.[53] The commonwealth, or *estado libre*, was created "within," or *dentro de*, Puerto Rico's union with the United States, meaning that the US constitutional framework of congressional supremacy over the territories remained intact. This arrangement was consistent with Congress's understanding; arguably, however, Puerto Rican voters expected the arrangement to yield a more balanced partnership, notwithstanding the immense power and resource disparities between Puerto Rico and the United States.

The staff of the *Puerto Rico Herald* emphasized the apparent disjunction between the parties' understandings in a retrospective written for the fifty-third anniversary of the Puerto Rican Constitution:

> While the Congress clearly understood what it was (and was not) granting to Puerto Rico, Muñoz Marin and the PDP (who had dominated the Constitutional Convention) were perhaps not so forthright in conveying that message to Puerto Rico's population. In one of the oddest and most confusing of word games, Puerto Rico's internal government adopted two completely different names, depending on the language. The English term of Commonwealth has a vague, innocuous sound to it. The Spanish term *Estado Libre Asociado* [*sic*], which translates to "Freely Associated State" in English, has another meaning entirely. Indeed, it refers back to Muñoz Marin's proposed status of "The Associated People of Puerto Rico," which had been ignored in Washington a few years earlier.
>
> Muñoz Marin, a poet, understood language, so he was thus able to make a subtle linguistic claim in Spanish that would have never been accepted in English. Confusion has reigned ever since.[54]

A similar point about language might be made of the statement in Public Law 600 that the law was being adopted "in the nature of a compact,"[55] given

---

53 Michael Reisman and I have suggested that commonwealth status lies somewhere on a "spectrum" of possible political arrangements between independence and integration. See Keitner and Reisman, "Free Association," 63. That said, Congress has made clear that "[t]he Commonwealth remains an unincorporated territory and does not have the status of 'free association' with the United States as that status is defined under United States law or international practice." United States-Puerto Rico Political Status Act, H.R. 856, 105th Cong. § 2(4) (1998), quoted in ibid., 22 n.129.

54 Puerto Rico Herald Staff, "A Brief History of the Puerto Rico Constitution," accessed Oct. 29, 2014, http://www.puertorico-herald.org/issues2/2005/vol09n28/HistPRConst.html.

55 Act of July 3, 1950, Pub. L. No. 81-600, § 1, 64 Stat. 319, 319 (codified at 48 U.S.C. §§ 731 et seq. (2013)).

that it was in fact adopted unilaterally by Congress. During the hearings on the Puerto Rican Constitution, Senator Guy Cordon asked but did not receive an answer to the question whether Puerto Rican political leaders who had campaigned for the constitution had represented that the proposed United States–Puerto Rico relationship could be modified only by mutual agreement.[56]

The US Congress approved the Puerto Rican Constitution in 1952, subject to three conditions, including reaffirming the continued application of the Federal Relations Act[57] and deleting references to certain economic and social rights.[58] The Senate report recommending approval of the constitution emphasized that

> [t]he enforcement of the Puerto Rican Federal Relations Act and the exercise of Federal authority in Puerto Rico under its provisions are in no way impaired by the Constitution of Puerto Rico, and may not be affected by future amendments to that constitution, or by any law of Puerto Rico adopted under its constitution.[59]

The report characterized Puerto Rico as neither a state of the United States nor an independent republic, but instead "a self-governing community bound by the common loyalties and obligations of American citizens living under the American flag and the American Constitution and enjoying a republican form of government of their own choosing."[60] The United States took the

---

56 Helfeld, "Congressional Intent and Attitude toward Public Law 600," 283. Helfeld takes the position that the adoption of the Puerto Rican Constitution did not change its status as a territory and that Congress "continues to possess plenary but unexercised authority over Puerto Rico." Ibid., 307. Gary Lawson and Robert Sloane note that it is "certainly arguable that a statute adopted either 'as' or 'in the nature of' a compact may not be modified unilaterally," but they indicate that the "unprecedented" nature of this formulation leaves much to "speculation." Gary Lawson and Robert D. Sloane, "The Constitutionality of Decolonization by Associated Statehood: Puerto Rico's Legal Status Reconsidered," *Boston College Law Review* 50 (2009): 1123-93, 1149. Public Law 600 described itself as being "in the nature of a compact," while Congress referred to the arrangement in 1952 "*as* a compact." Act of July 3, 1952, Pub. L. No. 82-447, pmbl., 66 Stat. 327, 327, quoted in ibid., 4 n.11.

57 Jones Act, Pub. L. No. 64-368, 39 Stat. 951 (1917), *amended by* Pub. L. No. 81-600, 64 Stat. 319 (1950), now known as the Puerto Rico Federal Relations Act of 1950 (codified at 48 U.S.C. §§ 731 et seq. (2013)).

58 Act of July 3, 1952, Pub. L. No. 82-447, 66 Stat. 327.

59 S. Rep. No. 82-1720, at 6 (1952).

60 Ibid., 7. Pedro Malavet has critiqued the misleading nature of the "commonwealth" label, indicating that "[t]o the extent that [commonwealth] was intended to suggest a relationship similar to that of the Commonwealth of Virginia or the

position that Puerto Rico, by adopting its own constitution, had achieved a "full degree of self-government" under international law, even though Puerto Rico remained within the scope of congressional authority under US domestic law. The question whether Puerto Rico should still be considered a non-self-governing territory turned on these apparently contradictory propositions.

After Congress approved the Puerto Rican Constitution, the United States sought to terminate its obligation to transmit information about Puerto Rico under article 73 of the UN Charter. In his letter transmitting the Puerto Rican Constitution to UN Secretary-General Trygve Lie, Ambassador Henry Cabot Lodge, Jr., emphasized:

> This is the kind of progress to self-government contemplated by the U.N. Charter. This is the democratic pattern of the free world—of goals set and hopes realized. The people of Puerto Rico expressed their view by resolution at their Constitutional Convention in the following words: "Thus we attain the goal of complete self-government, the last vestiges of colonialism having disappeared in the principle of Compact."[61]

During the ensuing discussions, Resident Commissioner Fernós Isern, who served as the US special representative in the UN General Assembly's Committee IV (Trusteeship), acknowledged that "[a] minority political party, the Independence Party, maintains that Puerto Rico has not yet achieved a full measure of self-government."[62] However, Fernós Isern countered that, on the contrary, "the people of Puerto Rico hold that the Constitution and the laws of the Commonwealth can be amended, suspended, or repealed only by their authority and that the compact between the United States and Puerto Rico can be amended or repealed only by mutual consent."[63] As indicated above, the interpretation that mutual consent would be required to amend the compact was shared by Governor Muñoz Marín.[64] It was reinforced by

---

Commonwealth of Massachusetts, the legal reality of Puerto Rico's continued territorial status makes it incorrect as applied to the island." Pedro A. Malavet, *America's Colony: The Political and Cultural Conflict between the United States and Puerto Rico* (New York: New York University Press, 2004), 43.

61 "Puerto Rico's New Self-Governing Status: U.S./U.N. Press Release Dated March 21," *Department of State Bulletin* 28 (Apr. 1953): 584.

62 "Statement by Dr. Fernós-Isern, U.S. Delegation Press Release Dated October 29 [Translation]," *Department of State Bulletin* 29 (Dec. 1953): 801.

63 Ibid.

64 As Governor Muñoz Marín wrote:

> The Commonwealth of Puerto Rico . . . reflects our own decision as to the type of institutions and the kind of relationship to the United States which we desire. There can be no doubt that in the full sense of the term, in form as well as in fact, the people of Puerto Rico are now self-governing. . . . Our status and the terms

statements made by Frances Bolton, representative of the United States to the General Assembly's eighth regular session, who indicated that Puerto Rico's "previous status was that of a territory subject to the full authority of the Congress of the United States" but that a new status had been created by "a compact of a bilateral nature whose terms may be changed only by common consent."[65] Based on these representations, the General Assembly voted to remove Puerto Rico from the list of non-self-governing territories and relieve the United States of its reporting requirements under article 73.[66]

---

of our association with the United States cannot be changed without our full consent.

"The Governor of Puerto Rico to the President of the United States: January 17, 1953," *Department of State Bulletin* 28 (Apr. 1953): 589.

65 See "November 3 Statement by Mrs. Bolton: U.S. Delegation Press Release Dated November 3," *Department of State Bulletin* 29 (Dec. 1953): 804. See also "October 30 Statement by Mrs. Bolton: U.S. Delegation Press Release Dated October 27," *Department of State Bulletin* 29 (Dec. 1953), 797; "Memorandum by the Government of the United States of America concerning the Cessation of Transmission of Information under Article 73(e) of the Charter with Regard to the Commonwealth of Puerto Rico," *Department of State Bulletin* 28 (Apr. 1953): 585; Lawson and Sloane, "The Constitutionality of Decolonization by Associated Statehood," 1150-51. A later attempt to codify this understanding in US law in the 1959 Fernós-Murray bill proved unsuccessful. See Laura Kalman, *Abe Fortas* (New Haven: Yale University Press, 1990), 173-74. The same is true of proposed compacts of "permanent union" between the United States and Puerto Rico. See *Hearing on H.R. 4751, Puerto Rico-United States Bilateral Pact of Non-Territorial Permanent Union and Guaranteed Citizenship Act, Committee on Resources,* 107th Cong. (2000) (discussing the possibility of an "enhanced commonwealth" status); *Compact of Permanent Union between Puerto Rico and the United States: Hearings before the Subcommittee on Territorial and Insular Affairs and the Committee on Territorial and Insular Affairs, H.R., on H.R. 11200 and H.R. 11201,* 94th Cong. (1976).

66 G.A. Res. 748 (VIII), U.N. GAOR, 8th Sess., Supp. No 17, at 25, U.N. Doc. A/2630 (Nov. 27, 1953). Ayala and Bernabe describe two positions on colonialism that emerged at the UN: the "subjective" perspective and the "objective" perspective. According to the subjective approach articulated by the US delegation, "no restrictions of Puerto Rico's sovereignty could be described as colonial if Puerto Rico had consented to them." Ayala and Bernabe, *Puerto Rico in the American Century,* 172. By contrast, delegates from India, Yugoslavia, Guatemala, Mexico, and Indonesia articulated an objective approach under which "the basic criteria was not—or was not only—the expression of consent but rather whether the new arrangement made it possible for the population concerned to govern itself." Ibid. Consistent with the latter position, Ediberto Román has remarked that "the international community has used the colonialism-by-consent defense to reconcile United States colonialism with the right to self-determination." Ediberto Román, *The Other American Colonies: An International and Constitutional Law Examination of the United States' Nineteenth and Twentieth Century Island Conquests* (Durham, NC: Carolina Academic Press, 2006), 59.

In finding that Puerto Rico had attained a full measure of self-government through the establishment of a "mutually agreed association" with the United States, the General Assembly

> expresse[d] its assurance that ... due regard will be paid to the will of both the Puerto Rican and American peoples in the conduct of their relations under their present legal statute, and also in the eventuality that either of the parties to the mutually agreed association may desire any change in the terms of this association.[67]

This understanding was bolstered by President Eisenhower's statement to the General Assembly, conveyed by Ambassador Lodge, that "if at any time the Legislative Assembly of Puerto Rico adopts a resolution in favor of more complete or even absolute independence, [Eisenhower will] immediately thereafter recommend to Congress that such independence be granted."[68] However, since Congress retains plenary power over Puerto Rico under the territory clause, "some have questioned whether Puerto Rico's [continued] status as a United States territory [under US domestic law] is consistent with statements that the United States made to the United Nations in 1953,"[69] and thus with the United States' obligations under the UN Charter.

Self-Determination and Free Association

On November 27, 1953, the UN General Assembly adopted Resolution 748 (VIII) terminating the United States' obligation to transmit information on Puerto Rico, on the grounds that Puerto Rico was no longer a non-self-governing territory.[70] On the same day, the General Assembly also adopted

---

67 G.A. Res. 748 (VIII), para. 9, U.N. GAOR, 8th Sess., Supp. No 17, at 25, U.N. Doc. A/2630 (Nov. 27, 1953).

68 G.A. Rep. of the Fourth Committee, para. 66, U.N. GAOR, 8th Sess., U.N. Doc. A/PV.459 (1953). Clark has noted that "this statement is probably binding on the United States as a matter of international law—though not as a matter of United States constitutional law." Clark, "Self-Determination and Free Association," 45 n.45. Lawson and Sloane have also observed that the United States "bound itself, in international law, to the particular understanding of the bilateral compact and associated state relationship expressed before the United Nations orally and in writing." Lawson and Sloane, "The Constitutionality of Decolonization by Associated Statehood," 1155.

69 Special Committee on the Situation with regard to the Implementation of the Declaration on the Granting of Independence to Colonial Countries and Peoples, Special Committee Decision of 18 June 2012 concerning Puerto Rico: Report Prepared by the Rapporteur of the Special Committee, Bashar Ja'afari (Syrian Arab Republic), para. 16, U.N. Doc. A/AC.109/2013/L.13 (2013).

70 G.A. Res. 748 (VIII), U.N. GAOR, 8th Sess., Supp. No 17, at 25, U.N. Doc. A/2630

Resolution 742 (VIII), enumerating "factors which should be taken into account in deciding whether a territory is or is not a territory whose people have not yet attained a full measure of self-government."[71] Clark notes that "[c]uriously, the General Assembly did not see fit to try to apply [these factors] in any detail to the case of Puerto Rico."[72] The factors are also somewhat confusing, as Clark points out. Part one lists factors indicating independence. Part two lists factors indicating "the attainment of other separate systems of self-government" and thus appears "to contemplate a situation of full internal self-government with some limitation, freely entered into, of the international personality of the territory."[73] This category is akin to the status known in international law as free association.[74] Part three enumerates factors indicating "the free association of a territory on equal basis with the metropolitan or other country as an integral part of that country or in any other form." The third part thus seems to be concerned, as Clark suggests, "primarily with union or integration (on either a unitary or a federal basis) with the metropolitan or another power."[75] As Clark indicates, the Puerto Rican situation did not fit into any of these categories.[76]

In 1960, the General Assembly clarified three alternatives for attaining the required "full measure of self-government." General Assembly Resolution 1541 (XV), which was passed the day after Resolution 1514 (XV) on the Granting of Independence to Colonial Countries and Peoples, provides

---

(Nov. 27, 1953). The resolution was ultimately adopted by a vote of twenty-six to sixteen, with eighteen abstentions. See Clark, "Self-Determination and Free Association," 41 n.250.

71 G.A. Res. 742 (VIII), annex, U.N. GAOR, 8th Sess., Supp. No. 17, at 21, U.N. Doc. A/2630 (Nov. 27, 1953). This resolution followed General Assembly Resolution 567 of the previous year, which had recommended establishing a list of such factors. See G.A. Res. 567 (VI), U.N. GAOR, 6th Sess., Supp. No. 20, at 60, U.N. Doc. A/2119 (Jan. 18, 1952). Resolution 567 envisioned that the "two principal forms of political advancement" were "(a) the attainment of independence or (b) the union of the territory on a footing of equal status with other component parts of the metropolitan or other country or its association on the same conditions with the metropolitan or other country or countries." This second alternative of "full integration" could take the form of a "federal or unitary relationship," provided that the territory was "on equal status with other component parts of the metropolitan or other country." Intervening Resolution 648 elaborated on "factors indicative of the free association of a territory with other component parts of the metropolitan or other country." See G.A. Res. 648 (VII), U.N. GAOR, 7th Sess., Supp. No. 20, at 33, U.N. Doc. A/2361 (Dec. 10, 1952).

72 Clark, "Self-Determination and Free Association," 42.

73 Ibid., 43.

74 Ibid., 44.

75 Ibid.

76 Ibid., 45-46.

guidance on the ways in which a former colony can implement its right to self-determination.[77] The options are "(a) Emergence as a sovereign independent State; (b) Free association with an independent State; or (c) Integration with an independent State." In Puerto Rico, the options of independence and US statehood each have fervent supporters. In addition, many on the island have proposed a form of "enhanced commonwealth" that would increase the benefits of union with the United States. It is highly unlikely, however, that the US Congress would accept a modified commonwealth arrangement, both because of its associated costs and because it arguably would require amending the US Constitution.[78]

Critics of congressional inertia have expressed the concern that

> [a]s long as Puerto Ricans remain divided as to the specific form in which a change of status should occur, the U.S. Congress seems to be more than happy to continue retaining its plenary powers and acting accordingly. . . . Acquiescence has become the justificatory principle of the relationship of domination.[79]

Other former US territories have entered into arrangements that fall into the recognized categories of independence, integration, and free association. The United States recognized the independence of the Republic of the Philippines on July 4, 1946,[80] and Hawaii became a state of the United States on August 21, 1959.[81] More recently, three of the former Trust Territories of the Pacific Islands entered into compacts of free association with the United States: the Federated States of Micronesia (1986), the Republic of the Marshall Islands

---

77 G.A. Res. 1541 (XV), U.N. GAOR, 15th Sess., Supp. No. 16, at 29, U.N. Doc. A/4684 (Dec. 15, 1960).

78 See, e.g., *Hearing on H.R. 4751, Puerto Rico-United States Bilateral Pact of Non-Territorial Permanent Union and Guaranteed Citizenship Act, Committee on Resources*, 107th Cong. (2000) (including skeptical testimony about the feasibility of an "enhanced commonwealth" status). Under the view currently held by the Justice Department and individual members of Congress, the inclusion of Puerto Rico within the scope of the territory clause (unless it becomes a US state, an independent country, or an independent country in free association with the United States) means that a future US Congress would always have the power to modify Puerto Rico's status unilaterally, making an enhanced relationship based on "mutual consent" unenforceable as a matter of US law. For a critique of this view, see *Hearing Before the Committee on Energy and Natural Resources on the Report by the President's Task Force on Puerto Rico's Status*, 109th Cong. 80-98 (2006) (statement of Charles J. Cooper, Brian S. Koukoutchos, and David H. Thompson, Cooper & Kirk).

79 Rivera Ramos, *The Legal Construction of Identity*, 232-33.

80 22 U.S.C. § 1394 (2006).

81 Hawaii Admission Act, Pub. L. No. 86-3, 73 Stat. 4 (1959).

(1986), and the Republic of Palau (1994).[82] These communities all confronted what Ponsa and Marshall have called "[t]he normative questions embedded in the status debate concern[ing] the kinds of trade-offs that distinct racial, ethnic, and cultural groups ought to be able to make in order to maintain their association with a larger polity while asserting and protecting their distinctive identities."[83] A free association arrangement—in more than name only—may offer one means to achieve this precarious balance.[84]

Free association entails the establishment of "formal and durable links between two independent states of unequal power.[85] Under international law, free association involves "the significant subordination and delegation of competence by one of the parties (the associate) to the other (the principal), but maintenance of the continuing international status of statehood of each component."[86] Importantly, "[t]he key to legality, and to an association's acceptance by the international decision-making process, is the substance of the relationship, not its label."[87] General Assembly Resolution 1541 (XV) provides:

> (a) Free association should be the result of a free and voluntary choice by the peoples of the territory concerned expressed through informed and democratic processes. It should be one which respects the individuality and the cultural characteristics of the territory and its peoples, and retains for the peoples of the territory which is associated with an independent State the freedom to modify the status of that territory

82　The Commonwealth of the Northern Mariana Islands (CNMI) opted for a closer relationship with the United States codified in the Covenant to Establish a Commonwealth of the Northern Mariana Islands in Political Union with the United States of America, Pub. L. No. 94-241, 90 Stat. 263 (1976). On the former Trust Territory of the Pacific Islands, see generally Keitner and Reisman, "Free Association," 33-61. The Ninth Circuit has held that the relationship between the CNMI and the United States is defined by the covenant rather than the territory clause, but this doctrinal distinction has not made a practical difference in the outcome of litigation challenging the validity of federal legislation affecting the CNMI. See United States ex rel. Richards v. De Leon Guerrero, 4 F.3d 749, 754 (9th Cir. 1993) (enforcing an administrative subpoena to compel release of CNMI tax records to the US Department of the Interior). Under the Ninth Circuit's framework, Congress may legislate on issues of federal interest even if they also affect the CNMI's internal affairs, as long as the degree of intrusion is warranted by the federal interest. Ibid., 755.

83　Duffy Burnett (Ponsa) and Marshall, "Between the Foreign and the Domestic," 23.
84　Manuel Rodríguez Orellana contemplated such an arrangement for Puerto Rico in a 1986 article. See Manuel Rodríguez Orellana, "In Contemplation of Micronesia: The Prospects for the Decolonization of Puerto Rico under International Law," *University of Miami Inter-American Law Review* 18 (1987): 457-90, 457.
85　See Keitner and Reisman, "Free Association," 5.
86　Ibid.
87　Ibid.

through the expression of their will by democratic means and through constitutional processes.

(b) The associated territory should have the right to determine its internal constitution without outside interference, in accordance with due constitutional processes and the freely expressed wishes of the people. This does not preclude consultations as appropriate or necessary under the terms of the free association agreed upon.[88]

Continued international scrutiny may be required even after the conclusion of a free association agreement, since associations involve unequal power relationships.[89] That said, power is unevenly distributed in the international system even among independent states; de facto power imbalances are impossible to avoid.[90]

International law recognizes a diverse array of actors with some degree of international legal personality. Freely associated states, unlike states in a federal union, are considered independent and are eligible for UN membership. The 1986 Compacts of Free Association between the United States and the Federated States of Micronesia and the Republic of the Marshall Islands provide that "the peoples of the Trust Territory of the Pacific Islands have and retain their sovereignty and their sovereign right to self-determination and the inherent right to adopt and amend their own Constitutions and forms of government."[91] If Puerto Rico were a freely associated state, its constitution would not be subject to approval or modification by the US Congress. After entering into a free association agreement, Puerto Rico and the United States could amend the agreement by mutual consent, or either party could terminate it unilaterally, subject to agreed-on survivability provisions.[92]

---

88 G.A. Res. 1541 (XV), annex, princ. VII, U.N. GAOR, 15th Sess., Supp. No. 16, at 29, U.N. Doc. A/4684 (Dec. 15, 1960).

89 Ibid.

90 See Keitner and Reisman, "Free Association," 4.

91 Compact of Free Association Act of 1985, Pub. L. No. 99-239, 99 Stat. 1770.

92 For example, certain terms of the agreements with the Federated States of Micronesia and the Republic of the Marshall Islands were renegotiated in 2003, with discussions including increased accountability for the use of US economic assistance and the scope of participation in federal services and programs. Compact of Free Association Amendments Act of 2003, Pub. L. No. 108-188, 117 Stat. 2720. For the text of the amended agreements, as well as the original compact, see http://www.uscompact.org. The Republic of the Marshall Islands submitted a "changed circumstances" petition in 2000 and again in 2001 to try to persuade Congress to increase the allotted compensation fund for US nuclear testing on the Bikini and Enewetak atolls in the 1940s and 1950s. See Thomas Lum et al., "CRS Report for Congress: Republic of the Marshall Islands *Changed Circumstances Petition* to Congress," May 16, 2005. In April 2014, the Republic of the Marshall Islands filed suit in a US federal court and before the International

The precise terms of a United States–Puerto Rico free association agreement would be determined through bilateral negotiations. The main features of the compacts of free association to which the United States is currently a party include the following:

1. *International legal personality of the associated state.* Unlike integration, both free association and independence involve the international personality of the associated state. The Republic of the Marshall Islands, the Federated States of Micronesia, and the Republic of Palau have all been admitted as members of the United Nations, and they participate in a wide range of international organizations.[93] In addition, the representatives exchanged between the associated states and the United States have ambassadorial rank.

2. *Full internal self-government for the associated state.* Although congressional approval was required to enact the compacts of free association, the US Congress does not have a veto over the constitutional provisions adopted by the freely associated states.[94]

3. *Authority and responsibility for security and defense matters delegated to the United States.* This was particularly important in the Micronesian Compact of Free Association

---

Court of Justice claiming that the United States and other countries have failed to comply with their obligations under the Treaty on the Non-Proliferation of Nuclear Weapons and seeking declaratory relief. See Lucy Westcott, "Marshall Islands Nuclear Lawsuit Reopens Old Wounds," *Newsweek*, Aug. 1, 2014, http://www.newsweek.com/marshall-islands-nuclear-lawsuit-reopens-old-wounds-262491.

93 See Keitner and Reisman, "Free Association," 59-61. Puerto Rico also participates in some international organizations, although to a more limited extent. For example, it is a member of the World Confederation of Labour, the Economic Commission for Latin America and the Caribbean, the World Health Organization, the World Federation of Trade Unions, and the Universal Postal Union; an associate member of the UN World Tourism Organization; a committee member of the International Olympic Committee; an observer in the Caribbean Community and Common Market and the Alliance of Small Island States; and a participant in INTERPOL and the Food and Agriculture Organization at the sub-bureau level.

94 This created a deadlock for many years over the adoption of the Compact of Free Association with Palau because the Constitution of Palau required the approval of 75% of voters (rather than a simple majority) of any arrangement that involved an asserted right of nuclear transit by the United States. See Keitner and Reisman, "Free Association," 50-51. Ultimately, the 75% requirement was amended, resulting in the approval of the compact by a 68% majority vote in 1993. See ibid.

because the United States' primary interest in Micronesia has been to exclude other powers from using the islands militarily.[95] This delegated power entails the United States' ability to establish and operate military facilities. Given the controversy surrounding the US Navy's use of the island of Vieques, the contours of this principle could appropriately form the subject of further negotiations in a United States–Puerto Rico free association agreement.

4. *Authority and responsibility for foreign affairs and marine resources retained by the associated state, with a commitment to consult with the United States.*[96]

5. *Ability of either party to terminate the agreement unilaterally, with continuation of certain elements of the agreement (notably, the security and defense provisions and the economic assistance provisions) for a defined period beyond the termination date.*[97]

The details of particular free association agreements can vary. Inhabitants of the Federated States of Micronesia and the Republic of the Marshall Islands are not US citizens, but they are exempted from the usual pre-admission requirements of non-US citizens when entering the United States.[98] Citizens of the freely associated states are eligible to receive Social Security Numbers and work in the United States, and they are entitled to request US consular assistance when travelling in countries where the Federated States of Micronesia and the Republic of the Marshall Islands do

---

95   Ibid., 35.

96   This stands in contrast to the CNMI's commonwealth arrangement, which vests responsibility for both foreign affairs and defense in the United States, and which the Ninth Circuit has held therefore entails US authority over seaward submerged lands whose ownership was disputed by the CNMI. See N. Mariana Islands v. United States, 399 F.3d 1057 (9th Cir. 2005).

97   The compacts require US consent to terminate the exclusivity or "denial" provisions excluding non-US military forces, even after termination. See Compact of Free Association: Federated States of Micronesia and Republic of the Marshall Islands, 48 U.S.C. §§ 1901-452(a)(3), -453(a)(2) (2013); Compact of Free Association: The Government of Palau, 48 U.S.C. §§ 1931-452(b), -453(a) (2013); Keitner and Reisman, "Free Association," 58.

98   Some of the migration provisions were subsequently revised, including by adding the requirement that visitors to the United States must hold a valid passport issued by the Federated States of Micronesia or the Republic of the Marshall Islands. See US Citizenship and Immigration Services, "Fact Sheet: Status of the Citizens of the Freely Associated States of the Federated States of Micronesia and the Republic of the Marshall Islands," Feb. 13, 2008, http://www.fsmgov.org/status.pdf.

not have diplomatic or consular representation. They may serve voluntarily in the US armed forces but are not subject to involuntary conscription. The freely associated states use the US dollar. They also benefit from various forms of US economic assistance and participate in designated federal programs and services, as provided in a number of subsidiary agreements.[99]

If Puerto Rico were to seek a free association arrangement with the United States, it should use the current allocation of federal funds for a plebiscite to establish whether the population supports pursuing such an arrangement. Representatives could then enter into bilateral negotiations, the result of which could be submitted to the Puerto Rican electorate for an up-or-down vote.

The ballot design for a plebiscite on status options is critical. Special attention should be given to translation in light of the linguistic complexity explored above. The most difficult question seems to be whether to include the status quo as an option or whether to include only the three options recognized as entailing a "full measure of self-government" under international law.[100] Taking the 1998 ballot as a model (without the status quo or "none of the above" options), and being careful to specify which options would require further US approval, one could envision a question along the following lines:

> International law recognizes three options for achieving a full
> measure of self-government: integration within an existing
> nation-state, free association with an existing nation-state, or
> independence as a separate nation-state. Puerto Rico's current

---

99 Entitlement to participate in federal programs has proved a major issue, particularly since one-third of the population of the Republic of the Marshall Islands has reportedly relocated to Hawaii, Guam, and the mainland United States. See Michael R. Duke, "Marshall Islanders: Migration Patterns and Health-Care Challenges," Migration Policy Institute, May 22, 2014, http://www.migrationpolicy .org/article/marshall-islanders-migration-patterns-and-health-care-challenges. See also Jon Letman, "U.S. Violating Compact of Free Association with Pacific Nations," IFG Asia-Pacific Program, Oct. 3, 2013, http://asiapacificifg.wordpress. com/2013/10/03/us-violating-compact-of-free-association-with-pacific-nations. In April 2014, the Ninth Circuit held that Hawaii is not required to fund Medicaid for migrants from the freely associated states whose federal health-care benefits were terminated as part of federal welfare reform. See Korab v. Fink, No. 11-15132 (9th Cir. Apr. 1, 2014), available at http://cdn.ca9.uscourts.gov/datastore/ opinions/2014/04/01/11-15132.pdf (finding that "Hawaii has no constitutional obligation to fill the gap left by Congress's withdrawal of federal funding for COFA Residents").

100 Including "none of the above" as an option in the December 13, 1998, Puerto Rico plebiscite seems to have compounded its inconclusiveness. See Chimène I. Keitner, "Associate Statehood: Principles and Prospects," *Faroese Law Review* 3 (2003): 13-40, 32-34.

status as a "commonwealth" (*estado libre asociado*) does not fall into any of these categories.

With the goal of promoting Puerto Rican dignity and a full measure of self-government, the following question asks you to select your preferred status for Puerto Rico. The United States would have to agree to implement any status modification other than independence.

INTEGRATION AS A STATE OF THE UNITED STATES. The admission of Puerto Rico into the United States of America as a state with rights, responsibilities, and benefits equal to those enjoyed by the rest of the states. The right to the presidential vote and equal representation in the Senate and proportional representation in the House of Representatives, with US citizenship provided by the Constitution of the United States of America.

ENTRY INTO A COMPACT OF FREE ASSOCIATION WITH THE UNITED STATES. The negotiation of a binding international agreement with the United States that recognizes the full authority and control of Puerto Rico over its internal self-government, with certain powers delegated to the United States as agreed by the parties. Provisions would likely include Puerto Rican citizenship instead of US citizenship for future generations, with the ability to travel to and work in the United States; foreign affairs conducted by Puerto Rico, with security and defense provided by the United States; continued use of the US dollar; and continued economic assistance from the United States. As a freely associated state (*estado libremente asociado*), Puerto Rico would be eligible for membership in the United Nations and other international organizations.

ESTABLISHMENT AS AN INDEPENDENT NATION-STATE. Declaration of independence and assertion of full control over economic, foreign affairs, security, and defense matters, as well as internal self-government. Membership in the United Nations and other international organizations. Cooperation with the United States to be determined by bilateral treaties between the United States and Puerto Rico.

If the status quo were included as an option on the grounds that voluntary continuation as a territory is consistent with the imperative of decolonization, the option could read as follows:

INDEFINITE CONTINUATION AS A US TERRITORY.
Continuation of the existing relationship with the United
States subject to the plenary authority of the US Congress
under the territory clause of the US Constitution, while
emphasizing the United States' commitment and obligation
under applicable US and international law to respect Puerto
Rican internal self-government.

Current debates about status options in Puerto Rico necessarily involve
speculation about the practical consequences of any new relationship, with
the understandable desire of all parties to maximize benefits and minimize
burdens. Some benefits and burdens—such as those relating to economic
assistance, taxation, and participation in federal programs—are quantifiable;
other implications of potential status options—such as those relating to
political and cultural identity—are less easily measured. The existing free
association arrangements with the Republic of the Marshall Islands, the
Federated States of Micronesia, and the Republic of Palau are far from
perfect, with continued struggles over certain issues, including entitlement
to compensation for nuclear testing and the receipt of federal health-care
benefits. That said, these agreements provide a legal framework for periodic
renegotiation and adjustment of the terms of these bilateral relationships free
from the constraints of the territory clause.

Conclusion

As a matter of US domestic law, the United States–Puerto Rico relationship
remains embedded in the conquest paradigm, reflected in the territory clause
of the US Constitution and the holdings of the Insular Cases. Meanwhile,
contemporary international law has replaced the prerogative of imperial
conquest with the imperative of popular consent. In the early 1950s, the
UN's application of the consent paradigm to Puerto Rico emphasized formal
acquiescence over substantive autonomy. At the same time, Puerto Rican
enthusiasm for the new constitutional arrangement may have been buoyed
by the belief that the island would have greater effective authority and more
significant input in relevant US policies than Congress intended to grant.
Subsequent discontent with the commonwealth model has not, however,
resulted in widespread agreement on how best to implement the consent
paradigm in both form and substance.

Genuine free association—the creation of an *estado libremente
asociado*—could present one viable option between integration as a US
state and full independence. It could address concerns that statehood, even
if accepted by Congress, would impair Puerto Rico's ability to preserve its

cultural and linguistic uniqueness and would impose an additional federal tax burden on the island's residents. At the same time, unlike the option of independence without association, it could offer an opportunity for Puerto Rico to negotiate long-term security and defense guarantees and economic assistance from the United States, while removing residual congressional authority over Puerto Rican affairs and enabling Puerto Rico to become a full-fledged member of the international community. No solution to Puerto Rico's status dilemma will garner uniform support, but genuine free association remains an option worth exploring.

CHAPTER SIX

The Insular Cases, Differentiated Citizenship, and Territorial Statuses in the Twenty-First Century

Rogers M. Smith*

Introduction

The Insular Cases are central to American political development because, in considering the applicability of the US Constitution to the territories acquired in the Spanish-American War, they addressed some of the most fundamental questions concerning appropriate forms of membership in modern republics. The answers they gave—that Congress had the power to decide whether residents of "unincorporated" territories would be US citizens, US "nationals," or perhaps something else—were and remain controversial.[1] In those cases, as in others of the Progressive Era (including ones scrutinizing race and gender classifications), the US Supreme Court upheld legislative powers to create what scholars have come to call "differentiated citizenship."[2] Several of the

---

*   I would like to thank Jaime Lluch and Gerald L. Neuman for helpful discussions of the themes of this chapter and Reed Smith for invaluable research assistance.

1   Bartholomew H. Sparrow, *The* Insular Cases *and the Emergence of American Empire* (Lawrence: University Press of Kansas, 2006), 215-16, 221-25.

2   The late political philosopher Iris Young probably did most to establish the term. See, e.g., Iris Marion Young, "Residential Segregation and Differentiated Citizenship," *Citizenship Studies* 3 (1999): 237-52.

most important forms of differentiated citizenship then sustained have since been repudiated as systems of unjust inequality.

But in the twenty-first century, many are contending that various contemporary forms of differentiated citizenship are necessary to achieve meaningfully equal membership statuses. These include distinct forms of territorial membership. And though all claims for particular types of differentiated citizenship are in some respects unique, they also make up a more general pattern that controversies over territorial membership can illuminate. That is because here—perhaps more starkly than in any other area of modern American citizenship laws—some of the most basic, enduring, and still unsettled questions of civic equality are again being explicitly contested. Disturbingly, many of the answers that still prevail with regard to territorial residents' rights of voting, expatriation, and birthright citizenship appear to do more to perpetuate past policies of inegalitarian differentiation than to establish statuses that are defensibly "different but equal." There are, however, also developments that provide legal support for the aspirations of many territorial residents to maintain distinct cultural identities while simultaneously being full American citizens. Whether these represent appropriate accommodations or abdications of core constitutional values remains deeply disputed.

The roots of these contested issues around civic equality are deep. However we view the complex history of political ideas that contributed to the rise of large-scale republics since the end of the eighteenth century, beginning with the American and French Republics, it is impossible to deny the existence of powerful strains insisting that the citizens of republics must be equal before the law, possessed of identical bundles of basic rights and duties. Those themes were robustly strengthened in the United States during the twentieth century by civil rights struggles against many forms of what came to be deemed second-class citizenship, especially for nonwhites and women but also for unpopular religious minorities, the disabled, the elderly, and people with unconventional sexual identities, among others. For a time, most of the intertwined versions of "liberalism," "democracy," and "republicanism" that became predominant in academia during the last half of the twentieth century, and to a lesser degree in mainstream political discourses, presumed that citizenship should, in principle and in practice, be a nearly or wholly universal status, and a nearly or wholly uniform status, for the residents of any and all liberal democracies or republics.[3]

Nonetheless, as many scholars are now stressing, that presumption has

---

3   I sketch these developments briefly in "Equality and Differentiated Citizenship: A Modern Democratic Dilemma in Tocquevillean Perspective," in *Anxieties of Democracy: Tocquevillean Reflections on India and the United States*, ed. Partha Chatterjee and Ira Katznelson (New Delhi: Oxford University Press, 2012), 90-99.

never matched the real structures of citizenship laws in the United States or, in varying ways, other modern democracies.[4] To grasp the character and significance of controversies over citizenship in the US territories today, it will be helpful to begin with a brief overview of the broader sources and types of civic differentiation, and to then lay out the main variations in modern territorial forms of political membership.

An Overview of Civic Differentiation

The specific sources of civic differentiation are as varied as its many forms, but they can be placed under four general headings:

1. *Remedial differentiations*: policies aimed at overcoming inegalitarian consequences of past unjust differentiations and at combating current forms of invidious discrimination, often by providing temporary special aid to long-disadvantaged groups.

2. *Accommodationist differentiations*: policies structured to give enduring legal recognition to various persons' and groups' distinctive senses of their identities, values, and interests by modifying legal regulations and public services so that these people can flourish in their own ways, yet equally with other citizens.

3. *Preservationist differentiations*: policies reflecting the desires of powerful political actors to distinguish—usually by limiting—the civic status of some who they see, for economic, national security, cultural, or ideological reasons, as threats to current arrangements that these powerful actors value. Proponents of preservationist differentiations are generally conservative opponents of remedial and accommodationist reform measures, but sometimes the preservation of their interests requires innovations in civic statuses to respond to new challenges.

4. *Legacy differentiations*: inherited policies created for reasons that today have lost force, so that these policies actually have few strong supporters. But in a path-dependent manner, these differentiations persist because no clear or intensely

---

4   See, e.g., Elizabeth F. Cohen, *Semi-Citizenship in Democratic Politics* (New York: Cambridge University Press, 2009); Kamal Sadiq, *Paper Citizens: How Illegal Immigrants Acquire Citizenship in Developing Countries* (New York: Oxford University Press, 2008).

motivated consensus on alternative policies exists that is capable of producing change. The contrasting views of the first three positions on which differentiations are appropriate can contribute to this kind of persistence, working against agreements on changes despite the lack of powerful contemporary advocates for the status quo. Such lack of consensus has arguably contributed to the perpetuation of the commonwealth status of Puerto Rico, for example. In three nonbinding referenda between 1967 and 1998, Puerto Ricans showed increasing dissatisfaction with remaining a commonwealth, but they were closely divided on what alternative to pursue.[5] In a fourth referendum in November 2012, for the first time, 54% of those voting opposed the status quo, and more than 61% of those who then chose between several status alternatives favored statehood.[6] The consequences of this vote remain to be seen.

The first two rationales, remedial and accommodationist, are often blended. Accommodations are often advocated for groups as a means of remedying past or current injustices against them, especially when it seems impractical to identify and correct every particular act of unjust discrimination. Still, they are analytically distinct. Special accommodations, such as exemptions from certain civic education requirements or the provision of multilingual ballots, have been provided in America to religious groups like the Amish and to recent European immigrants who have not experienced any substantial discrimination. The aim of special accommodations defended in modern multicultural theories and movements is often simply to enable distinctive groups to thrive as well as others while sustaining defining aspects of their group identities. Nonetheless, it is probably true that calls for special accommodations often garner broadest support when they are made on behalf of groups that have at least arguably been treated unfairly in the past—as in the case of persons who use wheelchairs, who were long unable to ride buses or enter public buildings because facilities had been designed without consideration for those who could not walk or climb stairs without aids beyond handrails.

But strikingly, although remedial arguments for policies of civic differentiation have long been persuasive to many ears, it is accommodationist

---

5   D.R., "Could Puerto Rico Become America's 51st State?," *The Economist*, Oct. 21, 2013, http://www.economist.com/blogs/economist-explains/2013/10/economist-explains-15.
6   Mariano Castillo, "Puerto Ricans Favor Statehood for First Time," CNN.com, Nov. 8, 2012, http://www.cnn.com/2012/11/07/politics/election-puerto-rico.

rationales, not remedial ones, that are multiplying and gaining broader support in the twenty-first century. They are the chief reason why the political phenomenon of differentiated citizenship is in many ways expanding beyond older "preservationist" and "legacy" forms, despite the popularity of ideals of uniform citizenship.

Among the contributing factors to this multiplication, two are especially pertinent here. First is the replacement of early twentieth-century doctrines and practices of imperialism by commitments to the rights of political self-determination for a wide range of groups defining themselves as "nations" or "peoples." The 1945 United Nations Charter committed its members who had responsibilities for "the administration of territories whose peoples have not yet attained a full measure of self-government" not only to provide for the interests of those peoples but "to develop self-government" according to "the particular circumstances of each territory and its peoples."[7] That goal suggested that self-governance, and thus citizenship rights, might take many different forms. Then, in 1960, the United Nations General Assembly adopted the Declaration on the Granting of Independence to Colonial Countries and Peoples, reasserting that "all peoples have the right to self-determination" and urging "immediate steps" to "transfer all powers to the peoples" of all "Non-Self-Governing" territories so that they could "enjoy complete independence and freedom."[8] That language appears to imply fully independent self-governance, but in practice it has often fostered varying degrees of greater autonomy for former colonies that retain many formal and informal affiliations with their former imperial metropole. The United States, which historically often justified its acquisitions of overseas territories as a means to provide tutelary preparation for self-governance, has long claimed that it seeks to adhere to these international commitments; however, in all the territorial cases considered here, since 1960, the United States has supported increases in self-governance but not full independence. The result has been dissimilar patterns of citizenship rights.

The second major contributor to that still-proliferating modern pattern is the continuing expansion of transnational networks of economic production and exchange, communications, transportation, social affiliation, and outright migration, including networks of actors and institutions promoting human rights goals—phenomena often collectively termed globalization. Somewhat paradoxically, by expanding the range of economic and political allies and options available to those discontented with their civic status quo, these developments have strengthened political movements to achieve greater devolution of political power to culturally distinct regions (such as Quebec,

---

7   United Nations Charter, art. 73.
8   G.A. Res. 1514 (XV), U.N. GAOR, 15th Sess., Supp. No. 16, at 66, U.N. Doc. A/4684 (Dec. 14, 1960).

Catalonia, Scotland, and many indigenous peoples and tribes) and also efforts to create new forms of transnational political communities (such as the European Union, the much less developed African Union, and the Union of South American Nations). They have thereby encouraged more widespread governmental acceptances of multilevel citizenships; dual or multinational citizenships for persons and corporations; policies of "quasi-citizenship" that extend special privileges to ethnic affiliates outside a nation's boundaries; "overseas citizens" statuses for former colonial subjects; and diverse policies of multiculturalism in many countries.[9]

Most of these developments have been promoted as methods of creating more meaningful equality of status and opportunities for persons while recognizing their distinct histories, aspirations, and needs, rather than as departures from norms of equal membership. But if they are forms of equal citizenship, they are also generally forms of differentiated citizenship. They mean that members of different nations within a transnational union; inhabitants of different locales in a country that offers special autonomous self-governing powers to some provinces, departments, states, or indigenous or immigrant communities; persons able to claim two or more national citizenships (in whole or in part); and members of religious and ethnic communities exempt from some general laws all possess bundles of rights and duties different from those of most other citizens in the states that issue their passports and promise protection in exchange for at least partial allegiance.

Territorial memberships are obviously among the forms of political membership that have been and are being transformed by these developments. Probably most significant has been the shift from the embrace of overtly imperialistic, if often professedly paternalistic, governance to varied forms of greater political autonomy and self-governance, amidst an international climate that teems with calls for further movement in those directions. But concerns to accommodate cultural differences and remedy injustices in ways that do not eradicate bases of common civic identity, as well as desires to

---

9   For pertinent recent discussions, see, e.g., David Cook-Martin, *The Scramble for Citizens: Dual Nationality and State Competition for Immigrants* (Stanford, CA: Stanford University Press, 2013); Kees Groenendijk, "The Status of Quasi-Citizenship in EU Member States: Why Some States Have 'Almost-Citizens,'" in *Acquisition and Loss of Nationality: Policy Trends in 15 European Countries*, vol. 1, ed. Rainer Baubock, Eva Ebersoll, Kees Groenendijk, and Harald Waldrauch (Amsterdam: Amsterdam University Press, 2007), 411-29; Will Kymlicka, *Multicultural Odysseys: Navigating the New International Politics of Diversity* (New York: Oxford University Press, 2007); Jean-Michel Lafleur, *Transnational Politics and the State: The External Voting Rights of Diasporas* (New York: Routledge, 2013); Willem Maas, ed., *Multilevel Citizenship* (Philadelphia: University of Pennsylvania Press, 2013).

preserve arrangements seen as beneficial to powerful interests, are also strongly at work. The next section maps out the differentiated forms of territorial citizenship that exist today in the United States. It is then followed by a brief comparison with France, the second-oldest modern republic and the one most avowedly committed to unitary citizenship.

The Differentiated Forms of Modern Territorial Membership

As Bartholomew Sparrow has noted, few though its territorial possessions may seem in comparison to past empires, the United States currently asserts sovereignty over more land outside its member states or provinces than any other country in the world. The list includes the Commonwealths of Puerto Rico and the Northern Mariana Islands, along with the territories of Guam, American Samoa, the US Virgin Islands, and some virtually and wholly uninhabited Pacific Islands.[10] Although the total population of these territories is just a little over four million people—a tiny portion of the US population of 317 million—the 2010 census showed Puerto Rico to be more populated than twenty-two states (though it has since lost residents rapidly).[11] Puerto Rico and Guam each have more citizens than the Federated States of Micronesia and Andorra, and every one of the inhabited US territories is more populous than Liechtenstein and Monaco.[12] Only China's territories have larger populations.[13]

The legacy of the Insular Cases is that all these entities under US sovereignty are "unincorporated" territories, a legal status that is now widely understood to mean territories for which Congress has never yet anticipated statehood.[14] Like other former colonial powers, the United States has been affected by, and indeed has sometimes led, the international movements to promote the rights of political self-determination for a wide range of communities, which began at the end of World War I and accelerated after

---

10   Sparrow, *The* Insular Cases *and the Emergence of American Empire*, 215.
11   Ibid.; Lizette Alvarez, "Economy and Crime Spur New Puerto Rican Exodus," *New York Times*, Feb. 9, 2014; US Census Bureau, "2010 Census Data," accessed Oct. 29, 2014, http://www.census.gov/2010census/data.
12   Cf. US Census Bureau, "Statistical Abstract of the United States: Section 29; Puerto Rico and the Island Areas," accessed Oct. 29, 2014, http://www.census.gov/prod/2011pubs/12statab/outlying.pdf; and World Atlas, "Countries of the World," accessed Oct. 29, 2014, http://worldatlas.com/aatlas/populations/ctypopls.htm.
13   Sparrow, *The* Insular Cases *and the Emergence of American Empire*, 216.
14   See, e.g., Examining Bd. of Engineers, Architects & Surveyors v. Flores de Otero, 426 U.S. 572, 600 n.30 (1976).

World War II. But as in other former empires, in the United States there has been no common path or solution to the forms of greater self-governance, or the forms of political membership, established for (and, to some disputed degree, by) the American territories. Congress has conferred—or in the eyes of some, imposed—US citizenship on most of the inhabitants of US territories, with the exception of American Samoans, who are designated US "nationals." Still, the rights and duties of US citizens in these territories vary from those of citizens in the states and from one another. A full mapping of the variations is unnecessary to show the prevalence of civic differentiation, but some contrasts are worth noting.

One of the two surviving Spanish-American War acquisitions, Puerto Rico became a "commonwealth" as a result of a process initiated by Congress in 1950 that included a constitution written and approved by Puerto Ricans but modified to satisfy congressional demands before it went into effect in 1952.[15] Puerto Rico now has broad powers of local self-governance; but in the eyes of the US government, including its courts, the island has these powers only at the sufferance of Congress. US citizens in Puerto Rico do not have voting representation in Congress, nor do they vote for the president. Partly in return, they also do not pay federal income taxes. Yet Puerto Rico is the only US territory that falls legally within the United States' customs borders: while goods entering it from outside the United States must pay US duties, its goods are not subject to tariffs when sent to the fifty states.[16]

Guam, in contrast, remains a territory broadly governed by Congress's 1950 Organic Act of Guam, which conferred American citizenship on Guamanians.[17] In 1968, as America's civil rights era reinforced international pressures for territorial self-governance, Congress authorized popular elections for the governors of Guam and the Virgin Islands. It provided both with nonvoting delegates to Congress in 1972. But in the late 1980s, the United States refused to approve Guam's efforts to gain commonwealth status with self-governing powers comparable to those of the territory's prospering neighbor, the Commonwealth of the Northern Mariana Islands.[18] Guam continues to be of significant strategic importance to the United States, and

---

15   T. Alexander Aleinikoff, *Semblances of Sovereignty: The Constitution, the State, and American Citizenship* (Cambridge, MA: Harvard University Press, 2002), 76-77.

16   Ibid.; Sparrow, *The* Insular Cases *and the Emergence of American Empire*, 226.

17   Organic Act of Guam, Pub. L. No. 81-630, 64 Stat. 384 (1950) (codified at 48 U.S.C. § 1421 (2013)); Robert F. Rogers, "Guam's Quest for Political Identity," *Pacific Studies* 12 (1988): 49-70, 49.

18   Arnold H. Leibowitz, *Defining Status: A Comprehensive Analysis of United States Territorial Relations* (Dordrecht: Martinus Nijhoff, 1989), 335-42; Dominica Tolentino, "Chammoro Quest for Self-Determination," *Guampedia: The Encyclopedia of Guam*, http://guampedia.com/chamorro-quest-for-self-determination.

many US officials have expressed concern that with greater autonomy, Guam might resist US military policies, especially because of the rising power of indigenous Chamorro activists in Guam's politics.[19] Some in Guam have also sought to have their citizenship status altered from congressionally based to constitutionally based through a declaration that their status derives from the citizenship clause in Section 1 of the Fourteenth Amendment, a position the United States has resisted.[20] As in the other territories, dissatisfactions and contestation over its status continues today.

The United States acquired the eastern group of the Samoan Islands via the 1899 Tripartite Convention with Germany and the United Kingdom.[21] President McKinley quickly issued an executive order proclaiming US authority over the American Samoan islands. But in 1900 and 1904, various chiefs of the eastern islands signed a "deed of cession" accepting US territorial status for "American Samoa" (and Congress added another privately owned Samoan island in 1925).[22] These agreements arguably made the process of Samoa's acquisition more consensual than in the other American territories: in all these measures, the rights of native Samoans to keep their lands for themselves and their posterity were repeatedly guaranteed.[23] The United States never passed an organic act for the islands, and many of its leaders have resisted efforts to incorporate American Samoa fully into the United States or to become US citizens instead of nationals. In 1967, Samoa adopted a constitution that has since structured its governance.[24] Nonetheless, the US secretary of the interior claims supervisory authority over all American Samoan governmental structures, a position that both Samoans and a leading scholar of American territories, Arnold H. Leibowitz, dispute.[25]

In still further contrast, the US Virgin Islands, purchased from Denmark in 1917 for their strategic value during World War I, are governed

---

19   Rogers, "Guam's Quest for Political Identity," 50, 56-67.
20   Leibowitz, *Defining Status*, 334. Guam Congresswoman Madeleine Z. Bordallo and former Guam Governor Carl Gutierrez both joined in a "Brief of *Amici Curiae* Certain Members of Congress and Former Governmental Officials" arguing on behalf of Fourteenth Amendment citizenship for those born in Guam in the now-pending case of *Tuaua v. United States*, discussed below. See Case No. 13-5272, U.S. Court of Appeals for the District of Columbia Circuit, Document #1492654, filed May 12, 2014.
21   Convention between the United States, Germany, and Great Britain to Adjust Amicably the Questions between the Three Governments in respect to the Samoan Group of Islands, Dec. 2, 1899, 31 Stat. 1878.
22   Leibowitz, *Defining Status*, 402-3, 414-15.
23   Ibid.
24   Sparrow, *The* Insular Cases *and the Emergence of American Empire*, 38; Rose Cuison Villazor, "Blood Quantum Land Laws and the Race versus Political Identity Dilemma," *California Law Review* 96 (2008): 801-37, 826.
25   Leibowitz, *Defining Status*, 418-21.

by the congressional Revised Organic Act of 1954,[26] modifying a 1936 act that
created a senate that makes up the islands' unicameral legislature. Like the
citizens of Guam, Virgin Islanders gained authority to elect their governor
and have a delegate to Congress in the early 1970s, following US promises of
movement toward greater self-governance.[27] But in part because of internal
disputes over who should count as a Virgin Islander and over the distribution
of power among the islands, four constitutional conventions from 1964 to
1980 failed to produce a popularly approved constitution for Congress to
approve.[28] In 2009, a fifth constitutional convention did produce a charter
that the Virgin Islands governor submitted to the US government, but in 2010
Congress sent it back for reconsideration, concerned that it inadequately
recognized US sovereignty and unduly favored persons of local birth and
ancestry, among other matters.[29]

The United States invaded its most recent territorial acquisition,
the Marianas, in 1944, when the islands were under Japanese control. The
United States then formally acquired the fifteen Northern Mariana Islands
in 1947, when the United Nations appointed it to serve as trustee for a trust
territory consisting of these and other Pacific Islands. In 1976, the United
States entered into a "covenant" that established the Commonwealth of the
Northern Mariana Islands (CNMI) in political union with the United States,
in part because the United States regarded the islands, like neighboring Guam,
as key to its strategic interests in the Pacific, and this change promised to still
discontents.[30] The new CNMI did well economically, and in 1986, after the
commonwealth had adopted and implemented its own constitution modeled
on that of the United States, President Reagan formally terminated the United
States' trusteeship over the islands. Most of its residents then became US
citizens, and they eventually gained an elected but, again, nonvoting delegate
to Congress.[31] Until 2009, the CNMI had its own immigration system, but

---

26 Revised Organic Act of the Virgin Islands, Pub. L. No. 83-517, 68 Stat. 497 (1954).
27 Leibowitz, *Defining Status*, 272-73.
28 Ibid., 276-78.
29 See Joint Resolution to Provide for the Reconsideration and Revision of the
Proposed Constitution of the United States Virgin Islands to Correct Provisions
Inconsistent with the Constitution and Federal Law, Pub. L. No. 111-194, 124
Stat. 1309 (2010). Virgin Islands Congresswoman Donna Christensen and former
Virgin Islands Governor Charles W. Turnbull also joined the "Brief of Amici
Curiae Certain Members of Congress and Former Governmental Officials" in
Tuaua v. United States, arguing for Fourteenth Amendment birthright citizenship
for all persons born in US territories.
30 Rogers, "Guam's Quest for Political Identity," 53-54.
31 See, e.g., Guerrero v. United States, 691 F. Supp. 260, 261-64 (D. N. Mar. I. 1988);
Lizabeth A. McKibben, "The Political Relationship between the United States and

in 2008 Congress imposed US immigration laws on it via the Consolidated Natural Resources Act.[32]

That last fact underlines the most salient political reality of the US territories: in the cases of the two commonwealths, the organized territories of Guam and the Virgin Islands, and what may be deemed the self-organized territory of American Samoa, the United States continues to assert its legal authority to engage in substantial administrative supervision and to legislate over many, if not all, territorial matters, including decisions on the scope of the US government's own authority. It does so ultimately on the basis of Congress's constitutional powers to "make all needful Rules and Regulations respecting the Territory or other Property belonging to the United States."[33] This includes the power to treat the citizens of territories differently from state citizens and from one another, and US statutes and judicial rulings often do so—in ways that many territorial inhabitants are contesting.

France in Comparison

Before turning to some of the most revealing of those contests, it is worth observing that although the United States, as the world's military superpower, may weigh strategic national security concerns in relation to its territories more heavily than any other nation, there is nothing unusual about its pattern of diverse territorial statuses and diverse political rights for many whom it proclaims to be its equal citizens. Probably no country in the world is more insistent on its dedication to equal citizenship for all members of its republic than France; yet French territories display a startling array of differences in their organization and rights that in some respects are being deliberately increased in the twenty-first century.[34]

Nathalie Mrgudovic notes that in 1962, France had eleven overseas territories—four overseas departments (DOMs, for their French acronym) (Martinique, Guadeloupe, French Guiana, and Réunion Island) largely identical in status to the *départements* in mainland France, and seven overseas territories (TOMs, for their French acronym) (New Caledonia, French

---

Pacific Islands Entities: The Path to Self-Government in the Northern Mariana Islands, Palau, and Guam," *Harvard International Law Journal* 3 (1990): 257-93, 271-75.

32 Consolidated Natural Resources Act of 2008, Pub. L. No. 110-229, §§ 701-18, 122 Stat. 754, 853-69.

33 U.S. CONST., art. IV, § 3, cl. 2.

34 Nathalie Mrgudovic, "The French Overseas Territories in Transition," in *The Non-Independent Territories of the Caribbean and the Pacific: Continuity of Change?*, ed. Peter Clegg and David Killingray (London: Institute of Commonwealth Studies, 2012).

Polynesia, Wallis and Futuna, the Comoros Islands, French Somaliland, the French Southern and Antarctic Lands, and Saint Pierre and Miquelon). The TOMs, unlike the DOMs, were guaranteed rights of "free-determination" expressed in diverse forms of relatively autonomous governing structures; and whereas the DOMs were treated almost the same as domestic *départements*, French national policy determined which otherwise generally applicable laws did and did not apply to particular TOMs.[35] Even so, all members of the DOMs and TOMs were French citizens, and they, in principle, enjoyed the same legal status as other French citizens—but in practice, they had a wide range of rights of political self-determination.[36]

Since then, the Comoros Islands have gained independence, though the island of Mayotte decided to remain French and become a CTOM, a status in between a DOM and a TOM; this status has since also been adopted by Saint Pierre and Miquelon.[37] The TOMs have also been subdivided into two new categories, and French officials have encouraged further redefinitions of statuses and self-governing powers.[38] They first sought to encourage DOMs to join in new regional entities, ROMs, so that they would be more economically self-supporting and require less aid from France. But the French Constitutional Council insisted that to be equal with metropolitan collectivities in France, they instead had to become Départements et Régions d'Outre-Mer, or DROMs.[39] How this solved the problem of equal status with French metropolitan regions is unclear.

In fact, the proliferation of statuses is greater than this listing of TOMs, DOMs, CTOMs, and DROMs indicates (there are also COMs). That is because French policy since 2000, largely in an effort to reduce the economic dependency of most territories on France, has held, in the words of President Chirac, that "uniform statuses are over and each overseas collectivity should evolve, if it so wishes, toward a somehow tailored status."[40] Chirac's successor, Nicolas Sarkozy, also contended that the "unity of the Republic does not imply a uniformity of its institutions," and he endorsed for each overseas territory "an organization adapted to its own characteristics as long as this does not affect the principle of unity of the Republic," which meant specifically that the "overseas territories are French and will remain French" (despite French commitments to their "free-determination").[41] But in 2010, more than 70% of voters in referenda in Martinique and French Guiana emphatically rejected Sarkozy's proposals to give their governments greater autonomy while

---

35   Ibid., 86-87.
36   Ibid., 87.
37   Ibid.
38   Ibid., 88-89.
39   Ibid., 90-91.
40   Ibid., 95.
41   Ibid., 95-96.

remaining part of France (and Guadeloupe refused to hold a referendum).[42] In 1998, New Caledonia independence supporters and French loyalists agreed to hold a similar status referendum between 2014 and 2018, and in the territory's 2014 parliamentary elections, independence supporters won twenty-five of fifty-four seats, a gain of two since the last election in 2009, while loyalists held the remaining twenty-nine.[43] This close division leaves the future status of New Caledonia very much in doubt.

Though arguments for greater French territorial autonomy and diversity are often cast in "accommodationist" rhetoric, stressing the desire to tailor policies to the distinct needs and aspirations of each locale, they are obviously also driven by a very strong "preservationist" motive—that is, the desire to keep France's wealth from draining into the territories. For the same reason, many territorial inhabitants resist them, believing that greater autonomy will leave them economically vulnerable. As in New Caledonia, exactly what all this means for the civic identities of the French territories is a contested, evolving work in progress. The point that these facts about France underline is that a wide array of varying forms of differentiated citizenship can be found everywhere—so the US territories are not exceptional in that regard. But what those forms should be remains unclear. Selecting from a range of possible topics, this chapter's analysis of contemporary struggles over US territorial citizenship will focus on four issues that have recently been subjects of litigation and continuing political battles.

Modern Controversies over Citizenship in the US Territories

The four issues are (i) whether US citizens in the territories possess constitutional rights to vote in American national elections; (ii) whether they can expatriate themselves from their US citizenship while retaining their territorial residences and citizenships; (iii) whether they are birthright citizens of the United States under the Fourteenth Amendment; and (iv) whether the US Constitution, especially its equal protection clause, permits them to maintain forms of owning and transmitting land that accord with their traditional customs, even when such land ownership would be deemed impermissible racial "restrictive covenants" within the fifty states. The answers that US officials and courts have given are that territorial citizens do not

---

42   Rodolphe Lamy, "French Guiana, Martinique reject autonomy proposal," *Boston.com*, Jan. 11, 2010, http://www.boston.com/cars/news/articles/2010/01/11/french_guiana_martinique_reject_autonomy_proposal.

43   "New Caledonia Elections: French Loyalists Win, Independence Supporters Gain Ground," *Australian Network News*, May 12, 2014, http://www.abc.net.au/news/2014-05-12/an-new-caledonia-elections/5445380.

possess a constitutional right to vote in federal elections, or any right to divest themselves of US citizenship without relinquishing residency in US territories and thus their territorial citizenship—nor are territorial citizens Fourteenth Amendment birthright citizens. Courts have held, however, in regard to both American Samoa and the Northern Mariana Islands, that it is constitutionally permissible for territories to maintain land laws and other culturally valued customs that would not be permissible in the states, regardless of whether territorial residents are US nationals or US citizens. These last rulings clearly represent "accommodationist" forms of differentiation, albeit controversial ones. The decisions on the first three topics, on the other hand, appear to be chiefly "preservationist" efforts to limit the rights and powers of territorial citizens relative to the US government.

Voting Rights

In 1994, Gregorio Igartúa de la Rosa began a series of cases in which he and other US citizens residing in Puerto Rico have claimed to have constitutional rights to vote for the president and for members of the House of Representatives—assertions that US courts have regularly rejected, though not without passionate dissents. Citing the rejection of an earlier similar claim by US citizens residing in Guam, federal courts have consistently held that the Constitution provides for the president to be elected by electors chosen by the states, and Puerto Rico is not a state.[44] In 2000, however, the United States District Court for the District of Puerto Rico ruled that the right to vote in national elections was a national right guaranteed by the First Amendment principle of freedom of association and the due process and equal protection clauses, and was not dependent on federalism. It also interpreted the congressional Uniformed and Overseas Citizens Absentee Voting Act[45] as confirmation that the right to vote rests on national citizenship, not residence in a state.[46] But that ruling was quickly overturned, with Circuit Judge Juan R. Torruella regretfully acknowledging that "the federal courts continue to recognize the almost absolute power of Congress to unilaterally dictate the affairs of Puerto Rico and her people," so that "the practicality of the matter is that Puerto Rico remains a colony."[47] He thought that this status violated "the very principles upon which this Nation was founded," but felt that the court's only recourse was to call on "the political branches of government" to correct

---

44   Igartúa de la Rosa v. United States, 32 F.3d 8 (1st Cir. 1994).
45   Uniformed and Overseas Citizens Absentee Voting Act of 1986, Pub. L. No. 99-410, 100 Stat. 924 (codified at 52 U.S.C. § 20301 (2013)).
46   Igartúa de la Rosa v. United States, 113 F. Supp. 2d 228, 232 (D.P.R. 2000).
47   Igartúa de la Rosa v. United States, 229 F.3d 80, 89 (1st Cir. 2000) (Torruella, C.J., concurring).

"what amounts to an outrageous disregard for the rights of a substantial segment of its citizenry."[48]

Igartúa de la Rosa pursued the litigation, adding claims that several treaties committing the United States to human rights and to rights of self-determination required recognizing the national voting rights of citizens; but the First Circuit Court of Appeals ruled that these treaties were incapable of overriding the constitutional structuring of presidential elections by states.[49] This time, Torruella, now senior circuit judge, dissented. He assailed the "unincorporated/incorporated" territorial distinction as a judicial invention rooted in racism, stressed that voting rights had long been judicially deemed "fundamental," and insisted that the treaties revealed "the emergence of a norm of customary international law" in favor of rights of political participation that has "an independent and binding juridical status."[50]

After that defeat, Igartúa returned with a slightly different argument. He contended that the language of Article I of the Constitution—which states that "[t]he House of Representatives shall be composed of Members chosen every second Year by the People of the several States"[51]—should be read as conferring voting rights on all who were part of "We the People of the United States," not simply people residing in "the several States."[52] The government of the Commonwealth of Puerto Rico added that because the US government has treated Puerto Rico as "the functional equivalent of a state" for many purposes, its citizens are entitled to representation in the House of Representatives in the manner of a state; and it added that the recent Supreme Court decision in *Boumediene v. Bush*[53] gives new recognition to the status claims of territories. The circuit court found nothing in that decision pertinent to voting rights, however.[54] Judge Torruella concurred in part and dissented in part, continuing to assail the "status of second-class citizenship" that he believed the courts had fostered through the Insular Cases' distinction between unincorporated and incorporated territories.[55] Igartúa has since continued to litigate without success. Throughout these cases both the Bush and Obama Justice Departments have filed briefs against him. Each administration has stressed that Puerto Ricans have had the opportunity to vote for statehood but have not yet committed to pursuing that option.[56]

---

48   Ibid., 89-90.
49   Igartúa de la Rosa v. United States, 417 F.3d 145, 147-49 (1st Cir. 2005).
50   Ibid., 169, 176 (Torruella, J., dissenting).
51   U.S. Const., art. I, § 2, cl. 1.
52   Igartúa v. United States, 626 F.3d 592, 596-97 (1st Cir. 2010).
53   Boumediene v. Bush, 553 U.S. 723 (2008).
54   Igartúa v. United States, 626 F.3d 592, 598 (1st Cir. 2010).
55   Ibid., 638 (Torruella, J., concurring in part and dissenting in part).
56   See Brief for the United States in Opposition at 8, Igartúa de la Rosa v. United

Administrations of both parties have thus argued in "accommodationist" or, at most, "legacy" terms: up into 2012, Puerto Ricans appeared to favor maintaining their distinctive status, or at least appeared to be too deeply divided regarding which option might be preferable for the United States to act on. The strong vote in favor of statehood in 2012, though still disputed, is spurring further action to gain that status. But even if Puerto Ricans persist in that pursuit, it is likely that Republicans in Congress will oppose it for "preservationist" reasons: statehood would probably increase the political power of Democrats.[57]

Expatriation

In response to being denied voting rights in US national elections, some Puerto Ricans have insisted that they should be allowed to give up the US citizenship conferred on them by Congress while continuing to reside in Puerto Rico and vote in Puerto Rico elections strictly as Puerto Rican citizens. The modern controversies stem chiefly from the 1994 decision of Puerto Rican independence activist Juan Mari Brás to renounce his US citizenship at the US Embassy in Caracas, Venezuela, and then return to Puerto Rico and participate in politics. The embassy gave him a "certificate of loss of nationality of the United States." But as other Puerto Ricans followed suit, the US State Department began refusing to permit persons to expatriate themselves from the United States while remaining Puerto Ricans, contending that expatriation requires giving up residence within the United States and its territories.[58]

The US government was concerned in part by the decision of the Supreme Court of Puerto Rico in 1997 that Mari Brás was in fact still a citizen of Puerto Rico, entitled to full political rights there, despite his renunciation.[59] Justice Fuster Berlingeri's opinion contended that when Puerto Rico gained commonwealth status from 1950 through 1952, "the public authority and governmental powers of the people of Puerto Rico were not, as before, merely delegated by Congress, but rather, *stemmed from itself and were free*

States, No. 05-650 (Sup. Ct. Feb. 2006); Brief for the Respondents in Opposition, Igartúa v. U.S., No. 11-876 (Sup. Ct. Apr. 2012).

57   Jason Koebler, "Despite Referendum, Puerto Rican Statehood Unlikely Until at Least 2015," *U.S. News and World Report*, Nov. 7, 2012, http://www.usnews.com/news/articles/2012/11/07/despite-referendum-puerto-rican-statehood-unlikely-until-at-least-2015.

58   I have previously discussed this case in "The Bitter Roots of Puerto Rican Citizenship," in *Foreign in a Domestic Sense: Puerto Rico, American Expansion, and the Constitution*, ed. Christina Duffy Burnett and Burke Marshall (Durham: Duke University Press, 2001), 373-74, 380-84.

59   Ramírez de Ferrer v. Mari Brás, Tribunal Supremo de Puerto Rico [Sup. Ct. of P.R.], No. CT-96-14 (Nov. 18, 1997).

from higher authority." Though Puerto Rican citizenship had been "initially established by federal law" of the United States, he maintained, "its legal foundation no longer rests on such federal law," stemming instead from the Constitution of the Commonwealth of Puerto Rico.[60] In a 2006 memorandum, Puerto Rico's secretary of justice affirmed the ruling's holding, and Mari Brás became the first—but not the last—person to receive a state certificate of Puerto Rican citizenship.[61]

Before then, however, the United States District Court for the District of Columbia had stated a different view, which the State Department has treated as authoritative. In 1996, Alberto O. Lozada Colón executed an oath renouncing his US citizenship at a US consulate in the Dominican Republic and, like Mari Brás, then resumed his residence in Puerto Rico. The following year, he sought to obtain a writ compelling the US State Department to supply him with a certificate of loss of nationality. The department refused to do so, and Colón sued. District Court Judge Stanley Sporkin upheld the department's decision, holding that while Colón claimed to be renouncing "all rights and privileges of United States citizenship," he in fact wished to "continue to exercise one of the fundamental rights of citizenship, namely the right to travel freely throughout the world and when he wants, to return and reside in the United States"—since "it is unmistakably clear that Puerto Rico is part of the United States."[62] Because Colón had not fully renounced his US citizenship, the State Department had no obligation to certify his expatriation.

Here, the United States opposed what, from the point of view of the litigants, amounted to a claim for a kind of "remedial" and "accommodationist" citizenship. Colón and Mari Brás thought that their US citizenship, with its limited political rights, was an unjust imperialist imposition, and they believed that the United States owed it to them to allow them to continue to be Puerto Rican citizens without having to pledge allegiance to the United States. The rejection of their claims by the State Department and US courts probably expressed, at least in part, worries that if these expatriations were upheld, increasing numbers of Puerto Ricans would profess loyalty to the commonwealth but not the United States, thereby threatening American civic unity and sovereignty. It is hard to describe this reasoning as anything other than "preservationist," regardless of whether one views it as right or wrong. The fact that Puerto Rican authorities have since rejected the US government's position shows that the issue is by no means settled. It may or may not be resolved by efforts to transform Puerto Rico's status after the 2012 referendum.

---

60   Ibid., 3-6, 14, 32.
61   Roberto J. Sánchez Ramos, letter to Fernando Bonilla, Oct. 13, 2006, http://derechoupr.com/dmdocuments/Opinion_2006_7.pdf.
62   Lozada Colón v. U.S. Dept. of State, 2 F. Supp. 2d 43, 45-46 (D.D.C. 1998).

Birthright Citizenship

While some Puerto Ricans wish to relinquish the US citizenship bestowed on them by Congress, other Puerto Ricans and many other territorial residents have long insisted that they are constitutionally entitled to it by virtue of Section 1 of the Fourteenth Amendment, which holds that "[a]ll persons born or naturalized in the United States and subject to the jurisdiction thereof, are citizens of the United States and the State wherein they reside."[63] In 1994, Senior Circuit Judge Thomas Tang wrote for the United States Court of Appeals for the Ninth Circuit in regard to the claim of Rodolfo Rabang and six others, all facing deportation proceedings, that they were constitutional birthright citizens because either they or their parents were born in the Philippines while it was still a US territory.[64] Noting that the courts had not previously decided this question, Tang followed the reasoning of the Supreme Court in *Downes v. Bidwell*[65] and contrasted the Fourteenth Amendment's wording with that of the Thirteenth Amendment, which bans slavery and involuntary servitude "within the United States, or any place subject to their jurisdiction."[66] The court reasoned that because the Fourteenth Amendment did not include any such reference, it meant to confine birthright citizenship to birth within the states, not any other places "subject to the jurisdiction" of the United States.

Circuit Judge Harry Pregerson dissented at length. He contended that the *Downes* court had been concerned with distinctions for the purposes of revenue laws, not citizenship; and he argued that the framers of the Fourteenth Amendment were focused not on the language of the Thirteenth Amendment but on longstanding common law views of birthright status going back to the 1608 *Calvin's Case*,[67] in which political membership at birth was understood to be assigned to all born within a sovereign's dominion and protection.[68] Pregerson also maintained that the Supreme Court's decisions in *Inglis v. Sailor's Snug Harbor*[69] in 1830 and *United States v. Wong Kim Ark*[70] in 1898 showed that it accepted these common law understandings extending

---

63   U.S. Const., amend. XIV, § 1. Former Puerto Rico Governor Pedro Roselló also joined the "Brief of Amici Curiae Certain Members of Congress and Former Governmental Officials" in *Tuaua v. U.S.*
64   Rabang v. Immigration and Naturalization Serv., 35 F.3d 1449 (9th Cir. 1994).
65   Downes v. Bidwell, 182 U.S. 244 (1901).
66   Rabang v. Immigration and Naturalization Serv., 35 F.3d 1449, 1452-53 (9th Cir. 1994).
67   Calvin v. Smith (1608), 77 Eng. Rep. 377 (K.B.).
68   Rabang v. Immigration and Naturalization Serv., 35 F.3d 1449, 1455, 1457 (9th Cir. 1994) (Pregerson, J., dissenting).
69   Inglis v. Trs. of Sailor's Snug Harbor, 28 U.S. 99 (1830).
70   United States v. Wong Kim Ark, 169 U.S. 649 (1898).

birthright citizenship to any territory under a sovereign's governance.[71] And Pregerson noted that the Insular Cases' efforts to distinguish the civic statuses of territorial inhabitants were based "in part, on fears of other races," which is why the modern court had recommended against giving their reasoning "any further expansion."[72] He also insisted that even if the Insular Cases were to be followed, birthright citizenship should be deemed one of the limited "fundamental rights" that applied to unincorporated territories as well as incorporated territories and states.[73] Tang's majority opinion replied that whether or not citizenship was a fundamental right for those who possessed it, territorial residents were not citizens under the Fourteenth Amendment.

Though the Ninth Circuit was thus divided on the issues, four years later, the United States Court of Appeals for the Second Circuit strongly endorsed Judge Tang's reasoning. In rejecting the claim of a Filipina, Rosario Valmonte, also seeking to resist deportation, this court, too, contrasted the language of the Thirteenth and Fourteenth Amendments to hold that the Fourteenth Amendment's citizenship clause is "limited to persons born or naturalized in the states of the Union."[74] Other circuits have followed suit, so there the issue has stood; but it is currently being litigated again in the case of *Leneuoti Fiafia Tuaua v. United States.*

In *Tuaua*, five American Samoans contend that they are not merely US nationals but US citizens under the Fourteenth Amendment's citizenship clause. They contrast their claims with those made in *Rabang* in part by contending that the United States had always intended to ultimately give independence to the Philippines, whereas American Samoa and the United States have agreed to an enduring union.[75] Judge Richard Leon of the United States District Court for the District of Columbia felt there was too much precedent against this claim and dismissed it, but it is currently under appeal.[76] One of the striking features of the case is that Congressman Eni F. H. Faleomavaega, the elected nonvoting representative of American Samoa to Congress, has filed repeated briefs in opposition to these other Samoans' claim to citizenship. Like many of his constituents, he is concerned that a

---

71 Rabang v. Immigration and Naturalization Serv., 35 F.3d 1449, 1458-60 (9th Cir. 1994) (Pregerson, J., dissenting).

72 Ibid., 1463-64.

73 Ibid., 1465.

74 Santillan Valmonte v. Immigration and Naturalization Serv., 136 F.3d 914, 919 (2d Cir. 1998).

75 Tuaua v. United States, 951 F. Supp. 2d 88, 94 (D.D.C. 2013).

76 Ibid., 93-98. I participated in two briefs filed in the pending appeal of this case: Brief of Amici Curiae Scholars of Constitutional Law and Legal History in Support of Neither Party, Tuaua v. United States, No. 13-5272 (D.C. May 12, 2014); and Brief of Citizenship Scholars as Amici Curiae in Support of Appellants and Urging Reversal, Tuaua v. United States, No. 13-5272 (D.C. May 12, 2014).

number of distinctive features of Samoans' customary ways of life, especially
their provisions for keeping land in the hands of native Samoans, might be
banned if they were deemed US citizens and fully subject to US constitutional
restrictions.[77] His position opposes those of the congressional representatives
of Guam and the Virgin Islands and many Puerto Rican officials, whose
constituents already have congressionally based US citizenship but wish to
see their citizenships granted constitutional status.[78]

This last birthright citizenship case, then, raises the question whether a
denial of citizenship that seems a "preservationist" form of civic differentiation,
born from racial fears and antagonisms as argued by Judge Pregerson, and
maintained against the claims of Filipinos whom the United States wished to
deport, may nonetheless be a desirable form of accommodation, at least in the
case of American Samoa. In the eyes of many Samoans, that is indeed the case.
It is hard, however, to make "accommodationist" defenses of the rejections
of claims by residents of the other American territories. Even in regard to
Samoa, the force of this accommodationist argument for not recognizing
birthright citizenship is less than clear, since courts have already ruled in
favor of claims of special accommodations for territorial land laws and other
cultural customs.

Customary Land Laws

In 1978, the Territorial Registrar of American Samoa refused to register
a deed that sought to convey land in Samoa to Douglas Craddick, a non-
Samoan American citizen married to a native Samoan wife. The registrar
asserted that the American Samoan Code banned the alienation of lands
there to non-Samoans.[79] The Craddicks contended that the code imposed
a racial restriction on economic rights in violation of the equal protection
and due process clauses of the US Constitution. The High Court of American
Samoa disagreed; while it accepted that equal protection and due process

---

77   Brief of the Honorable Eni F. H. Faleomavaega as Amicus Curiae in Support of
Defendants at 12-18, Tuaua v. United States, 951 F. Supp. 2d 88 (D.D.C. 2013).
78   Brief of Amici Curiae Certain Members of Congress and Former Governmental
Officials in Support of Plaintiffs-Appellants and in Support of Reversal, Tuaua v.
United States, 951 F. Supp. 2d 88 (D.D.C. 2013).
79   AM. SAMOA CODE ANN. § 37.0204(b) (2007) provides:
It is prohibited to alienate any lands except freehold lands to any
person who has less than one-half native blood, and if a person
has any nonnative blood whatever, it is prohibited to alienate
any native lands to such person unless he was born in American
Samoa, is a descendant of a Samoan family, lives with Samoans as
a Samoan, lived in American Samoa for more than five years and
has officially declared his intention of making American Samoa
his home for life.

applied to American Samoa and that racial classifications were suspect, it found "a compelling state interest in preserving the lands of American Samoa for Samoans and in preserving the Fa'a Samoa, or Samoan culture."[80] It noted that this policy was guaranteed in the Constitution of American Samoa and had been the policy of the Samoan government throughout its history; and, observing that American Samoa is only 76.2 square miles, it contended that "each acre is precious, and the government of American Samoa has a vital interest in protecting the Samoan people from improvident deprivation of their lands."[81]

Similarly, the United States Court of Appeals for the District of Columbia ruled in 1987 against land claims in American Samoa advanced by the Church of Jesus Christ of Latter-Day Saints.[82] Circuit Judge Douglas Ginsburg, a Republican appointee, specified that Congress, when acting under the authority of Article IV, could treat a territory "differently from States so long as there is a rational basis for its actions."[83] He therefore affirmed the legitimacy of the congressional policy of "preserving the Fa'a Samoa by respecting Samoan traditions concerning land ownership," a policy stated in the instruments of cession and in the Samoan Constitution, which "Congress may be viewed as having ratified . . . at least in principle."[84] The opinion thus suggested that US courts were actually willing to employ the deferential "rational basis" scrutiny for congressional accommodations of Samoa's distinctive customs.

Several years later, Concepcion S. and Elias S. Wabol sued to void a lease through which they had agreed to confer land in the Northern Mariana Islands to Philippine Goods, Inc. They contended that the lease violated article XII of the CNMI Constitution, which bans the sale of a freehold, or a leasehold exceeding forty years, to those not of CNMI descent. Philippine Goods responded that article XII violated the equal protection clause of the US Constitution, which had sovereign authority.[85]

The United States Court of Appeals for the Ninth Circuit ruled that in "the territorial context, the definition of a basic and integral freedom must narrow to incorporate the shared beliefs of diverse cultures."[86] The court was accordingly reluctant to restrict the powers of Congress "to accommodate the unique social and cultural conditions and values" of a particular territory.[87] It

---

80 Craddick v. Territorial Registrar of Am. Sam., 1 A.S.R.2d 11, 12 (App. Div. 1980).
81 Ibid., 14.
82 Corp. of Presiding Bishop of the Church of Jesus Christ of the Latter-Day Saints v. Hodel, 830 F. 2d 374 (D.C. Cir. 1987).
83 Ibid., 385 (quoting Harris v. Rosario, 446 U.S. 651 (1980)).
84 Ibid., 386.
85 Wabol v. Villacrusis, 908 F.2d 411, 413 (9th Cir. 1990).
86 Ibid., 421.
87 Ibid., 422.

added that, here, "the preservation of local culture and land . . . is a solemn and binding undertaking memorialized in the Trusteeship Agreement" through which the United States had acquired its authority over what had become the CNMI.[88] Since the court understood both Congress and the Trusteeship Agreement to have committed the United States to honoring the CNMI restrictions on land alienation, it also upheld those restrictions against this equal protection challenge. Circuit Judge Cecil Poole wrote that "interposing this constitutional provision would be both impractical and anomalous," for it "would hamper the United States' ability to form political alliances and acquire necessary military outposts" and would "operate as a genocide pact for diverse native cultures." The purpose of the equal protection clause, in his view, "was to protect minority rights, not to enforce homogeneity."[89]

In all of these cases, then—two involving American Samoa's US nationals and one involving the CNMI's US citizens—the courts ruled that ethnically or racially based land restrictions that would not be permissible in the states were valid, and, indeed, supported by compelling interests, in these territories. Those compelling interests included both preservationist US concerns to be able to take actions in the Pacific deemed necessary for national security and passionately worded commitments to accommodate practices deemed essential for the survival of distinctive territorial cultures. The rulings suggest that, at least when accommodationist and preservationist interests coincide, US courts and government officials have little difficulty sustaining differential customary rights for territorial residents, whether they are deemed US nationals or citizens, against constitutional challenges. Perhaps this situation might be altered if territorial residents were judged to be Fourteenth Amendment birthright citizens, not citizens granted that status by Congress. It is not evident, however, why treating their citizenship as constitutionally based would raise the bar against accommodationist policies.

Normative Reflections

American constitutional thought and political traditions include, among other elements, powerful strains holding that membership in a republic should arise from the explicit or implicit mutual consent of the existing citizenry and applicants for naturalization.[90] Most American citizens and many, if not most, academic theorists agree that current citizens can give weight to many considerations in their decisions on citizenship policies, including

---

88   Ibid., 423.
89   Ibid.
90   See generally Peter H. Schuck and Rogers M. Smith, *Citizenship Without Consent: Illegal Aliens in the American Polity* (New Haven: Yale University Press, 1985).

their economic, national security, foreign policy, law enforcement, and civil rights concerns. There is less agreement on whether Americans can or should create many forms of differentiated citizenship. But as the previous sections demonstrate, in fact they have always done so and continue to do so.

In recent writings, I have argued that one (but not the only) important moral consideration in American citizenship policies should be what I call, in an all-too-academic phrase, a "principle of coercively constituted identities."[91] The core argument begins with Abraham Lincoln's premise that America's constitutional democracy is best seen as dedicated to realizing the goals of the Declaration of Independence—securing the rights to life, liberty, and the pursuit of happiness—first for its citizens, and then for all of humanity insofar as possible. The second step is to accept the influential contention of Will Kymlicka that persons rarely can conceive of free, happy, and meaningful lives in ways that do not deeply reflect the values and traditions of the societies that have governed them, including the uses of public coercive powers to define the forms of educational, religious, cultural, familial, economic, and political activities that they can legitimately pursue.[92] The final step is to recognize that whenever the United States uses its coercive powers to shape persons' identities and aspirations—that is, their notions of how can they pursue happiness—its founding values require it to adopt policies consistent with their realization of those aspirations. Such policies may well include ones that offer these individuals the forms of citizenship they seek, including differentiated forms, if doing so does not unduly threaten other core American values and interests.

If we provisionally accept this understanding of the morality of American constitutionalism, what does it imply for the controversies over the territorial civic statuses just reviewed? There is little doubt that the US government has long coercively shaped many elements of the identities, interests, and aspirations of the inhabitants of its territories. It acquired Puerto Rico, Guam, and the Northern Mariana Islands through military actions, and it obtained the Virgin Islands and American Samoa through negotiations with other colonial powers. It has since claimed and often exerted powers to decide what political and legal rights, what kinds of economic endeavors, and what sorts of allegiances and political memberships the territorial inhabitants can have. It is true that American Samoa was also obtained in part through negotiations with Samoan leaders and that the US government has supported expanded powers of self-governance in all its territories over time. But in regard to

---

91 See, e.g., Rogers M. Smith, "Constitutional Democracies, Coercion, and Obligations to Include," in *The Limits of Constitutional Democracy*, ed. Jeffrey Tulis and Stephen Macedo (Princeton: Princeton University Press, 2010).

92 Will Kymlicka, *Multicultural Citizenship: A Liberal Theory of Minority Rights* (New York: Oxford University Press, 1995), 82-83.

these territories (including American Samoa), the United States has never relinquished the claim that Congress retains extensive, if not plenary, powers under Article IV to govern them as it wishes, in alliance with US executive officials and courts; and the US government has never ceased to exercise the powers it asserts over the territories on many vital matters.

As the preceding survey shows, although some American judges and officials have criticized the incorporated/unincorporated territories distinction and the differentiated civic statuses as partly originating in racism, the US government has rarely defined or defended its territorial citizenship policies in "remedial" terms. Instead, it has primarily stressed its "preservationist" interests in American national security, economic welfare, and law enforcement, on the one hand, while increasingly expressing willingness to accommodate the status desires of current territorial populations, on the other. Those emphases are understandable and I believe that they advance legitimate themes. Nonetheless, it is also appropriate for the US government to recognize that its policies have often worked to constrain profoundly, rather than to assist, the liberties and pursuits of happiness of many people in the territories it has governed for so long.

It therefore seems morally imperative, even if politically difficult, for the United States in the twenty-first century to seek as much as possible to allow territorial inhabitants to have the forms of citizenship they desire. There is no good reason why US citizens in the territories should not have the right to vote in elections for president and for full members of Congress, even if a constitutional amendment might be required to bring that about. It is wildly unlikely that doing so would give territorial citizens political power sufficient to threaten any American core interests. And this change would eliminate a form of civic differentiation that historically accompanied others that the nation has rightly repudiated. Ending it would expunge from American law the ugly taint of the origins of territorial residents' limited political statuses, the racist assertion that most are not capable of participating in self-governance on an equal basis with white Americans.

More controversial is the desire of some Puerto Ricans to be Puerto Rican citizens but not US citizens. I have long believed, however, that if citizenship by consent is to be a meaningful status, there must be practical opportunities to give up an undesired citizenship, as the American revolutionaries did, and as enshrined in the 1868 Expatriation Act.[93] Conditioning expatriation on the renunciation of every right conceivably associated with citizenship, including

---

93   Act concerning the Rights of American Citizens in Foreign States (1868 Expatriation Act), 15 Stat. 223. See Schuck and Smith, *Citizenship Without Consent*, 62, 86-88, 122-25.

rights held by resident aliens, amounts to a deliberate effort to prevent people from exercising expatriation rights they may reasonably see as vital to their pursuits of happiness, given their frustration with the statuses the United States has unilaterally imposed on them. It is chiefly Puerto Ricans who have sought to expatriate themselves in this way, and if their commonwealth status gives way to statehood and full political rights, there would likely be few who would still want this option. But it still seems a form of differentiated citizenship the United States should accept.

Most difficult are the current disputes over birthright citizenship, for two reasons. First, the recognition of Filipino claims to US citizenship would likely have a nontrivial impact on Filipino immigration to the United States, a development that many would see as threatening to American economic, if not cultural and political, interests. Second, the views of many American Samoans, including their elected congressman, that they do not wish to be seen as Fourteenth Amendment birthright citizens deserve respect, as much as the desires of other territorial residents for constitutional citizenship.

As much, but no more; and one of the difficulties here is that despite the different process of acquiring American Samoa and its considerable degree of autonomous self-governance, it is difficult to separate American Samoa's legal status from that of the other American territories, many of whose inhabitants do want Fourteenth Amendment–based US citizenship. The reality is that the United States claims the same ultimate sovereignty over American Samoa that it does over its other territories, even if many American Samoans and legal authorities disagree. So if the other territories should be deemed part of the United States and subject to its jurisdiction, making their residents Fourteenth Amendment birthright citizens, it seems the same should be true for American Samoa.

The rulings in the *Craddick* and *Wabol* cases, moreover, show that courts are already willing—indeed, rhetorically eager—to find that territorial inhabitants can be US citizens but differentiated citizens, entitled to maintain land laws and other practices vital to the survival of their distinct cultures that would otherwise not be constitutional. Undeniably, predominant judicial views can change; and there is also ample room for dispute about what differentiations are really necessary and appropriate accommodations, and which ones are simply unjust deprivations of due process, equal protection, or other rights. But those circumstances are true whether Samoans are deemed American nationals or whether they are American citizens. As the case law reviewed here shows, neither alternative is full proof against judicial rulings or American legislative and executive policies that contravene the perceived interests of members of the territories. Perhaps the only difference is that if territorial inhabitants were viewed as Fourteenth Amendment birthright citizens, it is inconceivable that they could be deprived of their US citizenship by Congress—something that is clearly legally possible, if politically difficult, at present.

The central arguments of Circuit Judge Pregerson's dissent in *Rabang* also seem compelling. My own studies of the Fourteenth Amendment and the surrounding case law on birthright citizenship suggest that when the amendment's framers wrote the amendment's citizenship clause, they had in mind primarily common law traditions, along with often dissonant international law traditions, rather than the wording of the Thirteenth Amendment. They did seek to deny birthright citizenship to those born into the native tribes, though they used language ill adapted to that purpose; and it is certainly possible to argue that the territories should be viewed as "domestic dependent nations," similar to the tribes. That is, in my view, the strongest argument for ruling against claims of Fourteenth Amendment birthright citizenship in the territories.

But the reality is that throughout much of the history of US territories, which were long administered by US-appointed governors, the territories were accorded even less recognition of their rights to autonomous self-governance than most of the native tribes. And in any case, as Judge Pregerson admonished, some features of US law, including some forms of civic differentiation, are so deeply tied to America's history of racial inequalities that they should not be interpreted expansively. The denial of birthright citizenship to those born into Native American tribes, like the Insular Cases' unincorporated/ incorporated distinction on which the courts have relied in the Fourteenth Amendment citizenship cases, is such a feature. It is the kind of invidious civic differentiation that Americans since World War II have sought to erase from their laws.

I conclude, then, that there are strong normative reasons for providing residents of US territories with the civic statuses many are contending for today—expanded political rights, the right to expatriate themselves without losing residency, constitutionally grounded citizenship, and accommodations of distinctive features of their ways of life that seem essential to their cultural survival. The safest empirical prediction, however, is that we will see continuing struggles over these civic statuses that will be heavily shaped by the preservationist concerns of powerful actors in the United States. And whatever the outcome, American law is still likely to display differentiated forms of territorial citizenship, with debates over which ones are and are not truly equal. Though in some ways unique, those disputes will echo contests over many other civic statuses in the American Republic and most nations of the modern world.

CHAPTER SEVEN

The Ideological Decolonization of Puerto Rico's Autonomist Movement

Rafael Cox Alomar

The Labyrinth

Perhaps not since the days when Major General Nelson A. Miles, at the helm of the Sixth Massachusetts Volunteer Infantry Regiment, led the US invasion of Puerto Rico in 1898[1] has the island received as much coverage from American media outlets as it does today. Not even the 1950 attempt on President Truman, at the hands of Puerto Rican Nationalists,[2] garnered as much mainland attention as Puerto Rico's current financial meltdown.

The colossal collapse of Puerto Rico's fiscal edifice—and, more importantly, the crisis's ever-increasing ripple effect on the pricing and financial viability of the United States' $4.3 trillion municipal bond market[3]—

---

1 See, e.g., "Our Flag Raised in Puerto Rico," *New York Times*, July 27, 1898.
2 See, e.g., Paul P. Kennedy, "Capital Startled; Police Swiftly Cordon Blair House," *New York Times*, Nov. 2, 1950; "Revolt Flares in Puerto Rico; Soon Quelled with 23 Dead," *New York Times*, Oct. 31, 1950.
3 Puerto Rico's default could potentially cost states and cities across the United States billions of dollars in additional interest rate charges. For a provocative argument, see Larry McDonald, "Could Puerto Rico Default Hammer the $3.7 Trillion U.S. Muni Bond Market in 2014?" *Forbes*, Jan. 3, 2014, http://www.forbes.com/sites/larrymcdonald/2014/01/03/puerto-rico-default-to-re-price-the-3-7-trillion-municipal-bond-market-in-2014.

has brought to bear not only the systemic infirmities of the island's archaic economic and governmental models but even more poignantly the inadequacy of its current neocolonial relationship with Washington. The commonwealth status, as it stands, does not serve the people of Puerto Rico well, and it certainly does not promote Washington's geopolitical interests in the Western Hemisphere, either.

It is no secret that Puerto Rico today is on the verge of virtual bankruptcy. And, yet, the writing has been on the wall for some time now. In the words of President Obama's Task Force on Puerto Rico's Status, "After several years of negligible growth, high unemployment, and deficit increases, the Puerto Rican economy started to slow as early as 2006 . . . leading to the sharpest economic contraction on the island since the late 1980s."[4]

The picture is bleak indeed. And all available economic indicators confirm it. By 2012, real gross national product (GNP) had shrunk by 10%, returning to its 2005 level.[5] GNP per capita, moreover, is roughly $15,000, "about one-third of the level on the U.S. mainland."[6] According to the US Bureau of Labor Statistics, between January 2013 and June 2014, Puerto Rico lost 35,873 net jobs.[7] Unemployment in the island is persistently higher than in any of the fifty states or the District of Columbia,[8] edging close to 16% in recent years,[9] while the labor participation index has recently fluctuated between 38% and 41%, among the lowest in the world.[10] Puerto Rico's chronic incapacity to generate jobs at home or to successfully compete in the global labor market is the most eloquent demonstration of the island's broken institutional repertoire. A decade of negative growth has led to widespread poverty, pervasive migration, and insurmountable levels of public debt. Close to 45% of Puerto Ricans live in poverty[11] (twice as many as in Mississippi, the

---

4   President's Task Force on Puerto Rico's Status, *Report by the President's Task Force on Puerto Rico's Status* (Washington, DC: White House, 2011), 38 [hereinafter President's Task Force, *2011 Report by the President's Task Force on Puerto Rico's Status*].

5   Federal Reserve Bank of New York, *Report on the Competitiveness of Puerto Rico's Economy* (New York: Federal Reserve Bank of New York, 2012), 4.

6   Ibid.

7   United States Department of Labor, Bureau of Labor Statistics, "Databases, Tables and Calculators by Subject," accessed Oct. 29, 2014, http://data.bls.gov.

8   President's Task Force, *2011 Report by the President's Task Force on Puerto Rico's Status*, 38.

9   Federal Reserve Bank, *Report on the Competitiveness of Puerto Rico's Economy*, 4.

10   Ibid.

11   D'vera Cohn, Eileen Patten, and Mark Hugo López, "Puerto Rican Population Declines on Island, Grows on U.S. Mainland," *Pew Research*, Aug. 11, 2014, http://www.pewhispanic.org/2014/08/11/puerto-rican-population-declines-on-island-grows-on-u-s-mainland.

poorest state in the United States), and 38% receive food stamps (three times as many as in the mainland).[12] Not surprisingly, these conditions have led to a massive exodus not seen since the days of Operation Bootstrap in the 1950s.[13] Puerto Rico's population decreased from 3.81 million in 2000 to 3.67 million in 2012. Between 2000 and 2012, 141,000 people left the island; in the last two years alone, Puerto Rico has lost 59,000 residents, or 1.5% of its population.[14]

And, to make matters worse, those who are leaving are precisely the ones Puerto Rico needs the most at this juncture: young, well-educated, productive professionals in their prime who cannot survive at home. This brain drain is, undoubtedly, one of the crisis's most tragic phenomena.

Puerto Rico, the third-largest municipal-bond issuer in the United States after New York and California,[15] has long enjoyed unencumbered access to the markets, due in no small measure to its bonds' high yields and triple exemption from federal, state, and local taxes.[16] Yet negative growth, together with uncontrolled deficit financing, has led to unmanageable levels of public debt. According to figures from the commonwealth's Government Development Bank, as of May 31, 2014, the total outstanding debt of the island's government (including its instrumentalities and municipalities) was $72.6 billion, "equivalent to approximately 103% of the Commonwealth's gross national product for fiscal year 2013."[17]

The deficits have become so pervasive, short-term financing and liquidity sources so scarce,[18] and the possibility of a default so real that by February 2014, the credit ratings of Puerto Rico's general-obligation bonds

---

12 Ibid.

13 During this period, approximately 500,000 people left the island for jobs on the mainland. See Michael A. Fletcher, "Puerto Rico, with At Least $70 Billion in Debt, Confronts a Rising Economic Misery," *Washington Post*, Nov. 30, 2013, http://www.washingtonpost.com/business/economy/puerto-rico-with-at-least-70-billion-in-debt-confronts-a-rising-economic-misery/2013/11/30/f40a22c6-5376-11e3-9fe0-fd2ca728e67c_story.html.

14 Maye Primera, "Puerto Rico se vacía lentamente," *El País*, Aug. 19, 2014, http://internacional.elpais.com/internacional/2014/08/18actuadad/1408390645_767393.html.

15 Close to 75% of US municipal bond funds own Puerto Rican bonds.

16 Fletcher, "Puerto Rico, with At Least $70 Billion in Debt."

17 Government Development Bank for Puerto Rico, *Commonwealth of Puerto Rico Quarterly Report Dated July 17, 2014* (San Juan: Government Development Bank for Puerto Rico, 2014), 6.

18 Ted Hampton, "Puerto Rico's Liquidity Remains at Risk Despite Recent Borrowings, Restructuring Law," *Moody's Investors Service*, Aug. 1, 2014, https://www.moodys.com/research/Moodys-Puerto-Ricos-liquidity-remains-at-risk-despite-recent-borrowings--PR_305269.

and commonwealth-guaranteed bonds were lowered to noninvestment grade (commonly known as "junk status") by Moody's Investors Service, Standard & Poor's Ratings Services, and Fitch Ratings.[19] Soon thereafter, in July 2014, each of the credit agencies lowered the commonwealth's ratings even further.[20]

So far, the pro-cyclical measures enacted by the insular authorities,[21] far from containing the crisis, have further arrested the island's economic development while "adversely affecting governmental revenues."[22]

A close perusal of the structural fundamentals of the island's economy shows that much has remained unchanged since, at least, the interwar period when Congress passed section 262 of the 1921 Revenue Act[23] (the precursor to the now-defunct section 936).[24] The island's economic model, for the most part, is still premised on similar variables: a sizeable proportion of internal production executed by US transnational companies, financed by US capital, buttressed by US technology, focused almost exclusively on exporting to the US market, and heavily dependent on the availability of profit-enhancing mechanisms exempting those companies from all applicable federal and local taxes. Congress's complete phaseout of section 936 by the end of 2005, however, brought this model to an abrupt halt, putting an end to the policy whereby Congress's unilateral control of all the economic variables affecting the island's sustainability was offset by an aggressive federal tax incentive program geared toward attracting American investment to the island. Consequently, Puerto Rico today bears the heavy brunt of all the regulatory costs flowing from the island's insertion into the US economy, without any control over such economic variables and, equally importantly, without any possibility of engineering yet another fiscal mechanism at the federal level for offsetting those costs.

---

19 Government Development Bank, *Commonwealth of Puerto Rico Quarterly Report*, 3.

20 Global Credit Research, "Rating Action: Moody's Negative Downgrades Puerto Rico GOs to B2 from Ba2, COFINA Senior-Sub to Ba3-B1," *Moody's Investors Service*, July 1, 2014, https://www.moodys.com/research/Moodys-downgrades-Puerto-Rico-GOs-to-B2-from-Ba2-COFINA--PR_303126.

21 See Ley Núm. 3-2013 [Law No. 3 of 2013], 2013 L.P.R.A. 3 (P.R.) (reform to the Employees' Retirement System); Ley Núm. 160-2013 [Law No. 160 of 2013], 2013 L.P.R.A. 160 (P.R.) (reform to Teachers' Retirement System); Ley Núm. 162-2013 [Law No. 160 of 2013], 2013 L.P.R.A. 162 (P.R.) (reform to Judiciary Retirement System); Ley Núm. 66-2014 [Law No. 66 of 2014], 2014 L.P.R.A. 66 (P.R.) (legislation approving sale of US$3.5 billion of general-obligation bonds); Ley Núm. 71-2014 [Law No. 71 of 2014], 2014 L.P.R.A. 71 (P.R.) (Puerto Rico Public Corporation Debt Enforcement and Recovery Act).

22 Government Development Bank, *Commonwealth of Puerto Rico Quarterly Report*, 5.

23 Revenue Act of 1921, Pub. L. No. 67-98, 42 Stat. 227.

24 Tax Reform Act of 1976, Pub. L. No. 94-455, 90 Stat. 1549.

From this unprecedented fiscal crisis, however, comes forth a unique opportunity for economic restructuring and politico-constitutional reengineering.

It is plainly clear that Puerto Rico's economic crisis is a reflection of a wider and equally pervasive political meltdown, as hinted by the President's Task Force on Puerto Rico's Status and the Federal Reserve Bank of New York.[25]

The perpetuation of a territorial relationship with Washington, fostering values of dependency while severely limiting the island's policy options, has no doubt exacerbated the catalysts behind the meltdown, making it even harder for Puerto Rico to overcome an endogenous economic depression in a weakened global economy.

Thus, the opportunity has arisen for turning around the economic collapse by way of addressing the island's status quagmire, particularly at a time when Congress and the federal judiciary have been revisiting a series of complex questions on the constitutional relationship between the federal government and special jurisdictions such as the unincorporated territories and the District of Columbia: Does the Commonwealth of the Northern Mariana Islands' right to local self-government, under the 1976 covenant, substantially limit Congress's legislative authority over it?[26] Does the Fourteenth Amendment's citizenship clause extend to American Samoa?[27] Are American Samoans US citizens at birth? Does the District of Columbia have the authority to spend its local tax and fee revenue without seeking an annual appropriation from Congress pursuant to its plenary power under Article I's district clause?[28]

Unsurprisingly, for the people of Puerto Rico, along with the political branches in Washington, the more pressing challenge is how best to craft a procedural mechanism that brings to life a legally viable and politically sound exercise of self-determination.

Hence, all roads must lead to Congress, where control over Puerto Rico's economic life is exerted without the express consent of the people of Puerto Rico. So far, Washington has been unable, perhaps unwilling, to articulate

---

25 President's Task Force, *2011 Report by the President's Task Force on Puerto Rico's Status*, 35-69; Federal Reserve Bank of New York, *An Update on the Competitiveness of Puerto Rico's Economy* (New York: Federal Reserve Bank of New York, 2014).

26 N. Mariana Islands v. United States, 670 F. Supp. 2d 65 (D.C. Cir. 2009).

27 Tuaua v. United States, 951 F. Supp. 2d 88 (D.D.C. 2013).

28 Council of D.C. v. Gray, No. 14-655, 2014 WL 2025078 (D.D.C. May 19, 2014) (appeal pending). Interestingly, these territorial ruminations follow *Boumediene v. Bush's* questionable granting of contemporary legitimacy to the extraterritorial doctrine flowing from the Insular Cases—a doctrine that is at odds with the philosophical underpinnings supporting a dignified disentanglement of the colonial web that today is zapping away Puerto Rico's ability to reinvent itself.

a coherent policy for addressing the Puerto Rican labyrinth.[29] However, no meeting of the minds will take place between Washington's political branches and Puerto Rico until the island's political leadership engages Congress from a platform of ideological clarity.

Therein lies the challenge. And the obvious question, then, is, where do things stand right now in Washington with respect to the Puerto Rican fiscal and political crisis?

Is There a Path for Disentangling the Status Knot?

On January 17, 2014, President Obama signed into law the 2014 Consolidated Appropriations Act,[30] which provides as follows with respect to Puerto Rico's political status question: "$2,500,000 is for objective, nonpartisan voter education about, and a plebiscite on, options that would resolve Puerto Rico's future political status, which shall be provided to the State Elections Commission of Puerto Rico."[31]

The Joint Explanatory Statement accompanying the Consolidated Appropriations Act of 2014[32] adopts by reference the language of House Report 113-171,[33] which preconditions the disbursement of the plebiscite funds as follows:

> The funds provided for the plebiscite shall not be obligated until 45 days after the Department [of Justice] notifies the Committees on Appropriations that it approves of an expenditure plan from the Puerto Rico State Elections Commission for voter education and plebiscite administration, including approval of the plebiscite ballot. This notification shall include a finding that the voter education materials, plebiscite ballot, and related materials are not incompatible with the Constitution and laws and policies of the United States.[34]

Thus, the island's political leadership must now decide how to approach the administration's latest overture without losing sight of the fact that the statutory language included in the Consolidated Appropriations Act leaves

---

29   Beyond uttering vague and sporadic statements in favor of providing technical assistance to local authorities, the political branches of Washington have yet to shoulder their part of the blame. See, e.g., Dereck Wallbank, "Congress Open to Puerto Rico Technical Aid, Hoyer Says," *Bloomberg*, July 8, 2014, http://www .bloomberg.com/news/2014-07-08/congress-open-to-puerto-rico-technical-aid-hoyer-says.html.

30   Consolidated Appropriations Act, Pub. L. No. 113-76, 128 Stat. 5 (2014).

31   Ibid., 61.

32   160 CONG. REC. H475-H1215 (daily ed. Jan. 15, 2014) (statement of Rep. Rogers).

33   H.R. Rep. No. 113-171 (2014).

34   Ibid., 53.

Congress, yet again, off the hook, as it does not bind Congress in any way to honor the will of the people of Puerto Rico.[35] The administration's suggested procedural path, moreover, is at odds with the campaign pledge made to the people of Puerto Rico by the island's governing party (the pro-commonwealth Popular Democratic Party, or PDP) during the 2012 election cycle for the convening of a constitutional convention in the event that Congress failed to pass a self-executing status bill during 2013. The apparent change of heart of the PDP's governing board, as announced by Governor Alejandro García Padilla on July 16, 2014, embracing the president's nonbinding plebiscite proposal, signals the beginning of a new round of byzantine discussions in the local legislature and among (and within) the political movements on the island. And while the PDP attempts to elucidate its internal strategic and ideological dissonances, the pro-statehood New Progressive Party (NPP), encouraged by statehood's alleged victory in the controvertible 2012 local plebiscite, has been able to introduce two admission bills in Congress.[36] Neither bill, however, has received attention, nor have hearings been scheduled in the US House or Senate—unsurprisingly, since there appears to be a clear consensus in Washington that, contrary to what the pro-statehood leadership incessantly suggests, statehood does not command the support of an overwhelming majority of the Puerto Rican people and that given Puerto Rico's severe economic downturn, this is not a path worth plodding along.[37]

If seen in light of other attempts at unraveling the status impasse since the days of the Eisenhower administration, the most sensible procedural path for propelling a serious exercise of self-determination and directly engaging Congress is for the people of Puerto Rico themselves to convene a constitutional convention, which would in turn negotiate with Congress with one voice and pursuant to a direct mandate from the Puerto Rican people. It is by far the most decisive mechanism for, firstly, directly engaging Congress; secondly, openly considering the more intractable legal and policy issues surrounding this jigsaw puzzle (as the drafters of the 2011 *Report by the President's Task Force on Puerto Rico's Status* openly suggest);[38] thirdly, extricating the island's electoral politics from the status negotiations; and, fourthly, guaranteeing to all political and nonpolitical actors from the various ideological movements

---

35 Arguably, an independence request, as opposed to a petition for admission into the Union or the forging of a treaty relationship, would be acted on by Congress in a forthright manner.

36 Puerto Rico Status Resolution Act, H.R. 2000, 113th Cong. (2013); Puerto Rico Status Resolution Act, S. 2020, 113th Cong. (2014).

37 General Accountability Office "Information on How Statehood Would Potentially Affect Selected Federal Programs and Revenue Sources," Mar. 4, 2014, http://www.gao.gov/products/gao-14-31.

38 President's Task Force, *2011 Report by the President's Task Force on Puerto Rico's Status*, 28-29.

a more inclusive and arguably more representative platform from which to participate in the negotiations with Washington's political branches.

Puerto Rico, in all likelihood, will not arrive at the substantive (and, perhaps, more crucial) stage of defining *in extenso*, together with Congress, the legal and economic conditions surrounding each status formula (i.e., statehood, independence, commonwealth, and free association) until the procedural path is cleared.

Substantively, however, one of the more complex issues besieging the Puerto Rican landscape is how to bring about ideological clarity to the PDP's pro-commonwealth camp. More so than arriving at a mutually agreeable understanding with Congress on the specifics behind statehood or independence, this has become by far a more elusive and more problematic proposition because the PDP's ideological crisis has become an albatross around the neck of any plausible path for undoing the status knot. Senator Ron Wyden's admonition at the most recent status hearing before the US Senate Committee on Energy and Natural Resources, held in August 2013, deserves particular attention:

> Two out of 3 of you seem to believe that the current status and enhanced Commonwealth are no longer options. . . . So looking forward it seems to me that it's especially important to see if the 3 of you can come to an agreement on the language of a ballot that, in effect, has 2 remaining options: statehood, or sovereignty as an independent or freely associated State. Absent an agreement of the 3 of you it seems that this will just go round and round some more.[39]

The PDP's leadership must openly acknowledge that, as a matter of US public policy, the so-called enhancement or perfection of commonwealth status can flourish only outside the US Constitution's territory clause.[40] This goes right to the essence of the problem.

It is clear from the congressional record that in passing Public Law 600 in 1950,[41] Congress did not intend to alter the fundamental nature of Puerto Rico's legal status with respect to the United States. Antonio Fernós Isern, the

---

39   *Puerto Rico: Hearing before the Committee on Energy and Natural Resources, United States Senate, One Hundred Thirteenth Congress, First Session, to Receive Testimony on the Nov. 6, 2012, Referendum on the Political Status of Puerto Rico and the Administration's Response*, 113th Cong. 35-36 (2013).
40   U.S. Const., art. IV, § 3, cl. 2.
41   Act of July 3, 1950, Pub. L. No. 81-600, 64 Stat. 319 (codified at 48 U.S.C. §§ 731 et seq. (2013)).

then resident commissioner, summed it up best in his testimony before the Senate Committee on Interior and Insular Affairs in May 1950 (less than two months before President Truman signed Public Law 600):

> As already pointed out, S. 3336 would not change the status of the island of Puerto Rico relative to the United States. It would not commit the United States for or against any specific form of political formula for the people of Puerto Rico. It would not alter the powers of sovereignty acquired by the United States over Puerto Rico under the terms of the Treaty of Paris.[42]

The PDP's leadership must come to terms with this inescapable reality. There will be no resolution of the status conundrum so long as Puerto Rico's sovereignty remains in the hands of Congress. Far from becoming an agent for historical transformation, the PDP will add further confusion to the status quicksand to the extent that it pays heed to those voices advocating for an enhanced or perfected commonwealth status (premised on Congress's devolution to the island of further administrative authority over a limited array of issues) while shying away from the sovereignty question. Anything short of that is tantamount to beating around the bush because none of the autonomist movement's historical aspirations (e.g., the inapplicability of federal legislation without Puerto Rico's express consent and the authority to enter into international agreements, to participate in international organizations, and to regulate commerce free from the strictures of the dormant commerce clause) will be achieved under the current territorial condition. This also helps explain why, to date, all efforts to enhance or perfect commonwealth status—the 1959 Fernós-Murray bills, the 1975 Compact of Permanent Union put forward by the Ad Hoc Advisory Group on Puerto Rico, and the 1989 Johnston bills in the US Senate—have foundered.

This asymmetry between the movement's aspirations and the path chosen for achieving them comes to light most patently in the party leadership's failure to cogently describe what an enhanced commonwealth would look like and how, if at all, it would fit within the United States' federal superstructure. A recent exchange between Governor García Padilla and Senators Lisa Murkowski (R-Alaska) and Martin Heinrich (D-New Mexico) speaks volumes:

---

42 *Hearing before a Subcommittee of the Committee on Interior and Insular Affairs, United States Senate 81st Congress, 2nd Session, on S. 3336, A Bill to Provide for the Organization of a Constitutional Government by the People of Puerto Rico*, 81st Cong. 4 (1950).

Senator Murkowski. Since we're talking about definitions here and whether or not they cause some confusion. Governor, can you define exactly what enhanced Commonwealth really means because I'm not sure that I understand it.

Mr. Padilla. Thank you, Senator, for that question. It is a very valid one. A good example of serious consideration by Congress of the enhanced development of Commonwealth may be found in the legislative process between 1989 and 1991 and during the 1975 ad hoc procedure. But in 1975 a young fellow of the Department of Justice quote in a letter. "The proposed compact would without altering the fundamental nature of Puerto Rico's Commonwealth status provides [sic] substantially increased autonomy to the island's government and its people." We can talk about for example, those processes that have been already studied by Congress and by the Commonwealth to see what [federal laws] apply to Puerto Rico that cannot damage the possibility of economic development of Puerto Rico or the language in [federal] courts in Puerto Rico that should be Spanish. . . .

Senator Murkowski. Governor, what I'm trying to understand is exactly what enhanced Commonwealth is and the question really here is whether or not it's consistent with the U.S. Constitution. Now I understand that your legislature has passed this resolution that, when we're talking about the plebiscite it says, incorporates all options including the enhanced Commonwealth. But if our Department of Justice should determine that enhanced Commonwealth does not, in fact, meet with the definitions within our U.S. Constitution, doesn't fit within that. We've got a situation here where you're going to have a plebiscite that, again, is not going to be followed or upheld. So what I'm trying to understand is how we're defining this and is it consistent with our Constitution.

. . .

Senator Heinrich. Thank you, Mr. Chairman. I want to ask Governor Garcia Padilla, under what you're calling an enhanced Commonwealth would Puerto Rico be subject to all the Federal laws that the Congress, House and Senate, signed by the President are passed or would you pick and choose which laws under—

Mr. Padilla. No, no one is trying to mislead you. If anyone tell you that we want to pick. What had been studied in 1975 process, with approval of the Department of Justice, but what state to Congress in 1989 to 1991 process and passed the House unanimously was the process between Congress and Puerto Rico. Both will agree if there's any Federal law that can damage in a different way without damaging the effect of that law in the states, damage the possibility of the economy of Puerto Rico to move on. So it's the process between the Congress and the people of Puerto Rico, not a picking process.

SENATOR HEINRICH. So, Governor, what exactly is an enhanced Commonwealth?

MR. PADILLA. Let's go for example. It has been studied very well. As I told you it passed the House already once in the state here, in the Senate. We can arrange that way where Federal laws which apply to Puerto Rico, but in a mutual, working together, with Congress not Puerto Rico alone. We can talk about Federal courts in Puerto Rico not about the application of the Federal court to Puerto Rico, but the language there. The Federal courts in Puerto Rico is struggling with the language in Puerto Rico because most of Puerto Ricans speak Spanish. There you have two examples.[43]

It is precisely this degree of ambiguity, substantive equivocation, and faulty reading of the constitutional text and the legislative history leading to the founding of commonwealth status in 1952 that has made the territorial enhancement construct utterly untenable.

Against this background, a number of questions immediately arise. First, what is the nature of the legal and policy arguments leveled in Washington against the proposition that commonwealth status can evolve to a greater degree of autonomy within the federal superstructure? Second, are these arguments consistent with a sound reading of the constitutional text and public policy of the United States? Finally, how relevant is the ideological crisis at the heart of the pro-commonwealth PDP to the overall resolution of Puerto Rico's status question?

A closer look at these issues requires an in-depth scrutiny of the philosophical tenets and historical trajectory of Puerto Rico's autonomist movement and, at the same time, a contemporaneous understanding of the acute internal cleavages that today have come to divide the movement between so-called *autonomistas* and *soberanistas*,[44] bearing in mind that the

---

43 *Puerto Rico: Hearing before the Committee on Energy and Natural Resources, United States Senate, One Hundred Thirteenth Congress, First Session, to Receive Testimony on the Nov. 6, 2012, Referendum on the Political Status of Puerto Rico and the Administration's Response*, 113th Cong. 26-29 (2013).

44 *Autonomista* is commonly used to describe the more conservative voices

economic meltdown, together with the realization that the territorial praxis leads nowhere, has led important elements of the PDP's rank and file to transition to the *soberanista* camp.

The Philosophical Values of the Autonomist Movement

Puerto Rico's autonomist movement came to life in the wake of the Napoleonic Wars. The fall of the Bourbons' absolutist rule in Spain in 1808,[45] together with the proclamation of the 1812 Cádiz Constitution,[46] opened the floodgates of revolution across Spanish America. More specifically, in Puerto Rico, the inauguration of Spain's short-lived constitutional experiment led to the election—for the first time in 300 years of Spanish rule—of a Puerto Rican delegate to the Cortes[47] and to the devolution to the island of limited authority over issues of local governance.[48]

However, the Bourbons' restoration to the Spanish throne following Napoleon's expulsion from the Iberian Peninsula in 1814 and the concomitant strengthening of Spain's rule in Puerto Rico under the reigns of Ferdinand VII

within the PDP who cling to the traditional framework of organically growing commonwealth status within the strictures of the territory clause. *Soberanista* is used to refer to those within the PDP who support the forging of a treaty relationship with the United States, whereby Puerto Rico as a sovereign would delegate some of its authority to Congress while retaining for itself the panoply of political prerogatives emanating from its inherent powers as a sovereign state.

45 In May 1808, after forcing the abdication of Charles IV and Ferdinand VII along with the surrendering of their respective dynastic rights, Napoleon imposed on Spain his own rule (by appointing his brother Joseph as king) and a constitution of his own making. For the text of this constitution, see Jorge de Esteban, *Las Constituciones de España*, 3rd ed. (Madrid: Centro de Estudios Políticos y Constitucionales, 2012), 109-23.

46 The Cádiz Constitution was proclaimed on March 18, 1812. The return of Ferdinand VII to Madrid in 1814, following Napoleon's abdication pursuant to the 1814 Treaty of Fontainebleau, put an end to the Cádiz liberal experiment, turning the wheel back to absolutist rule. For the text of the Cádiz Constitution, see Esteban, *Las Constituciones de España*, 125-64.

47 For the election of delegates from the overseas colonies, see article 37 of the Cádiz Constitution. For a detailed analysis of the process leading to the election on April 16, 1810, of Ramón Power y Giralt (1775-1813) as Puerto Rico's only delegate to the Cortes in Cádiz, see Lidio Cruz Monclova, *Historia de Puerto Rico (Siglo XIX)*, 2nd ed., vol. 1 (Río Piedras: Editorial de la Universidad de Puerto Rico, 1958), 30-39.

48 For the internal governance of provinces and municipalities under the 1812 Cádiz Constitution, see articles 309-37.

and Isabella II[49] abruptly arrested the incipient flourishing of the autonomist ideal among the island's endogenous economic and intellectual elite.

It was not until the 1880s that Puerto Rico witnessed the emergence of a politically organized and ideologically sound autonomist movement. A combination of economic maladies[50] and incessant dissatisfaction with Spain's harsh colonial dictatorship[51] served as a catalyst for the island's more progressive movements to embrace an openly autonomist agenda. Under the charismatic leadership of Román Baldorioty de Castro, such an agenda, initially expounded in a manifesto entitled *El Plan de Ponce*,[52] led to the founding of Puerto Rico's first authentic political party, the Partido Autonomista Puertorriqueño, in 1887.[53]

Ideologically, however, the philosophical underpinnings of Puerto Rico's autonomist movement are found in the dominion status relationship that Canada and the British Crown inaugurated in 1867,[54] pursuant to the

---

49 Both Ferdinand VII (1814-1833) and his daughter Isabella II (1833-1868) stifled Spain's liberal movement by annulling the Cádiz Constitution and subsequently passing the 1834 Royal Statute and the 1845 Constitution, respectively. Esteban, *Las Constituciones de España*, 165-68, 171-78.

50 Among these maladies were Spain's devaluation of the circulating currency on the island, the obsolescence of Puerto Rico's sugar industry, and the absence of political liberties. See, e.g., Astrid Cubano Iguina, "El autonomismo en Puerto Rico, 1887-1898: Notas para la definición de un modelo de política radical," in *La nación soñada: Cuba, Puerto Rico y las Filipinas ante el 98*, ed. Consuelo Naranjo (Madrid: Doce Calles, 1995), 408-9.

51 The 1876 Spanish Constitution made it clear that Cuba and Puerto Rico would be governed pursuant to "special legislation" in matters pertaining to individual rights and civil liberties. CONSTITUCIÓN DE 1876 [CONSTITUTION OF 1876], art. 89 (Spain).

52 *El Plan de Ponce* advocated for the concession of greater autonomy to the municipalities and provinces in areas such as tax, industrial, financial, educational, and agricultural policies, but always within the "national union" with Spain. It also called for universal male adult suffrage. See José A. Gautier Dapena, *Baldorioty, Apóstol* (San Juan: Instituto de Cultura Puertorriqueña, 1970), 135-44. See also Lidio Cruz Monclova, *Historia de Puerto Rico (Siglo XIX)*, 2nd ed., vol. 3 (Río Piedras: Editorial de la Universidad de Puerto Rico, 1958), 33-36.

53 For a description of the proceedings, see Pilar Barbosa de Rosario, *De Baldorioty a Barbosa: Historia del autonomismo puertorriqueño* (San Juan: Instituto de Cultura Puertorriqueña, 1957), 107-21; and Cruz Monclova, *Historia de Puerto Rico*, vol. 3, 49-59.

54 For an analysis of the influence the Canadian model exerted on Baldorioty de Castro's thinking, see Gautier Dapena, *Baldorioty, Apóstol*, 128-29; and Cruz Monclova, *Historia de Puerto Rico* vol. 3, 51-52.

British North America Act of that same year.[55] It is essential to note that Puerto Rico's autonomist movement has always sought intellectual refuge in European conceptions of autonomy, such as those available in the Charter of Autonomy granted to Puerto Rico in 1897 by the Spanish Crown,[56] the 1931 Statute of Westminster,[57] the 1954 Charter for the Kingdom of the Netherlands (as amended by the 2010 Kingdom Act with respect to Curaçao and Sint Marteen's achievement of *status aparte*),[58] the 1967 West Indies Act,[59] the 1978 Spanish Constitution,[60] the 1991 Åland Autonomy Act,[61] the 2009 Greenland Self-Government Act,[62] and the European Union treaties (i.e., the 1992 Maastricht Treaty and its progeny)[63]—notions that have been largely unavailable in American constitutionalism, particularly following

---

55   Constitution Act, 1867, 30 & 31 Vict., c. 3 (U.K.), *reprinted in* R.S.C. 1985, app. II, no. 5 (Can.).

56   Carta Autonómica de 1897 [Charter of Autonomy of 1897] (Spain). The "autonomy" construct, in principle, ran counter to the post-1875 restoration project that the monarchical political parties in Madrid had engineered under the leadership of Antonio Cánovas del Castillo and Práxedes Mateo Sagasta to restore the Bourbons to the Spanish throne. Alfonso XII, son of Isabella II, entered Madrid as king on January 14, 1875. The 1876 Constitution, moreover, established a centralized monarchical state where notions of regionalization, decentralization, and, hence, autonomy had no ascendancy. The geopolitical imperatives of the late 1890s, however, brought about a complete volte-face that in turn led to the proclamation on November 25, 1897, of the Charter of Autonomy for Puerto Rico. For the text of the charter, see Antonio Fernós López Cepero, *Documentos históricos-constitucionales de Puerto Rico* (San Juan: Ediciones Situm, 2005), 21-37. For an analysis of the substantive provisions of the charter, see José Trías Monge, *Historia constitucional de Puerto Rico*, vol. 1 (Río Piedras: Editorial de la Universidad de Puerto Rico, 1980), 90-134; and José Julián Álvarez, "El viejo pacto: El elemento de la bilateralidad en la Carta Autonómica de 1897," *Revista Jurídica de la Universidad de Puerto Rico* 67 (1998): 983-1001.

57   Statute of Westminster, 1931, 22 & 23 Geo 5, c. 4 (Eng.).

58   Statuut voor het Koninkrijk der Nederlanden [Charter for the Kingdom of the Netherlands], Stb. 1954 503, *amended by* Decree of Nov. 1, 2010, Sb. 2010, 775 (Neth.).

59   West Indies Act 1967, 11 & 12 Eliz. 2, c. 4 (Eng.).

60   CONSTITUCIÓN ESPAÑOLA [SPANISH CONSTITUTION] (1978) (Spain).

61   Act on the Autonomy of Åland, 1991/1144 (1991) (Fin.).

62   Act on Greenland Self-Government, Act No. 473 of June 12, 2009 (Green.).

63   Treaty on European Union (Maastricht Treaty), Feb. 7, 1992, 1992 O.J. (C191) 1; Treaty of Amsterdam, Amending the Treaty on European Union, the Treaties Establishing the European Communities and Certain Related Acts, Oct. 2, 1997, 1997 O.J. (C 340); Treaty of Nice Amending the Treaty on European Union, the Treaties Establishing the European Communities and Certain Related Acts, Feb. 26, 2001, 2001 O.J. (C80) 1; Treaty of Lisbon Amending the Treaty on European Union and the Treaty Establishing the European Community, Dec. 13, 2007, 2007 O.J. (C 306) 1.

the demise of the Indian treaty system[64] during the Reconstruction period[65] and the hyper-federalization of US governance in the aftermath of the civil rights movement.

Any detailed analysis of the various European modalities of autonomy brings to the surface the common features of this political construct and lays bare the ideological bedrock of Puerto Rico's autonomist movement. If looked at collectively, continental autonomy models have historically been predicated, albeit to varying degrees, on the following principles: political union between the metropolis and the autonomous jurisdiction, shared nationality through common citizenship, bilateralism by means of mutual consent arrangements, participation in the metropolis's politico-constitutional processes, allocation of concentric areas of legislative authority between the contracting parties, devolution of political authority to engage in transnational economic relationships with other sovereigns, and legal recognition by the metropolis of the distinct sociological and linguistic inheritance of the peripheral political entity. These European tenets, in turn, have constituted for over a century the unfulfilled aspirations of Puerto Rico's autonomist movement.

The 1867 British North America Act made it clear that even in the face of the substantial political authority that the British Crown had devolved to Canada,[66] the new dominion's union to the British Crown would remain

---

64 A common feature of the relationship that soon ensued between the Native American nations in North America and their European colonizers was the practice of treaty-making, in an effort to regulate their uneasy coexistence. Both the British and the French developed, as a matter of course, a network of treaties with the several Native American nations. Critics of the Indian treaty system have pointed out the pathological nature of such agreements, in light of the bad-faith tactics often employed by the European colonizers in their efforts to breach their obligations. It is essential, however, to point out that Chief Justice John Marshall, in the eponymous Marshall Trilogy (i.e., *Johnson v. M'Intosh*, 21 U.S. 543 (1823), *Cherokee Nation v. Georgia*, 30 U.S. 1 (1831), and *Worcester v. Georgia*, 31 U.S. 515 (1832)), held that the Indian nations had retained for themselves an inherent right to self-government that had never been extinguished.

65 In 1871, by way of a rider to the 1871 Indian Appropriations Act, Congress ended the practice of entering into treaties with the Indian nations. According to the rider, Indian nations were not entities "with whom the United States may contract by treaty." 25 U.S.C. § 71 (1871). Contrary to what some think, the demise of the treaty-making policy did not respond to constitutional impermissibility but to political tinkering in Congress at the heyday of the Reconstruction period. For a closer look at the Indian treaty system, see Henry F. De Puy, *A Bibliography of the English Colonial Treaties with the American Indians* (New York: Lennox Club, 1917); Robert A. Williams, Jr., *Linking Arms Together* (New York: Oxford University Press, 1997); and Francis Paul Prucha, *American Indian Treaties: The History of a Political Anomaly* (Berkeley: UCLA Press, 1994).

66 The act defined Canada as "one Dominion" made up of the provinces of Canada,

unaltered.[67] Both the 1926 Imperial Conference Report[68] and the 1931 Statute of Westminster, while extolling the dominions' unprecedented autonomy in domestic and external affairs, made explicit reference to the fact that Canada, Australia, New Zealand, South Africa, the Irish Free State, and Newfoundland remained "united by a common allegiance to the Crown."[69] Article 1 of the Charter for the Kingdom of the Netherlands establishes in no uncertain terms the unitary nature of The Hague's relationship with its former Caribbean colonies: "The Kingdom shall consist of the Countries of the Netherlands, Aruba, Curaçao and Sint Marteen."[70] Similarly, both the 2009 Act on Greenland Self-Government and the 2004 Act on Danish Nationality characterize the political relationship between Denmark and Greenland (and the Faroe Islands) as unitary in nature,[71] despite the substantial installments of political authority devolved to Greenland's Naalakkersuisut (government). Greenland's self-government act states that "the partnership between Denmark and Greenland is based on a wish to foster equality and mutual respect."[72] The 1991 Act on the Autonomy of Åland, together with the 2011 Finnish Nationality Act, confirms the Åland Islands' unitary bond to Finland.[73] Even Puerto Rico's 1897 Charter of Autonomy and the 1876 Spanish Constitution underlying it were predicated on the unitary nature of the Spanish Kingdom, including with respect to the overseas autonomous regions (namely, Puerto Rico and Cuba).[74] Today, the 1978 Spanish Constitution states that "[t]he Constitution is based on the indissoluble unity of the Spanish nation . . . ; it recognizes and guarantees the right to autonomy of the nationalities and regions of which it is composed, and the solidarity amongst them all."[75]

Nova Scotia, and New Brunswick. Constitution Act, 1867, 30 & 31 Vict., c. 3, § 3 (U.K.), *reprinted in* R.S.C. 1985, app. II, no. 5 (Can.).

67   Ibid., pmbl. This was similar to the conception of legal union ingrained in the 1707 Treaty of Union between the Kingdoms of England and Scotland.

68   United Kingdom Parliament, *Report of the Inter-Imperial Relations Committee at Imperial Conference*, Cmd. 2768 (London: Her Majesty's Stationery Office, 1926).

69   Statute of Westminster, 1931, 22 & 23 Geo 5, c. 4, pmbl., para. 2 (Eng.).

70   Statuut voor het Koninkrijk der Nederlanden [Charter for the Kingdom of the Netherlands], Stb. 1954, art. 1(1) (Neth.).

71   See Act on Greenland Self-Government, Act No. 473 of June 12, 2009, pmbl. (Green.); Consolidated Act on Danish Nationality, Consolidation Act No. 422 of June 7, 2004, § 3 (2004) (Den.).

72   Act on Greenland Self-Government, Act No. 473 of June 12, 2009, pmbl. (Green.).

73   Act on the Autonomy of Åland, 1991/1144 ch. 1, § 1 (1991) (Fin.); Nationality Act, Act 579/2011 (2011) (Fin.).

74   Carta Autonómica de 1897 [Charter of Autonomy of 1897] (Spain); CONSTITUCIÓN DE 1876 [CONSTITUTION OF 1876] (Spain).

75   CONSTITUCIÓN ESPAÑOLA [SPANISH CONSTITUTION], art. 2 (1978) (Spain).

It is essential to note, moreover, that in all these instances, the unitary nature of the political relationships between the various metropolitan centers and their respective autonomous partners has been bound even further by a shared legal citizenship. The 1967 West Indies Act made it clear that "in relation to an associated state the British Nationality Acts 1948 to 1965 shall have effect."[76] According to the Charter for the Kingdom of the Netherlands, Dutch nationality falls under "Kingdom affairs," making the nationality available in each of the constituent countries of the kingdom—namely, the Netherlands, Aruba, Curaçao and Sint Marteen.[77] Furthermore, the charter requires that all ministers plenipotentiary from the Caribbean countries be of Dutch nationality.[78] The 2004 Act on Danish Nationality has full force and effect in both Greenland and the Faroe Islands, thus making those born in either territory natural-born Danish nationals.[79] Equally, Finland's 2011 Nationality Act has full force and effect in the Åland Islands, making those born in Ålander territory natural-born Finnish nationals.[80] Likewise, the legal status of Puerto Ricans as Spanish nationals, as was provided under article 1(1) of the 1876 Spanish Constitution, was not modified by the entry into force in 1897 of the Charter of Autonomy.

Perhaps the key element in all these European autonomic constructs has been their bilateral nature—namely, the safeguards ingrained in each of the applicable legal instruments for balancing the often complex interactions between two concentric sovereigns.

The Statute of Westminster provided:

> No law and no provision of any law made after the commencement of this Act by the Parliament of a Dominion shall be void and inoperative on the ground that it is repugnant to the law of England, or to the provisions of any existing or future Act of Parliament of the United Kingdom, or to any order, rule or regulation made under such Act.[81]

With the exception of statutory instruments implicating defense and foreign affairs, the West Indies Act established that "no Act of the Parliament of the United Kingdom . . . shall extend . . . to an associated state as part of its law,

---

76   West Indies Act 1967, 11 & 12 Eliz. 2, c. 4, § 12 (Eng.).
77   Statuut voor het Koninkrijk der Nederlanden [Charter for the Kingdom of the Netherlands], Stb. 1954, art. 3 (Neth.).
78   Ibid., art. 8.
79   See Consolidated Act on Danish Nationality, Consolidation Act No. 422 of June 7, 2004 (2004) (Den.).
80   Nationality Act, Act 579/2011 (2011) (Fin.).
81   Statute of Westminster, 1931, 22 & 23 Geo 5, c. 4, § 2.2 (Eng.).

unless it is expressly declared in that Act that that state has requested and consented to its being enacted."[82]

Not only do the Dutch, Danish, Finnish, and even the Spanish autonomic models provide for a clear demarcation between the legislative powers distributed to the metropolitan jurisdiction and those distributed to the autonomous jurisdictions,[83] but, equally importantly, each of them has set in place institutional consultation mechanisms between the contracting parties prior to the enactment of metropolitan legislation (including treaties with foreign sovereigns) that could affect the welfare of the associated jurisdiction and, additionally, allows representatives from the autonomous entities to sit in the metropolitan parliamentary institutions. Pursuant to the Charter for the Kingdom of the Netherlands, both the Council of Ministers and the Council of State at The Hague include members from Aruba, Curaçao and Sint Marteen.[84] Furthermore, Greenland and the Faroe Islands are separate Danish constituencies, each with individual representation in Denmark's Parliament, while the Åland Islands constitute a separate district with representation in the Finnish Parliament. Along similar lines, the 1876 Spanish Constitution, in full force and effect by the time the 1897 Charter of Autonomy came into existence, provided for the representation of Puerto Rico (and Cuba) in Madrid's Cortes.[85]

In the realm of foreign affairs, moreover, continental arrangements have tended to provide a wide latitude, particularly in areas pertaining to the economic variables that potentially impinge on the economic welfare of the associated state.

Even before the enactment of the Statute of Westminster in 1931, the old dominions already enjoyed considerable authority on transnational issues. Canada, Australia, New Zealand, South Africa, the Irish Free State, and Newfoundland were empowered to negotiate freely with foreign powers; dispatch their own diplomats, including representatives to the League of Nations, without interference from the British Cabinet; and declare neutrality

---

82   West Indies Act 1967, 11 & 12 Eliz. 2, c. 4, § 3 (Eng.). Under the Statute of Westminster and the 1967 British West Indies Act, both the Colonial Courts of Admiralty Act (53 & 54 Vict., c. 27) and the Merchant Shipping Act (57 & 58 Vict., c. 6) no longer applied to the dominions or to the associated states, respectively.

83   See, e.g., Statuut voor het Koninkrijk der Nederlanden [Charter for the Kingdom of the Netherlands], Stb. 1954, art. 3 (Neth.); Act on Greenland Self-Government, Act No. 473 of June 12, 2009, chs. 2, 3 (Green.); Act on the Autonomy of Åland, 1991/1144, §§ 7, 18, 27, 44 (1991) (Fin.); Carta Autonómica de 1897 [Charter of Autonomy of 1897], arts. 32-35, 39 (Spain); CONSTITUCIÓN ESPAÑOLA [SPANISH CONSTITUTION], arts. 148-49 (1978) (Spain).

84   Statuut voor het Koninkrijk der Nederlanden [Charter for the Kingdom of the Netherlands], Stb. 1954, arts. 7, 13 (Neth.).

85   CONSTITUCIÓN DE 1876 [CONSTITUTION OF 1876], art. 89 (Spain).

in the face of a declaration of war issued by the British Parliament.[86] Under the West Indies Act, moreover, Antigua, Saint Kitts and Nevis, Dominica, Saint Lucia, Saint Vincent, and Grenada were endowed with the authority to apply for full or associate membership in United Nations specialized agencies and other international organizations;[87] arrange state visits by representatives of such organizations; and, more importantly, sign trade treaties with independent countries and sign financial, technical, cultural, and scientific agreements with member states of the British Commonwealth and with the United States.

The Charter for the Kingdom of the Netherlands bestows on Aruba, Curaçao, and Sint Marteen the authority to conclude international economic and financial agreements and to accede to membership in international organizations, while enabling each of the kingdom's Caribbean countries to waive the enforceability on its soil of treaties ratified by the Netherlands if these treaties are detrimental to its interests.[88] Similarly, the Act on Greenland Self-Government establishes that Greenland may "negotiate and conclude agreements under international law with foreign states and international organizations, including administrative agreements which exclusively concern Greenland and entirely relate to fields of responsibility taken over."[89] Meanwhile, "[a]greements under international law which are of particular importance to Greenland must, before they are concluded or terminated, be submitted to Naalakkersuisut [the Government of Greenland] for comments."[90] The act also states that representatives of Greenland "shall be appointed to the diplomatic missions of the Kingdom of Denmark to attend to Greenland interests within fields of responsibilities that have been entirely assumed by the Self-Government authorities."[91] For its part, the Act on the Autonomy of Åland mandates that "[t]he Government of Åland may propose negotiations on a treaty or another international obligation to the appropriate State officials."[92] It furthermore states that "[i]f a treaty or another international obligation binding on Finland contains a term which under this

---

86 See British Foreign Office Papers, FO 371/A 1017/55 (UK National Archives Centre, Kew Gardens).

87 See British Cabinet Papers, CAB 148/27, UK National Archives Centre, Kew Gardens. See also Rafael Cox Alomar, *Revisiting the Transatlantic Triangle: The Constitutional Decolonization of the Eastern Caribbean* (Miami: Ian Randle, 2009), 202.

88 Statuut voor het Koninkrijk der Nederlanden [Charter for the Kingdom of the Netherlands], Stb. 1954, arts. 25, 26, 28 (Neth.).

89 Act on Greenland Self-Government, Act No. 473 of June 12, 2009, § 12(1) (Green.).

90 Ibid., § 13(4).

91 Ibid., § 15.

92 Act on the Autonomy of Åland, 1991/1144, § 58 (1991) (Fin.).

Act concerns a matter within the competence of Åland, the Åland Parliament must consent to the statute implementing that term in order to have it enter into force in Åland."[93]

In the particular contexts of Greenland and the Åland Islands, their legal instruments also provide for linguistic, and thus cultural, autonomy. The Act on Greenland Self-Government establishes that "Greenlandic shall be the official language in Greenland."[94] Due in great part to Åland's complex geopolitical trajectory, the Act on the Autonomy of Åland requires that Swedish, as opposed to Finnish, be the official language in Åland, including in all proceedings before the Supreme Court and the Evangelical Lutheran Church.[95] The act also mandates that Swedish be the language of public instruction throughout the islands.[96]

Against this background, one can safely conclude that if seen from a holistic perspective, the cardinal elements of these European modalities of autonomy have so far eluded Puerto Rico's autonomist movement.

The demobilization of the Spanish colonial project in Puerto Rico, following Madrid's decisive defeat at the hands of the United States in 1898, led to a dramatic realignment of the island's autonomist forces—an ideological recalibration that, on the one hand, swayed the movement's trajectory for the foreseeable future and, on the other, left out in the open the hold that European notions of autonomy still exerted over the ideological discourse of Puerto Rico's autonomists, even after the entrenchment of American rule on the island.

The ideological heirs of Baldorioty de Castro, now at the helm of a fractured autonomist movement, at first glance perceived turn-of-the-century American federalism as an arrangement whereby the United States amounted to a *república de repúblicas*[97] in which the several states enjoyed considerable internal authority relative to the federal government. And it was, to a great degree, in light of that perception of the United States' federal system that the two old autonomist parties under Spain refashioned their respective platforms and political ideologies following the signing of the Treaty of Paris. On the one hand, the *autonomistas ortodoxos* led by José Celso Barbosa founded the Puerto Rican Republican Party on July 4, 1899.[98] Having discarded the viability of any attempt to superimpose a Canadian-style autonomy model on the US federal landscape, the Republicans set their sights on Puerto Rico's sociological

---

93   Ibid., § 59.
94   Act on Greenland Self-Government, Act No. 473 of June 12, 2009, § 20 (Green.).
95   Act on the Autonomy of Åland, 1991/1144, ch. 6, § 36 (1991) (Fin.).
96   Ibid., § 40.
97   See Luis Muñoz Rivera's manifesto on the founding of the Federal Party of Puerto Rico, dated October 1, 1899, in Bolívar Pagán, *Historia de los partidos políticos puertorriqueños* (San Juan: Editorial Campos, 1959), 46.
98   This was the precursor to Puerto Rico's New Progressive Party.

and institutional assimilation into the United States as a means of achieving incorporation into the Union—first as an organized territory and, ultimately, as a state. On the other hand, the *autonomistas liberales*, under the leadership of Luis Muñoz Rivera, initially regrouped on October 1, 1899, under the new and short-lived American Federal Party, which advocated for the concession to Puerto Rico of home rule under the American flag. Reorganized in 1904 under the Union Party, Muñoz Rivera and his fellow *unionistas* reaffirmed the ideological compass of their movement. No longer committed to the autonomic formula as the end goal, the movement's immediate objective became the achievement of self-government under the unincorporated territory formulation in preparation for either statehood or independence; as they saw it, under either formula, Puerto Rico would remain self-governing.[99] In the words of Muñoz Rivera, "como medida temporal y transitoria el *home rule*; como aspiraciones finales, la estadidad o la independencia."[100] During the first period of US rule in Puerto Rico, up until the end of World War II, the island's political leadership, regardless of party allegiance, no longer saw the autonomy ideal as a permanent status formula.

Decades later, the postwar period brought with it yet another turnaround in the island's autonomist discourse. With the "iron curtain descending across Europe"[101] and the "winds of change"[102] undoing the old European empires throughout the developing world,[103] the autonomic formula began to be perceived in both Washington and San Juan as a permanent solution to Puerto Rico's colonial condition. The introduction of the 1945 Tydings-Piñero bill[104]—which advocated for a plebiscite in which dominion status appeared as a permanent formula[105]—and the subsequent inauguration, seven years later, of commonwealth status must then be seen as by-products of this complex geopolitical tapestry.[106] A rigorous look at the legislative history leading to

---

99   See *base quinta* of the Union Party's manifesto, published on February 19, 1904, in Pagán, *Historia de los partidos políticos*, 107.

100 Luis Muñoz Rivera, letter to José de Diego, July 25, 1913, in Muñoz Rivera, *Campañas políticas*, vol. 3 (Madrid: Editorial Puerto Rico, 1925), 155 ("as a temporary and transitory measure, home rule; as an ultimate goal, statehood or independence").

101 Winston Churchill, speech (Westminster College, Fulton, MO, Mar. 5, 1946).

102 Harold Macmillan, speech (Cape Town, South Africa, Feb. 3, 1960).

103 Undoubtedly, Puerto Rico's constitutional evolution must be seen in light of the constitutional transformations that were already taking place in the British, Dutch, and French Caribbean during this same period.

104 A Bill to Provide for the Submission to the People of Puerto Rico of Alternative Forms of Political Status, H.R. 3237, 79th Cong. (1945).

105 For the writings of one of the first proponents of dominion status for Puerto Rico, see Theodore Roosevelt, Jr., *Colonial Policies of the United States* (New York: Doubleday, 1937), 117.

106 The following statement by then assistant secretary of state Jack K. McFall brings to the surface how Cold War considerations swayed this process:

the enactment of Public Law 600, as well as the corpus of jurisprudence that soon emerged, brings to life the competing catalysts enabling the Truman and Muñoz Marín administrations' discursive metamorphosis with respect to the meaning of the autonomic formula.[107] No longer a temporary solution, the autonomic formula had become a permanent solution in and of itself.

The Genesis of the Commonwealth Relationship

From the time of the American invasion on July 25, 1898, until the signing of the Foraker Act on May 1, 1900, Puerto Rico was under the supreme command of military governors.[108] President McKinley's signing of the Foraker Act put an end to military rule.[109] A civilian governor was now chief executive,[110] while a so-called executive committee made up of six Americans and five Puerto Ricans, some of whom would also sit in the governor's cabinet, constituted the island's upper legislative chamber.[111] Both the governor and the members of the executive committee were appointed by the president, with the advice and consent of the US Senate.[112] A house of delegates (elected every other year and made up of thirty-five members), together with the executive committee, made up the local legislative assembly.[113] This first organic act, moreover,

---

> The achievement of self-government by Puerto Rico will be a matter of great interest to members of the UN in their discussions of the political progress of non-self-governing territories. It will be a convincing answer to attacks by those who have charged the US Government with imperialism and colonial exploitation, and it should be warmly welcomed by members who have a sincere interest in the political advancement of dependent peoples.

S. Rep. 82-1720, 82d Cong. (1952). See also letter from Jack K. McFall, Assistant Secretary of State, to Senator Joseph C. O'Mahoney, Chairman of the Committee on Interior and Insular Affairs (Apr. 25, 1950), in Hearing before a Subcommittee of the Committee on Interior and Insular Affairs, United States Senate 81st Congress, 2nd Session, on S. 3336, A Bill to Provide for the Organization of a Constitutional Government by the People of Puerto Rico, 81st Cong. 4 (1950).

107 The Cold War scenario did not go unheeded by the founders of commonwealth status in their efforts to impress on the American political branches the geopolitical significance of strengthening the commonwealth relationship.

108 For the military general orders governing Puerto Rico during this period, see *Laws, Ordinances, Decrees and Military Orders Having the Force of Law, Effective in Porto Rico*, H.R. Doc. No. 1484, pt. 4, 2177 (1909).

109 Organic Act of 1900 (Foraker Act), ch. 191, 31 Stat. 77 (1900) (codified as amended in scattered sections of 48 U.S.C. (2013)).

110 Ibid., § 17.

111 Ibid., § 18.

112 Ibid., §§ 17-18.

113 Ibid., § 27.

established the United States District Court for the District of Puerto Rico[114] and called for the election, every other year, of a resident commissioner to the United States who would act on behalf of the people of Puerto Rico before federal authorities in Washington.[115]

A year after the Foraker Act was signed into law, the US Supreme Court laid down the legal framework for regulating the relationship between the federal government and its recently acquired Caribbean territory. Unlike the organized territories incorporated pursuant to the Northwest Ordinance (1787),[116] the Louisiana Purchase (1803),[117] the Adams-Onís Treaty (1819),[118] the Oregon Treaty (1846),[119] the Treaty of Guadalupe Hidalgo (1848),[120] and the Alaska Purchase (1867),[121] among others, Puerto Rico, along with the Philippines and Guam, was now "a territory *appurtenant* and *belonging to* the United States, but not a part of the United States."[122] More specifically, with respect to the international personality of the newly minted unincorporated territory, the Supreme Court held:

> The result of what has been said is that whilst in an international
> sense Porto Rico was not a foreign country, since it was subject to the
> sovereignty of and was owned by the United States, it was foreign to
> the United States in a domestic sense, because the island had not been
> incorporated into the United States, but was merely appurtenant thereto
> as a possession.[123]

Nearly two decades later, Congress passed a second organic act effecting minor administrative modifications while at the same time conferring US

---

114 Ibid., § 34. For a relevant discussion of the process leading to the 1899 inauguration of the US Provisional Court, predecessor to the Foraker Act's United States District Court for the District of Puerto Rico, see Carmelo Delgado Cintrón, *Derecho y Colonialismo* (Río Piedras: Edil, 1988), 221-77.

115 Organic Act of 1900 (Foraker Act), ch. 191, § 39, 31 Stat. 77 (1900) (codified as amended in scattered sections of 48 U.S.C. (2013)).

116 An Act to Provide for the Government of the Territory of the United States North-West of the River Ohio, ch. 8, 1 Stat. 50 (1789).

117 Louisiana Purchase Agreement, U.S.-Fr., Apr. 30, 1803, 8 Stat. 200.

118 Treaty of Amity, Settlement, and Limits between the United States of America and His Catholic Majesty, U.S.-Spain, Feb. 22, 1819, 8 Stat. 252.

119 Treaty Establishing the Boundary in the Territory on the Northwest Coast of America Lying Westward of the Rocky Mountains, U.S.-Gr. Brit., June 15, 1846, 9 Stat. 869.

120 Treaty of Peace, Friendship, Limits, and Settlement with the Republic of Mexico, U.S.-Mex., Feb. 2, 1848, 9 Stat. 922.

121 Convention Ceding Alaska, U.S.-Russ., Mar. 30, 1867, 15 Stat. 539.

122 Downes v. Bidwell, 182 U.S. 244, 287 (1901) (emphasis added).

123 Ibid., 341-42.

citizenship on Puerto Ricans. The 1917 Jones Act[124] included a bill of rights; abolished the executive committee, replacing it with a locally elected senate; and established a two-chamber legislative assembly whose members were elected for four-year terms.[125] The veto power over local legislation, however, remained in the hands of the appointed governor and, ultimately, the US president.[126] Along these lines, all key executive appointments—including the governorship, cabinet positions, judgeships in the insular Supreme Court, and even the chancellorship of the University of Puerto Rico—still came from Washington. This new organic act, as the Taft court would soon hold in *Balzac v. Porto Rico*, left untouched the island's status with respect to Congress. Puerto Rico remained an unincorporated territory, even after the 1917 concession of US citizenship to its inhabitants.[127]

Thirty years later, in 1947, President Truman signed Public Law 362,[128] which granted Puerto Ricans the right to directly elect their governor.[129] And soon thereafter, in 1950, the president signed Public Law 600, providing "for

---

124 Jones Act, Pub. L. No. 64-368, 39 Stat. 951 (1917) (codified at 48 U.S.C. §§ 731 et seq. (2013)).

125 Ibid., §§ 2-11, 25.

126 Ibid., § 34. In the event that both houses of the local legislature overrode the governor's veto, the bill would then go to the US president, who would have the last word.

127 In *Balzac v. Porto Rico*, Chief Justice Taft, writing for the majority, found:

> Had Congress intended to take the important step of changing the treaty status of Porto Rico by incorporating it into the Union, it is reasonable to suppose that it would have done so by plain declaration, and would not have left it to mere inference. It is true that, in the absence of other and countervailing evidence, a law of Congress or a provision in a treaty acquiring territory, declaring an intention to confer political and civil rights on the inhabitants of the new lands as American citizens, may be properly interpreted to mean an incorporation of it into the Union, as in the case of Louisiana and Alaska. This was one of the chief grounds upon which this court placed its conclusion that Alaska had been incorporated in the Union. But Alaska was a very different case from that of Porto Rico. It was an enormous territory, very sparsely settled and offering opportunity for immigration and settlement by American citizens. It was on the American Continent and within easy reach of the then United States. It involved none of the difficulties which incorporation of the Philippines and Porto Rico presents.

Balzac v. Porto Rico, 258 U.S. 298, 306 (1922).

128 Act of Aug. 5, 1947 (Elective Governor Act), Pub. L. No. 80-362, 61 Stat. 770.

129 For the reaction of Governor Muñoz Marín, the island's first elected governor, to the enactment of this statute, see Luis Muñoz Marín, *Memorias*, vol. 2 (San Germán: Universidad Interamericana, 1992), 188-89.

the organization of a constitutional government by the people of Puerto Rico."[130] Congress adopted this statute "in the nature of a compact so that the people of Puerto Rico may organize a government pursuant to a constitution of their own adoption."[131] Public Law 600 was accepted by the people of Puerto Rico in a referendum held in June 1951, after which delegates to a constitutional convention were selected by the local electorate to draft a constitution. This constitution was ratified by the Puerto Rican people in a referendum held in March 1952 and subsequently transmitted to Congress for approval.[132] On July 3, 1952, Congress finally sanctioned the new constitution, but not without first modifying several of its provisions.[133] The new internal constitutional framework came to life under the name Estado Libre Asociado, intentionally translated into English as "commonwealth," on July 25, 1952.[134] Meanwhile, the provisions of the Foraker and Jones Acts perpetuating the island's political and economic subordination to Washington continued in force and effect under a new statutory instrument known as the Puerto Rico Federal Relations Act.[135]

Soon, Puerto Rico's autonomist movement, emboldened by the commonwealth's removal from the United Nations' list of non-self-governing territories in 1953,[136] characterized the overall political relationship between

---

130 Act of July 3, 1950, Pub. L. No. 81-600, 64 Stat. 319 (codified at 48 U.S.C. §§ 731 et seq. (2013)).

131 Ibid., § 1.

132 The Constitution of Puerto Rico was approved by 80% of voters. See Constitutional Convention, *Res. No. 34 of July 10, 1952* (1952) (P.R.) (codified in P.R. Laws Ann. tit. 1, at 144-46 (1982)).

133 United States v. Acosta Martínez, 106 F. Supp. 2d 311, 313 (D.P.R. 2000). For the congressional act approving the 1952 constitution, see Pub. L. No. 82-447, 66 Stat. 327 (1952). Congress eliminated section 20 of the commonwealth's constitution, which, modeled after the Universal Declaration of Human Rights, elevated the rights to free education, work, and adequate living standards, among others, to the rank of constitutional rights. See José Trías Monge, *Historia Constitucional de Puerto Rico*, vol. 3, 270-312.

134 See Constitutional Convention, *Resolution No. 22 of February 4, 1952* (1952) (P.R.).

135 See 48 U.S.C. § 731(b) (2013).

136 See G.A. Res. 748 (VIII), U.N. GAOR, 8th Sess., Supp. No 17, at 25, U.N. Doc. A/2630 (Nov. 27, 1953). The representations made by the US delegation with respect to Puerto Rico's new constitutional arrangement at the United Nations must be seen in light of the acute imperatives of the Cold War. Moreover, the Puerto Rican leadership did pay attention to these geopolitical imperatives. In a letter to Henry Cabot Lodge, Jr., the United States' ambassador to the United Nations, Governor Muñoz Marín made it abundantly clear that "Puerto Rico can be a weapon of some significance in the psychological warfare in which the free world under American leadership is engaged in the defense of human freedom." Luis Muñoz Marín, letter to Henry Cabot Lodge, Jr., May 25, 1953.

the people of Puerto Rico and Congress as one premised on a bilateral compact, unalterable unless by mutual consent, following "the precedent established by the Northwest Ordinance."[137]

Thus, the compact mythology was born, notwithstanding the fact that Public Law 600 did not modify "the status of the island of Puerto Rico relative to the United States,"[138] as Resident Commissioner Fernós Isern had clearly forewarned during the congressional hearings that preceded the passing of Public Law 600.[139]

Such mythology, however, has failed to dissipate the almost-universal consensus on the pathological nature of the 1952 bilateral compact theory, particularly if seen in light of the applicability to Puerto Rico of the US Constitution's supremacy clause.[140] Under this clause, any federal law openly conflicting with the island's constitution overrides it (in obvious violation of the compact's alleged bilateral nature),[141] and any federal legislation applies to Puerto Rico in its entirety, unless Congress unilaterally decides otherwise. The unavailability of a bilateral consultation mechanism enabling Puerto Rico to participate in Congress's statutory, regulatory, and treaty-making processes as concerns the island's welfare flies in the face of the bilateral compact theory.

Since the rendering of the Insular Cases, the US Supreme Court has seldom addressed the Puerto Rican status question; and on the few occasions that it has referred to it, the court has approached the issue largely through dicta.

---

137 *Hearing before a Subcommittee of the Committee on Interior and Insular Affairs, United States Senate 81st Congress, 2nd Session, on S. 3336, A Bill to Provide for the Organization of a Constitutional Government by the People of Puerto Rico,* 81st Cong. 4 (1950). For a compact in the early days of the Thirteen Colonies, see the 1620 Mayflower Compact.

138 Ibid.

139 The US House's report on Public Law 600, consistent with the resident commissioner's proposition, stated that "[i]t is important that the nature and general scope of S. 3336 be made absolutely clear. The bill under consideration would not change Puerto Rico's fundamental political, social and economic relationship to the United States." H.R. REP. No. 81-2275 (1950).

140 U.S. CONST., art. 6, cl. 2.

141 See, e.g., United States v. Acosta Martínez, 252 F.3d 13 (1st Cir. 2001) (reversing lower court's holding that the federal death penalty act was locally inapplicable in Puerto Rico under art. II, § 7 of the Puerto Rican Constitution); United States v. Quiñones, 758 F.2d 40 (1st Cir. 1985) (holding that although contrary to the mandate of art. II, § 10 of the Puerto Rican Constitution, wiretapping under 18 U.S.C. § 2510 was appropriate in Puerto Rico because the adoption of its constitution in no way altered the applicability of US laws and federal jurisdiction to Puerto Rico).

For instance, in *Rodríguez v. Popular Democratic Party*, the court found that "Puerto Rico, like a state, is an autonomous political entity, sovereign over matters not ruled by the Constitution."[142] In *Examining Board of Engineers, Architects and Surveyors v. Flores de Otero*, the court noted that "Congress relinquished its control over the organization of the local affairs of the island and granted Puerto Rico a measure of autonomy comparable to that possessed by the States."[143] In *Calero-Toledo v. Pearson Yacht Leasing Co.*, the court suggested that "Puerto Rico is a political entity created by the act and with the consent of the people of Puerto Rico and joined in union with the United States of America under the terms of the compact."[144] None of these dicta, however, alter the court's decision in *Harris v. Rosario*, which held that

> Congress, which is empowered under the Territory Clause of the Constitution . . . to "make all needful Rules and Regulations respecting the Territory . . . belonging to the United States" may treat Puerto Rico differently from the States so long as there is a rational basis for its actions.[145]

The *Harris* decision was arguably a regurgitation of the court's holding in *Califano v. Torres*, where the court had held that treating Puerto Rico differently from the several states was rationally grounded.[146] And while the *Harris* and *Califano* holdings were specifically tailored to address disparate treatment under federal welfare programs, the seminal problem with the court's discreet ruminations on the Puerto Rican status labyrinth remains because little stands in the way of Congress's plenary authority under the territory clause to unilaterally impinge on Puerto Rico's collective political right to internal self-government under Public Law 600, the Federal Relations Act, and its local constitution. While in an abstract juridical sense Puerto Rico in 1952 ceased to be an unincorporated territory subject to Congress's plenary powers, the unavoidable reality is that Congress's unilateral authority over Puerto Rico remains utterly unbridled—on the one hand demystifying the

---

142 Rodríguez v. Popular Democratic Party, 457 U.S. 1, 8 (1982) (holding that the voting rights of Puerto Ricans are constitutionally protected to the same extent as those of all other citizens of the United States).

143 Examining Bd. of Engineers, Architects & Surveyors v. Flores de Otero, 426 U.S. 572, 597 (1976) (holding that Puerto Rico is a state rather than a territory for the purposes of section 1983 jurisdiction).

144 Calero-Toledo v. Pearson Yacht Leasing Co., 416 U.S. 663, 672 (1974) (holding that the statutes of Puerto Rico are state statutes under the Three Judge Court Act (28 U.S.C. § 2281)).

145 Harris v. Rosario, 446 U.S. 651, 652 (1980).

146 Califano v. Torres, 435 U.S. 1 (1978).

bilateral compact theory and, on the other, taking the wind out of the viability of any enhancement formula predicated under the territory clause.

An Ideological Crisis in the Autonomist Movement

Not surprisingly, all attempts at endowing the commonwealth relationship with legal and political attributes commensurate to those enjoyed by European autonomous jurisdictions have blatantly failed.

The first effort to enhance the commonwealth arrangement crystallized in March 1959, when Resident Commissioner Fernós Isern introduced a bill in the US House of Representatives to "amend the compact between the people of Puerto Rico and the United States." H.R. 5926 was soon referred to the House Committee on Interior and Insular Affairs, under the chairmanship of Wayne N. Aspinall (D-Colorado). Two months later, Senator James E. Murray (D-Montana), chairman of the Senate Committee on Interior and Insular Affairs, introduced a sister bill, S. 2023, in the Senate.[147] Hearings on S. 2023 were held in June 1959, at which time oral testimony was offered by Fernós Isern and Governor Muñoz Marín, while written testimony was provided by the Bureau of the Budget, the Department of Agriculture, and the Department of Labor.[148] In the succeeding months, additional federal agencies would also report on the Fernós-Murray bill. These agencies included the Department of Justice; Department of State; Administrative Office of the US Courts; Department of Health, Education, and Welfare; Civil Service Commission; Federal Communications Commission; Department of the Navy; and Department of the Interior. H.R. 5926 and S. 2023 would undergo amendments following the Senate hearings; consequently, substitute bills were introduced in both the House and Senate in September 1959, as H.R. 9234 and S. 2708, respectively.[149]

Conceived, in the words of Governor Muñoz Marín, as legislation "to clarify as precisely and unequivocally [sic] as possible, the relations between the Commonwealth of Puerto Rico and the Federal Government,"[150] the main thrust of the Fernós-Murray bill was to amend Public Law 600 by devolving

---

147 A Bill to Provide for Amendments to the Compact between the People of Puerto Rico and the United States, S. 2023, 86th Cong. (1959).

148 *Puerto Rico Federal Relations Act: Hearing before the Committee on Interior and Insular Affairs, United States Senate, Eighty-Sixth Congress, First Session on S. 2023,* 86th Cong. 3-6 (1959).

149 A Bill to Provide for Amendments to the Compact between the People of Puerto Rico and the United States, and Related Legislation, H.R. 9234, 86th Cong. (1959); A Bill to Provide for Amendments to the Compact between the People of Puerto Rico and the United States, S. 2708, 86th Cong. (1959).

150 Luis Muñoz Marín, letter to Wayne N. Aspinall, May 3, 1960, Fernós Isern Papers, Faculty of Law, Interamerican University of Puerto Rico.

to the people of Puerto Rico powers of self-government in areas critically important for the island's long-term economic growth.[151] It sought to do all of this without undoing Congress's firm grip on the island's sovereignty under the 1898 Treaty of Paris.[152]

The Fernós-Murray bill provided that "[a]t the request of the Commonwealth of Puerto Rico, the President of the United States may, within the limits of the President's authority under applicable Federal law, negotiate trade and commercial agreements."[153] It also established a mechanism for the federal government to gradually transfer to Puerto Rican authorities "responsibility for specific functions, duties and services performed by the federal government in Puerto Rico except those which the federal government should retain in order to fulfill the nature of the permanent association."[154] Further, it mandated the US government to convey to the commonwealth legal title to all former Spanish Crown lands belonging to it under the Treaty of Paris, as well as all existing harbor areas, navigable streams, bodies of water, and submerged lands in the territory.[155] More importantly, under the Fernós-Murray bill, the "[s]tatutory laws of the United States hereafter enacted shall not be deemed to be applicable to the Commonwealth of Puerto Rico unless specifically made applicable by Act of Congress, by reference to Puerto Rico or to the Commonwealth of Puerto Rico by name."[156] And contrary to the Federal Relations Act, the bill specifically provided for the resident commissioner's membership in the US House of Representatives.[157] Moreover, the United States District Court for the District of Puerto Rico could, subject to its discretion, "conduct any trial or proceeding . . . in the Spanish language."[158] Finally, in a calculated attempt to strengthen the legitimacy of the bilateral compact theory, the drafters of the Fernós-Murray bill included the following language: "This Act and any amendments thereto enacted by the Congress

---

151 Paul D. Shriver, memorandum to Wayne N. Aspinall and Leo O'Brien, Apr. 11, 1960, Fernós Isern Papers, Faculty of Law, Interamerican University of Puerto Rico.

152 *Hearing before a Subcommittee of the Committee on Interior and Insular Affairs, United States Senate 81st Congress, 2nd Session, on S. 3336, A Bill to Provide for the Organization of a Constitutional Government by the People of Puerto Rico*, 81st Cong. 4 (1950) (statement of Fernós Isern).

153 A Bill to Provide Amendments to the Compact between the People of Puerto Rico and the United States, H.R. 5926, 86th Cong. art. IV(f) (1959).

154 Ibid., art. VI.

155 Ibid., art. VII.

156 Ibid., art. IX(c).

157 Ibid., art. XI. Section 36 of the Federal Relations Act provides for the election of a resident commissioner but, unlike the Fernós-Murray bill, does not specifically provide for the commissioner's membership in the US House of Representatives. The commissioner's current position in the US House is not statutorily protected but rather has been granted on the basis of the House's internal rules.

158 Ibid., art. XIII(b).

shall become effective when approved by a majority of the qualified voters of Puerto Rico participating in a referendum."[159]

The archival record shows that the Fernós-Murray bill faced a barrage of substantive opposition in Washington circles; not surprisingly, Governor Muñoz Marín formally requested its withdrawal in May 1960.[160]

The Fernós-Murray legislation was bound to fail from the outset because at no point was there a meeting of the minds between the bill's proponents and the political branches in Washington; complete and utter disagreement over the constitutional viability of a bilateral compact that neither contracting party could modify without the consent of the other hung like the Sword of Damocles over the bill's fate. The argument made by Governor Muñoz Marín, Abe Fortas, and others to the effect that without "complete and absolute bilateralism Puerto Rico was a colony" was unpersuasive.[161] Voices in the Eisenhower administration were adamant to counter that under the Fernós-Murray bill, Puerto Rico was effectively asking Congress for a "blank check" and that Congress "could not give up its power."[162] Other federal agencies—the Department of State; Department of the Treasury; Department of Health, Education, and Welfare; Department of Agriculture; Department of Commerce; Civil Service Commission; and the Administrative Office of the US Courts—expressed acute misgivings with devolving authority to Puerto Rico on issues ranging from foreign and trade issues, tariff matters, Crown lands, the administration of social security laws, and even the use of the Spanish language in federal court proceedings.[163] More importantly, the US Department of Justice, in its report on H.R. 9234,[164] while suggesting that "a theory might be constructed that the United States may, as an implied aspect of sovereignty, enter into arrangements with the people of a formerly dependent territory to determine the status of that territory . . . in a manner

---

159 Ibid., § 3.

160 Muñoz Marín, letter to Wayne N. Aspinall.

161 Minutes of meeting between Abe Fortas and Phillip Hughes, Sept. 3, 1959, Fernós Isern Papers, Faculty of Law, Interamerican University of Puerto Rico.

162 Ibid.

163 Minutes of meeting between Luis Muñoz Marín and Secretary of the Treasury, Mar. 29, 1960; Secretary of the Treasury, letter to James E. Murray, Jan. 12, 1960, Fernós Isern Papers, Faculty of Law, Interamerican University of Puerto Rico; *Puerto Rico Federal Relations Act: Hearing before the Committee on Interior and Insular Affairs, United States Senate, Eighty-Sixth Congress, First Session on S. 2023,* 86th Cong. 2-16 (1959).

164 The Department of Justice rendered its report on H.R. 9234 on February 16, 1960. *Hearing before a Special Subcommittee on Territorial and Insular Affairs of the Committee on Interior and Insular Affairs, United States House of Representatives, Eighty-Sixth Congress, First Session on H.R. 9234,* 86th Cong. 802-15 (1960).

permanent and binding upon both parties," shied away from adopting a definitive view regarding "whether the foregoing theories would ultimately be accepted by the courts."[165] In addition, the Department of Justice was uneasy with the possibility that the granting of additional powers of self-government to Puerto Rico could mean that the island was no longer subject to the same limitations as the several states.[166]

The scenario in Congress with respect to the Fernós-Murray bill was equally clouded. In the words of Senator Henry M. Jackson (D-Washington), "the heart of the problem"[167] for the members of the Committee on Interior and Insular Affairs was determining whether Congress had "the ability to set up a Commonwealth and to delegate in perpetuity power which Congress has previously retained."[168] In the final analysis, strong opposition in Congress to the bilateral compact theory led the Fernós-Murray bill to a quiet death.

Four years later, in 1963, in an attempt to resurrect a seemingly modified version of the Fernós-Murray bill, Congressman Aspinall introduced a bill calling for the establishment of a joint United States–Puerto Rico compact commission to draft "a compact of permanent union" between both parties.[169] After a rough ride in the Committee on Interior and Insular Affairs, where the same legal and policy arguments leveled against the Fernós-Murray bill resurfaced yet again, a watered-down version of the Aspinall bill was signed into law by President Johnson the following year.[170] Retracting from its original intention of redrawing the compact, the Aspinall legislation was limited to establishing a United States–Puerto Rico commission with the oblique mandate of studying "all factors ... which may have a bearing on the present and future relationship between the United States and Puerto Rico."[171] In its report, published in August 1966, the commission recommended holding a plebiscite allowing Puerto Ricans to choose between commonwealth, statehood, and independence, and, contingent on the plebiscite's outcome, convening a joint United States–Puerto Rico "advisory group" to consider either "appropriate transition measures" to statehood or independence or "proposals conducive to Commonwealth growth."[172] Despite commonwealth's robust victory in the

165 Ibid., 810.

166 Shriver, memorandum to Wayne N. Aspinall and Leo O'Brien.

167 *Puerto Rico Federal Relations Act: Hearing before the Committee on Interior and Insular Affairs, United States Senate, Eighty-Sixth Congress, First Session on S. 2023,* 86th Cong. 11 (1959).

168 Ibid.

169 To Establish a Procedure for the Prompt Settlement, in a Democratic Manner, of the Political Status of Puerto Rico, H.R. 5945, 88th Cong. (1963).

170 Act of Feb. 20, 1964, Pub. L. No. 88-271, 78 Stat. 17.

171 Ibid.

172 United States–Puerto Rico Commission on the Status of Puerto Rico, *Report of the*

plebiscite, which was held in 1967,[173] the much-heralded bilateral advisory group would come to life only after a six-year hiatus, in 1973. Only then would the second substantive effort at enhancing commonwealth status come to fruition, with the appointment by President Nixon and Governor Rafael Hernández Colón of the members of the Ad Hoc Advisory Group of Puerto Rico, co-chaired by Senator Marlow Cook (R-Kentucky) and former governor Muñoz Marín.[174]

In 1975, the Ad Hoc Advisory Group on Puerto Rico transmitted its final report, entitled *Compact of Permanent Union between Puerto Rico and the United States*, to President Ford.[175] The advisory group's proposal trod, for the most part, along the same path that the Fernós-Murray bill had already traversed.

The overarching principle behind it was to provide Puerto Rico "with a greater degree of self-government and self-determination within the existing framework of common defense, common market, common currency and common citizenship."[176] Hence, the 1975 compact initiative, as the preceding 1959 Fernós-Murray effort, amounted to an attempt to achieve the permanent transfer of political authority to Puerto Rico within the traditional territorial framework, seeking doctrinal refuge in the infirm bilateral compact theory.

Similarly to the Fernós-Murray bill, the Compact of Permanent Union would have granted Puerto Rico the authority to conclude financial and commercial agreements with foreign countries and to participate in the specialized agencies of international organizations;[177] legal title to Crown lands and navigable waters;[178] exemption from US tax revenue laws;[179] and a mechanism for gradually transferring to Puerto Rico those "functions vested in the United States"[180] and for determining the applicability of federal legislation to the island.[181]

United States–Puerto Rico Commission on the Status of Puerto Rico (Washington, DC: Government Printing Office, 1966), 9.

173 Results of 1967 plebiscite: commonwealth, 60.4%; statehood, 39%; and independence, 0.6%. The Puerto Rican Independence Party boycotted the plebiscite.

174 See Ad Hoc Advisory Group on Puerto Rico, *Compact of Permanent Union between Puerto Rico and the United States* (Oct. 1, 1975).

175 Ibid. The proposal outlined in the report was introduced in the US House of Representatives later that year by Resident Commissioner Jaime Benítez. To Approve the Compact of Permanent Union between Puerto Rico and the United States, H.R. 11200, 94th Cong. (1975).

176 Jim Cannon, memorandum to Gerald Ford, Oct. 28, 1976, Ford Presidential Library.

177 To Approve the Compact of Permanent Union between Puerto Rico and the United States, H.R. 11200, 94th Cong. § 2(d) (1975).

178 Ibid., § 3.

179 Ibid., § 4.

180 Ibid., § 13.

181 Ibid., § 12.

Unlike the drafters of the Fernós-Murray bill, however, the drafters of the compact requested the devolution to Puerto Rico of a more robust repertoire of political powers. More specifically, the compact provided that those provisions related to common citizenship, security and defense, currency, common market, title to Crown lands, applicability of federal laws, and Puerto Rico's representation in Congress could not be amended without the consent of the Puerto Rican electorate.[182] While Puerto Rico would be given authority to "levy, increase, reduce or eliminate tariffs and quotas on articles imported directly from foreign countries or transshipped through the United States," the island would be able to import, duty-free, from other countries materials and articles for subsequent shipment and sale to other parts of the United States' customs area, provided that the shipment price contained at least 35% value added in Puerto Rico.[183] Furthermore, the compact made it clear that

> [p]rior to final passage of any legislation applicable to the Free Associated State, the Governor or Resident Commissioner thereof shall be entitled to submit to the Congress objections as to the applicability of said legislation to the Free Associated State, whereupon the Congress shall specifically act upon those objections so as to determine whether the proposed law is essential to the interest of the United States and is compatible with the provisions and purposes of this Compact. If the respective committee or committees by vote express agreement with the objections, the Free Associated State will be held exempt from those affected provisions of the proposed law in the event of its final enactment: Provided, That this paragraph shall not apply to proposed laws which directly affect the rights and duties of citizens, security and common defense, foreign affairs, or currency.[184]

It also established that "rules, regulations and orders issued by the departments and agencies of the United States . . . shall apply to Puerto Rico unless and except to the extent they are incompatible with this Compact."[185] Further, it provided for the establishment of a joint commission on United States–Puerto Rico relations endowed with authority to recommend to the US president and the governor of Puerto Rico the modification or discontinuance of existing federal laws applicable to Puerto Rico.[186] With respect to the resident commissioner and the United States District Court for the District of Puerto Rico, the proposed compact of 1975 went somewhat further than the Fernós-Murray bill. On the one hand, it would have granted representation to Puerto Rico not only in the US House of Representatives but also in the

---

182 Ibid., § 21.
183 Ibid., § 9(e).
184 Ibid., § 12(d).
185 Ibid., § 12(e).
186 Ibid., § 14.

US Senate; and on the other, it mandated that "the procedures, pleadings and records shall be in Spanish, unless the Court . . . shall otherwise determine in particular cases."[187]

Like the Fernós-Murray bill, the Compact of Permanent Union faced decisive opposition from the White House, federal agencies, and Congress. Unresolved legal questions—such as whether the people of Puerto Rico had sufficient authority to delegate to the United States "the power and attributes specified in the Compact"[188]—and complex policy questions on the nature of US federalism[189] led to the ultimate undoing of the compact.[190]

Serious consideration by the political branches in Washington of yet another formulation of commonwealth enhancement under the territory clause came forth between 1989 and 1991, with the introduction of three bills: S. 712; its successor, S. 244; and H.R. 4765.[191] Although not identical, these three bills stood for the same substantive proposition as their precursors—namely, the so-called organic growth of the alleged bilateral compact under the territory clause. And although H.R. 4765, which included a perfected commonwealth formula loosely defined as a permanent relationship that could be altered only by "mutual consent,"[192] passed the US House of Representatives, the available record shows that its constitutionality and viability as a matter of policy were clearly under attack, as the debates in the US Senate surrounding S. 244 would soon demonstrate.[193]

These later initiatives, which coincided with the end of the Cold War,

---

187 Ibid., §§ 11(a), 16(b).
188 Mitchell McConnell, letter to Marlow Cook, May 12, 1975, 4.
189 See, e.g., Jim Cannon, memorandum to Gerald Ford, Mar. 1, 1976, Ford Presidential Library; Brent Scowcroft, memorandum to Jim Cannon, Nov. 15, 1976, Ford Presidential Library.
190 Following his defeat at the polls, President Ford discarded the Compact of Permanent Union and announced his support for Puerto Rico's statehood. See White House, "Statehood for Puerto Rico," press release, Dec. 31, 1976. See also Gerald Ford, letter to the Speaker of the House, Jan. 14, 1977, Ford Presidential Library.
191 To Provide for a Referendum on the Political Status of Puerto Rico, S. 712, 101st Cong. (1989) (S. 712, if compared to the Compact of Permanent Union and S. 244, provided for additional powers of self-government in areas ranging from aviation (subpart 5), to intellectual property (subpart 10), to the management of federal grant-in-aid programs (subpart 11)); Puerto Rico Status Referendum Act, S. 244, 102d Cong. (1991) (S. 244 also included a provision mandating the US president to consult with the governor of Puerto Rico with respect to the appointment of federal personnel to the various US agencies operating in the island); To Enable the People of Puerto Rico to Exercise Self-Determination, H.R. 4765, 101st Cong. (1990).
192 To Provide for a Referendum on the Political Status of Puerto Rico: Hearings before the Senate Committee on Energy and Natural Resources on S. 244, 102d Cong. 70 (1991).
193 Ibid., 210-11.

suffered the same fate as their predecessors, with the daunting aggravation that the Department of Justice's institutional attitude had considerably changed in regard to the legal viability of any formula of commonwealth enhancement premised on a mutual consent arrangement under the territory clause.

A closer look at the various legal opinions rendered by the Justice Department's Office of Legal Counsel between the introduction of the Fernós-Murray bill in 1959 and the publication in 2011 of the *Report by the President's Task Force on Puerto Rico's Status* reveals that the department's legal posture concerning the commonwealth question has indeed evolved.[194] From the 1950s to this day, the Justice Department has plodded along an evolutionary continuum with regard to the nature and plausible growth of the commonwealth arrangement. Long gone are the days when the department shied away from confirming or denying the alleged bilateral nature of the step that Puerto Rico and Congress took in 1952. Since the early 1990s, the Justice Department has become a consistent detractor of any enhancement proposition resting on the notion that a bilateral compact of mutual consent is available to Puerto Rico and Congress.

Contrary to its earlier, more pragmatic reading of the proprietary rights doctrine and its extension to the political field—as evidenced, for example, in memoranda from the Office of Legal Counsel from 1963, 1971, and 1975[195]—the department's more recent legal opinions have embraced the view that proprietary rights protected under the due process clause of the Fifth Amendment do not vest in political status arrangements.[196] Henceforth, the Justice Department has invariably adhered to this position, as demonstrated by the legal conclusions of the 2005, 2007, and 2011 reports of the President's Task Force on Puerto Rico's Status.[197]

---

194 It goes without saying that the Department of Justice's internal inconsistencies with respect to these questions have added confusion to the status debate in Puerto Rico.

195 Office of Legal Counsel, "Memorandum Re: Power of the United States to Conclude with the Commonwealth of Puerto Rico a Compact Which Could Be Modified Only by Mutual Consent," July 23, 1963; Office of Legal Counsel, "Memorandum Re: Micronesian Negotiations," Aug. 18, 1971; Mitchell McConnell, letter to Marlow Cook, May 12, 1975. See also Edward Levy, "Memorandum for the Honorable James E. Connor, Secretary to the Cabinet, Re: Report of the Ad Hoc Advisory Group on Puerto Rico," Nov. 21, 1975, Ford Presidential Library.

196 See, e.g., Teresa Wynn Roseborough, memorandum to the Special Representative for Guam Commonwealth, July 28, 1994. See also Robert Raben, letter to Frank Murkowski, Jan. 18, 2001.

197 President's Task Force on Puerto Rico's Status, *Report by the President's Task Force on Puerto Rico's Status* (Washington, DC: White House, 2005), 6-7; President's Task Force on Puerto Rico's Status, *Report by the President's Task Force on Puerto*

The department's evolution has, no doubt, coincided with a sweeping rearrangement of the United States' geopolitical imperatives following the end of the Cold War. Therefore, policy issues, more so than legal ones, have arguably led to the obliteration of any self-determination path for Puerto Rico premised on the traditional framework of commonwealth enhancement.

Thus, the transformation of the autonomic paradigm, both substantively and discursively, is of the essence if there is any hope of unraveling the status labyrinth.

Lessons Learned for the Road Ahead

The time is ripe for Puerto Rico's autonomist movement—and in particular for its most outspoken political standard-bearer, the PDP—to take stock of the seminal lessons stemming from the long string of failed attempts at enhancing commonwealth status.

The first lesson that must be clearly understood is that the step taken in 1952 did not alter the fundamentals of the relationship between Puerto Rico and the United States. Sovereignty over Puerto Rico rests squarely in Congress's hands. In that respect, nothing has changed since 1898.

The second lesson that cannot go unheeded is Congress's historical aversion to partial dispositions of its sovereignty—let alone permanent ones. The PDP's ideological project will be doomed to failure to the extent that its leadership does not assimilate this lesson. Making the enhancement of commonwealth contingent exclusively on congressional delegations of political authority in economic and foreign affairs under the territory clause is not the right approach, if seen in light of history and experience.

Even assuming, *arguendo*, that there is no constitutional impediment for Congress to delegate in perpetuity such authority to Puerto Rico, there are grave policy considerations making this approach patently unworkable for both parties, as seen by the fate suffered by the Fernós-Murray bill, the Compact of Permanent Union, and the Johnston bills. More so, recent decisions of the federal courts on the compact of the Northern Mariana Islands highlight the deleterious effects of the congressional delegation method.

The third lesson that must be observed is that as long as the PDP remains fixated on the syllogism that Puerto Rico, like a state, is sovereign over matters not ruled by the Constitution,[198] its timid demands for the devolution of even more political authority than that enjoyed by the several states may fall on deaf ears.

Rico's Status (Washington, DC: White House, 2007), 7; President's Task Force, *2011 Report by the President's Task Force on Puerto Rico's Status*, 26.
198 Rodríguez v. Popular Democratic Party, 457 U.S. 1, 8 (1982).

The fourth lesson is that under any future relationship between Puerto Rico and the United States, the source of local authority on the island must emanate not from a congressional delegation of political power but from Puerto Rico's inherent authority as a sovereign. Under such an arrangement, Puerto Rico would be the entity delegating or surrendering authority to Congress under a treaty or other international instrument, doing away with the colonial vestiges that currently surround the commonwealth relationship. Under this approach, moreover, Congress would have no residual authority over Puerto Rico, except that expressly delegated to it by the people of Puerto Rico.

The fifth lesson is that the resolution of Puerto Rico's status is not so much a legal issue as a political one. This is not a legal question for the US Supreme Court to decide but rather a political question that will require a political compromise between Congress and the people of Puerto Rico.

The sixth lesson is that, simply put, statehood for Puerto Rico is not (and has never been) in the cards for Washington. Superimposing the Alaska and Hawaii case studies on the Puerto Rican landscape is misguided, considering the fact that statehood has never commanded the levels of electoral support in Puerto Rico that it did in those two territories and that both Alaska and Hawaii had the fiscal wherewithal to bear the economic burdens of statehood. Only an association relationship, premised on Puerto Rico's inherent authority as a sovereign, meets both Washington's and San Juan's overall imperatives.

The seventh lesson is that a new procedural approach is required to fully engage Congress. The time for nonbinding local plebiscites and reports from high-ranking advisory groups is over. To jumpstart Puerto Rico's self-determination process, only a constitutional convention (or status assembly), with equitable participation from all Puerto Rican stakeholders, will command sufficient legitimacy in Washington, San Juan, and around the world.

The eighth lesson is that no substantive meeting of the minds will take place between the island's leadership and the political branches in Washington until a procedural consensus has been reached in Puerto Rico. Hence, no progress will be achieved so long as the political leadership in Puerto Rico carries on its petty cannibalistic infighting.

The ninth lesson is that the political branches in Washington will not engage Puerto Rico on the status debate unless and until it becomes absolutely necessary. Only in times of crisis have Congress and the White House proven inclined to act with respect to Puerto Rico. The Jones Act of 1917 (granting US citizenship to Puerto Ricans), the Elective Governor Act of 1947,[199] and the inauguration of commonwealth status in 1952 are the most eloquent illustrations of this phenomenon. The crisis of our times is Puerto Rico's

---

199 Act of Aug. 5, 1947 (Elective Governor Act), Pub. L. No. 80-362, 61 Stat. 770.

economic pandemic and its effects on the United States' municipal bond market and hemispheric interests at a time of renewed global upheaval. Only the politico-constitutional reengineering of Puerto Rico's relationship with the United States will lead to the systemic transformation the island requires and, in turn, bolster the shared interests of the people of Puerto Rico and the political branches of Washington.

The tenth lesson is that no period in recent memory has offered as fertile a terrain as this one for disentangling Puerto Rico's status labyrinth. Thus, in the final analysis, the decolonization of the autonomist movement's ideological discourse constitutes an indispensable first step in the right direction.

CHAPTER EIGHT

Our Journey Is Not Complete

Andrés W. López*

The American territory of Puerto Rico faces a crisis of unprecedented proportions. The steady stream of national news coverage—also unprecedented in scope—has cast a spotlight on the serious problems that have brought the United States' oldest territory to the brink of insolvency.[1] By

---

*   I thank Martha Minow, Gerald L. Neuman, Tomiko Brown-Nagin, and everyone responsible for organizing the "Reconsidering the Insular Cases" conference. This event marked the first time in Harvard's history that the institution has formally reconsidered the Insular Cases. Dean Minow's inspiring leadership gives hope that just as Harvard played an all-too-prominent role in paving the way for the Insular Cases in the twentieth century, Harvard and its modern-day alumni can help eradicate the dishonorable legacy of the Insular Cases in the twenty-first century.

1   The media attention given to Puerto Rico's deepening crisis has no parallel in history. See, e.g., Andrew Bary, "Troubling Winds in Puerto Rico," *Barron's*, Aug. 26, 2013, http://online.barrons.com/news/articles/SB5000142405274870471920457902 2892632785548; Mary Williams Walsh, "Worsening Debt Crisis Threatens Puerto Rico," *New York Times*, Oct. 7, 2013, http://dealbook.nytimes.com/2013/10/07/ worsening-debt-crisis-threatens-puerto-rico; "Puerto Pobre," *The Economist*, Oct. 26, 2013, http://www.economist.com/news/finance-and-economics/21588364-heavily-indebted-island-weighs-americas-municipal   bond-market-puerto-pobre; "Puerto Rico's Sinking Economy Needs Help," *Washington Post*, Nov. 6, 2013, http://www.washingtonpost.com/opinions/puerto-ricos-sinking-economy-needs-help/2013/11/06/35b93dac-4327-11e3-8b74-d89d714ca4dd_story.html;   Lizette Alvarez, "Economy and Crime Spur a New Puerto Rican Exodus," *New York Times*, Feb. 8, 2014, http://www.nytimes.com/2014/02/09/us/economy-and-crime-spur-new-puerto-rican-exodus.html?_r=0; Francesca Trianni, "The Next Financial Catastrophe You Haven't Heard About Yet: Puerto Rico," *Time*, Mar. 12, 2014, http://

now, the crippling effects of the crisis are well known: multiple downgrades of Puerto Rico's debt to junk status; a mountainous debt obligation exceeding $70 billion, by far the largest in the United States; and a correspondingly massive migration wave from Puerto Rico to the US mainland—at a pace of almost 1,000 Puerto Ricans leaving *every week*—that shows no real signs of abating.[2] Amid this "ticker tape of woes," as the *New York Times* calls it,[3] there are two concurrent positive developments that provide grounds for optimism and a foundation on which to build a lasting solution to Puerto Rico's crisis.

First, there is now a wide-ranging consensus regarding the root cause of Puerto Rico's economic problems. As the *Washington Post* recently wrote, "Puerto Rico's economic and financial woes are structural—traceable, ultimately, to its muddled political status," which remains unresolved after 116 years.[4] And now, for the first time in history, this consensus has become US national policy. After decades of delays and failed experiments by previous administrations, the Obama administration has taken a "fresh look" at the issue of Puerto Rico.[5] Upon doing so, it has concluded that the failure to resolve Puerto Rico's political status has held Puerto Rico back and that Puerto Rico's economic success is intimately linked to an expeditious resolution of its status issue. The idea that resolving Puerto Rico's economic problems *requires* resolving Puerto Rico's status problem is a groundbreaking policy shift. Instead of trying to separate the territory's structural economic problems from its unresolved political status problem, as some have done in the past, the Obama administration believes that the two are, in fact,

time.com/20416/the-next-financial-catastrophe-you-havent-heard-about-yet-puerto-rico; "Neither a State nor Independent," *The Economist*, July 5, 2014, http://www.economist.com/news/united-states/21606319-how-territory-falls-between-bankruptcy-regimes-neither-state-nor-independent.

2   Cindy Y. Rodriguez, "Why More Puerto Ricans Are Living in Mainland U.S. Than in Puerto Rico," CNN.com, Mar. 24, 2014, http://edition.cnn.com/2014/03/22/us/puerto-rico-migration-economy/index.html; D'Vera Cohn, Eileen Patten, and Mark Hugo Lopez, *Puerto Rican Population Declines on the Island, Grows on U.S. Mainland* (Washington, DC: Pew Research Center, 2014). US Census Bureau data shows a net migration total of 144,000 Puerto Ricans arriving to the US mainland between mid-2010 and 2013. This alarming pace of migration has resulted in Puerto Rico's first sustained population decline in its history as a US territory.

3   Alvarez, "Economy and Crime Spur a New Puerto Rican Exodus."

4   "Puerto Rico's Sinking Economy Needs Help," *Washington Post*.

5   President's Task Force on Puerto Rico's Status, *Report by the President's Task Force on Puerto Rico's Status* (Washington, DC: White House, 2011) [hereinafter President's Task Force, *2011 Report by the President's Task Force on Puerto Rico's Status*].

inextricably intertwined. Indeed, it argues that "the most effective means of assisting the Puerto Rico economy *depends* on resolving the ultimate question of status."[6] This welcome policy change clears the way for a meaningful long-term resolution of both problems.

Second, in the aftermath of the federal policy change, the people of Puerto Rico took to the polls and loudly called for status change. After the Obama administration stated that "immediate and true forward movement on the issue of status" would greatly benefit Puerto Rico, it invited concrete action by declaring that "it is time for Puerto Rico to take the *next step* in the history of its status and its relationship to the rest of the United States."[7] In 2012, Puerto Rico did just that. In a referendum featuring massive electoral participation (almost 80%), Puerto Rico took a decisive "next step," resoundingly rejecting its crumbling territorial status and choosing equality as the path forward.[8] The White House validated Puerto Rico's historic vote, affirming that "the results were clear, the people of Puerto Rico want the issue of status resolved, and a majority chose statehood in the second question."[9] Now, the Obama administration has become the first in American history to confront an awkward reality. A country founded on the concept of the *consent of the governed* faces a sharp rebuke from its oldest territory and its citizens—all of whom are *natural-born American citizens*—who have used the power of the ballot box to say that they do not consent to their inherently unequal territorial status.

Today's crisis provides us with an opportunity for reconsideration—literally, to consider again decisions of the past—and ask ourselves if we would do things the same way again. For example, if we had to do it again,

---

6   Ibid., 33 (emphasis added). See also 2012 Democratic Platform, "Greater Together: Strengthening the American Community," accessed Oct. 29, 2014, http://www.democrats.org/democratic-national-platform.

7   President's Task Force, *2011 Report by the President's Task Force on Puerto Rico's Status*, 24 (emphasis added).

8   Caitlin Dewey, "Puerto Rico Approves Statehood," Washington Post, Nov. 7, 2012, http://www.washingtonpost.com/blogs/post-politics/wp/2012/11/07/puerto-rico-approves-statehood; Mariano Castillo, "Puerto Ricans Favor Statehood for First Time," CNN.com, Nov. 8, 2012, http://www.cnn.com/2012/11/07/politics/election-puerto-rico; R. Sam Garrett, Puerto Rico's Political Status and the 2012 Plebiscite: Background and Key Questions (Washington, DC: Congressional Research Service, 2013).

9   Byron Tau, "White House Clarifies Puerto Rico Stance," *Politico.com*, Dec. 4, 2012, http://www.politico.com/politico44/2012/12/white-house-clarifies-puerto-rico-stance-151019.html.

would we create an inherently unequal American territory whose very structure undermines the concept of the consent of the governed, and hold it in seeming perpetuity? By like token, would we demean the concept of American citizenship by inventing a second category of citizens without the same constitutional rights as every other citizen? I do not think so. If we are to change the course of history, then, our goals must be clear: America cannot hold territories indefinitely, and America cannot have second-class citizens. Our goal must be equality.

If Puerto Rico's structural problem is its fundamental inequality, today's crisis shows the consequences of sustained inequality. Puerto Rico's territorial status has impaired its ability to develop economically, politically, and socially. It begs the question, were territories meant to last *as territories* for over one hundred years? After 116 years of kicking that can, we know the answer. We must step back and reconsider everything from the start.

If we are going to start at the beginning, we must begin at Harvard. It is impossible to overstate Harvard's role in laying the groundwork for the Insular Cases—that empire-minded vision, fueled by prejudice, that America could hold territories indefinitely and create a subcategory of citizens.[10] Some of that breathtaking chutzpah no doubt stems from the notion (thankfully a relic today) that only Anglo-Saxon males could be trusted with the duties of self-government. After all, this was the age of separate but equal, where women could not vote, and there was no marriage equality.

Of all the *Harvard Law Review* authors who wrote about America's new possessions, none was more influential than my fellow Harvard Law alumnus Abbott Lawrence Lowell.[11] Fittingly, Lowell became a government professor

---

10   Juan R. Torruella, *The Supreme Court and Puerto Rico: The Doctrine of Separate and Unequal* (Río Piedras: Editorial de la Universidad de Puerto Rico, 1985). Several scholarly publications have examined and painstakingly detailed the political climate that led to the Insular Cases. One of the best and most comprehensive efforts is Circuit Judge Juan R. Torruella's analysis, which led him to conclude that the Supreme Court's novel rulings in the Insular Cases created the doctrine of "separate and unequal," a close relative of the "separate but equal" doctrine that the Supreme Court invented in *Plessy v. Ferguson*, 163 U.S. 537 (1896).

11   As José Trías Monge writes:

>   Professor Abbott Lawrence Lowell of Harvard, later its president, was the principal exponent of a third view, the one espoused by the administration, with somewhat less precision, and eventually adopted by the Supreme Court. Lowell thought that the Constitution allowed for two kinds of territories: those that were part of the United States and those that were not part of but were instead possessions of the United States.

José Trías Monge, *Puerto Rico: The Trials of the Oldest Colony in the World* (New

at Harvard in 1898, the year the United States acquired Puerto Rico. The next year, Lowell published his infamous article entitled "The Status of Our New Possessions: A Third View," which persuaded the Supreme Court to invent the "unincorporated territory" category.[12] Lowell later became president of Harvard, and as a student here I benefitted from some of his reforms. As a Puerto Rican, I (and millions like me) have been disproportionately affected by one of his greatest mistakes.

Before the Insular Cases, the acquisition of a territory meant eventual equality, without exception.[13] Moreover, the grant of American citizenship *always* meant equality.[14] Before Lowell's "third view" article, the notion that Congress could hold territories indefinitely ran counter to the very principles that led to America's existence. And yet, Lowell concluded that applying the US Constitution fully in the new territories would lead to an "irrational result."[15] That peculiar phrase becomes easier to understand after one learns of other "irrational results" that Lowell sought to avoid. To note just one example documented in Harvard Law School Professor Kenneth W. Mack's wonderful book *Representing the Race*, Lowell thought it irrational to require that white Harvard students live together with their black counterparts in Harvard's dormitories.[16] Unlike in the Insular Cases, Lowell's view did not carry the day. While we have largely erased the stain of this type of insidious prejudice, the Insular Cases and their rationale still stand today as remnants of a bygone era that the United States has left behind.

Lowell's "third view" allowed for the creation—by judicial fiat—of a new category of American jurisdiction that was neither a state nor a territory like all others. His *Harvard Law Review* article provided the Supreme Court with the intellectual cover to treat the new American territories unequally. In this new category of American territories, unlike all other territories, the

---

Haven: Yale University Press, 1997), 44.

12   Abbott Lawrence Lowell, "The Status of Our New Possessions: A Third View," *Harvard Law Review* 13 (1899): 155-76.

13   Since the founding of the Republic, all thirty-seven American territories that have sought equality have achieved it. All thirty-seven were admitted to the Union as states.

14   The first case in American history to decide otherwise was *Balzac v. Porto Rico*, 258 U.S. 298 (1922). In *Balzac*, the Supreme Court created a second class of American citizens by holding that even though Puerto Ricans living in the "third view" American territory of Puerto Rico had become American citizens by birth, they still could not enjoy the full spectrum of constitutional and civil rights as every other American citizen.

15   Lowell, "The Status of Our New Possessions," 157.

16   Kenneth W. Mack, *Representing the Race: The Creation of the Civil Rights Lawyer* (Cambridge, MA: Harvard University Press, 2012), 34-35.

US Constitution would not apply fully.[17] Even after Puerto Ricans became American citizens in 1917, the Supreme Court continued to apply Lowell's reasoning to invent what one might call the light-switch theory of American constitutional law. In *Balzac v. Porto Rico*,[18] the Supreme Court declared that there was a second class of American citizen who, despite being born American, could not enjoy the full spectrum of constitutional and civil rights like every other American. The second-class American citizens living in the "third view" American territory of Puerto Rico would have to travel to the US mainland to have their full panoply of civil rights "turned on," as if by a magical constitutional light switch. Conversely, their return to the American territory of Puerto Rico would "turn off" their civil rights, restoring them to their truncated version. Well over a century later, Lowell's "third view," and the structural inequality it has wrought, is still the law of the land in America's oldest territory.

Even Lowell's "third view," however, did not envision the creation of an American territory in perpetuity. Indeed, the Supreme Court of that time seemed to concede that the *permanent* segregation of an American territory comprising American citizens would be distinctly un-American. Justice John Marshall Harlan's prescient admonition that the creation of indefinitely held American territories would usher in "a colonial system entirely foreign to the genius of our Government and abhorrent to the principles that underlie and pervade our Constitution" appears to have prompted an attempt to impose a time limit on the "third view" experiment.[19] For example, in the seminal Insular Case of *Downes v. Bidwell*, decided at the turn of the twentieth century, the Supreme Court unabashedly sought to justify the "third view" status for the new American territories by claiming that "[a] false step *at this time* might be fatal to the development of what Chief Justice Marshall called the American Empire."[20] As a result, because the court believed that the administration of government and justice in the new territories—inhabited by "alien races"—might be impossible "for a time," the court wondered

---

17   The first and perhaps most infamous Insular Case to so decide was *Downes v. Bidwell*, 182 U.S. 244 (1901).

18   Balzac v. Porto Rico, 258 U.S. 298 (1922).

19   Justice Harlan's powerful dissent in the Insular Case of *Downes v. Bidwell* has stood the test of time:

>   The idea that this country may acquire territories anywhere upon the earth, by conquest or treaty, and hold them as mere colonies or provinces—the people inhabiting them to enjoy only such rights as Congress chooses to accord them—is wholly inconsistent with the spirit and the genius, as well as with the words of the Constitution.

Downes v. Bidwell, 182 U.S. 244, 375-91 (1901) (Harlan, J., dissenting).

20   Ibid., 286 (majority opinion) (emphasis added).

"whether large concessions ought not to be made *for a time,*" at least until a final decision was made regarding the new territories' status.[21]

By 1957, more than fifty years after *Downes,* the Supreme Court would say without a trace of irony that the Insular Cases were designed to assert congressional power over the "third view" American territories "temporarily"—even though, by then, Puerto Rico had been a territory for almost sixty years.[22] Most recently, in 2008, the court would again use the word "temporarily," but would also conspicuously open the door for change.[23] While justifying the territorial incorporation doctrine "[a]t least with regard to the Philippines,"[24] a territory to which the United States always intended to grant independence, the Supreme Court—in an obvious reference to Puerto Rico, by then an American territory for *110 years*—openly signaled change by using the concept of time in Puerto Rico's favor: "It may well be that *over time* the ties between the United States and any of its unincorporated Territories strengthen in ways that are of constitutional significance."[25] Months later, a federal judge in Puerto Rico published a comprehensive chronicle of the "monumental constitutional evolution" that has taken place in the century-plus relationship between the United States and Puerto Rico, arguing that the ties have indeed strengthened in constitutionally significant ways.[26] The stage is now set for a court challenge on the basis of the Supreme Court's invitation.

---

21 Ibid., 287 (emphasis added). As the court wrote:

> Whatever may be *finally decided* by the American people as to the status of these islands and their inhabitants—whether they shall be introduced into the sisterhood of States or be permitted to form independent governments—it does not follow that, *in the meantime,* awaiting that decision, the people are in the matter of personal rights unprotected by the provisions of our Constitution, and subject to the merely arbitrary control of Congress.

> Ibid., 283 (emphasis added).

22 Reid v. Covert, 354 U.S. 1, 14 (1957).

23 Boumediene v. Bush, 553 U.S. 723, 759 (2008).

24 Ibid., 757.

25 Ibid., 758 (emphasis added).

26 Consejo de Salud Playa de Ponce v. Rullán, 586 F. Supp. 2d 22, 43 (D.P.R. 2008). The federal judge, Gustavo A. Gelpí, is a full-fledged Article III judge sitting in the United States District Court for the District of Puerto Rico. This would surely come as a shock to Chief Justice William Howard Taft and the majority in the Insular Case of *Balzac v. Porto Rico,* 258 U.S. 298, 312 (1922), who argued that one of the reasons for treating Puerto Rico unequally—despite the fact that all Puerto Ricans were American citizens by then—was that Puerto Rico did not have a "true" Article III court. In 1966, a federal law made Puerto Rico one of the ninety-four Article III judicial districts in the country, and the only American territory to hold such a distinction. See Act of Sept. 12, 1966, Pub. L. No. 89-571, 80 Stat. 764. Today, Puerto Rico has a "true" Article III federal court.

Can terms like "for a time" and "temporarily" possibly mean anything close to 116 years, especially given the constant development of Puerto Rico's relationship with the United States? There is no more time for delay. It is time for equality.

The United States cannot hold territories indefinitely in an unequal state. And Puerto Rico's current crisis provides Harvard with an opportunity to say just that. Harvard should play a leading role, as it did back then, but this time to help put an end to this shameful legacy of discrimination. As we reconsider Harvard's role in the Insular Cases and in Puerto Rico's future, we must ask ourselves this: Would Harvard endorse Lowell's views today? Would it support such aberrational notions of inequality? I am convinced that it would not. Lowell got it wrong in the twentieth century. Harvard can get it right in the twenty-first century.

That is Harvard's challenge. First, Harvard should say that America cannot hold territories indefinitely. That is not America. That is not who we are. A country founded on the concept of the consent of the governed cannot keep a territory in a perpetual state of limbo. Second, Harvard should say, as Chief Justice Margaret Marshall did in her landmark ruling on marriage equality, that the US Constitution *forbids* the creation of second-class citizens.[27] Harvard should say, as Justice Harlan did in *Plessy v. Ferguson*, that the Constitution neither knows nor tolerates classes among its citizens.[28] The time has come for Harvard to vindicate Justice Marshall's and Justice Harlan's views. And the time has come to consign Lowell's misguided view to the dustbin of history.

Today's crisis also presents a unique opportunity for President Obama. I am proud to have played a role in his two historic elections. I am prouder still that President Obama has changed the United States' national policy with respect to Puerto Rico for the better. Thanks to the work of the President's Task Force on Puerto Rico's Status and the Democratic Party's platform committee, the course of action for the president's second term signals an urgent need for change. Today, the country's forward-looking policy on Puerto Rico is rooted in a trilogy of principles: first, that the failure to resolve the status problem has held Puerto Rico back; second, that Puerto Rico's economic success is inextricably linked to a prompt resolution of the status issue, and that the best way of moving Puerto Rico's economy forward depends on solving the status problem; and third, that the time has come for Puerto Rico to take the next step in its relationship to the rest of the United States, and that the White

---

27   Goodridge v. Dep't of Pub. Health, 798 N.E.2d 941, 948 (Mass. 2003).
28   Plessy v. Ferguson, 163 U.S. 537, 559 (1896).

House specifically commits to moving the status issue forward with the goal of resolving it expeditiously.[29]

Taken together, these three bedrock principles make up a fundamental policy change. By concluding that resolving Puerto Rico's economic problem depends on solving Puerto Rico's status problem, the Obama administration has provided cause for optimism that we will finally get Puerto Rico back on the path to equality. The federal policy shift acknowledges an indisputable truth: a century-plus of experiments and "third way" theories have not resolved the problem. Now, the people of Puerto Rico have given a clear mandate: *no more territory status.* As we reconsider the decisions of the past and look to resolve the current crisis, we must ask ourselves, would we do things the same way again? We must learn from history.

In 1917, the United States passed a law granting American citizenship to Puerto Ricans.[30] In the aftermath of that crucial milestone, and for over two decades, the Democratic Party policy platforms expressly supported a path of equality for Puerto Rico.[31] After the grant of American citizenship, the Democratic Party consistently and specifically supported "ultimate statehood for Puerto Rico, accorded to all territories of the United States since the beginning of our government."[32] The Democratic Party's platform language throughout these decades left no room for doubt:

1920 Platform
We favor granting to the people of Porto Rico the traditional territorial form of government, *with a view to ultimate statehood, accorded to all territories of the United States since the beginning of our government,* and we believe that the officials appointed to administer the government of such territories should be qualified by previous bona-fide residence therein.[33]

1928 Platform
We favor granting to Puerto Rico such territorial form of government as

---

29 2012 Democratic Platform, "Greater Together"; President's Task Force, *2011 Report by the President's Task Force on Puerto Rico's Status*, 33.

30 Jones Act, Pub. L. No. 64-368, 39 Stat. 951 (1917) (codified at 48 U.S.C. §§ 731 et seq. (2013)).

31 Since the focus of this chapter is on President Obama's opportunity to help bring about change, I will highlight the Democratic Party's views on the issue of Puerto Rico equality.

32 American Presidency Project, "Democratic Platform of 1928," accessed Oct. 29, 2014, http://www.presidency.ucsb.edu/ws/index.php?pid=29594.

33 American Presidency Project, "Democratic Platform of 1920," accessed Oct. 29, 2014, http://www.presidency.ucsb.edu/ws/index.php?pid=29592 (emphasis added).

would meet the present economic conditions of the island, and provide for the aspirations of her people, *with the view to ultimate statehood accorded to all territories of the United States since the beginning of our government*, and we believe any officials appointed to administer the government of such territories should be qualified by previous bona fide residence therein.[34]

1932 Platform
Independence for the Philippines; ultimate *statehood for Puerto Rico*.[35]

1940 Platform
We favor a larger measure of self-government leading to statehood, for Alaska, Hawaii *and Puerto Rico*.[36]

As can be seen, certain platforms specifically aligned Puerto Rico with Alaska and Hawaii, which became states in 1959 and 1961, respectively. By like token, certain platforms specifically distinguished Puerto Rico from the Philippines, which became independent in 1946, and whose residents never became American citizens.[37] With regard to Alaska, Hawaii, and Puerto Rico, the Democratic Party constantly and unwaveringly (until 1940) supported equality, the path accorded to *all* territories since the beginning of America.

What happened in 1940? That year saw the ascent to power of Luis Muñoz Marín, who would become Puerto Rico's longest-serving governor and gain a stranglehold at the top of Puerto Rico's politics for the next three decades. That sea change derailed Puerto Rico from its path to equality and took Puerto Rico down a hazardous path on which no American territory had yet traveled. Under the slogan "el status no está en *issue*" ("status is not the issue"), Muñoz Marín argued that Puerto Rico should focus on solving its economic problems first and should defer solving the status problem

---

34   American Presidency Project, "Democratic Platform of 1928" (emphasis added).
35   American Presidency Project, "Democratic Platform of 1932," accessed Oct. 29, 2014, http://www.presidency.ucsb.edu/ws/index.php?pid=29595 (emphasis added).
36   American Presidency Project, "Democratic Platform of 1940," accessed Oct. 29, 2014, http://www.presidency.ucsb.edu/ws/index.php?pid=29597 (emphasis added).
37   The 1924 and 1936 Democratic platforms do not mention Puerto Rico, nor do they suggest a departure from the Democratic Party's pro-equality policy toward Puerto Rico. See American Presidency Project, "Democratic Platform of 1924," accessed Oct. 29, 2014, http://www.presidency.ucsb.edu/ws/index.php?pid=29593; American Presidency Project, "Democratic Platform of 1936," accessed Oct. 29, 2014, http://www.presidency.ucsb.edu/ws/index.php?pid=29596.

until a later time.[38] This experiment—which dovetailed nicely with Lowell's "third view" theory—kept Puerto Rico as an American territory and delayed resolution of its status problem.[39] By 1944, in a historic error, the Democratic Party platform moved away from its decades-long policy of favoring equality for Puerto Rico.[40] The detour proved quite costly in the long run.

Over time, the shortcomings of this experimental approach became painfully apparent. Public discontent with the experiment steadily eroded, culminating in November 2012, when Puerto Rico massively rejected territorial status. By then, the Democratic Party platform had also evolved to reflect an unavoidable reality: the failure to resolve Puerto Rico's territorial status was *the* issue. The White House recognized the vote's historic impact, saying that the results of the vote were clear, that the people of Puerto Rico wanted to resolve their status, and that statehood—the people's choice for a path forward—had prevailed. In early 2014, President Obama signed into law a bill providing for a $2.5 million allocation and a process to "resolve" Puerto Rico's status.[41] And the chorus for change keeps growing louder in Congress: Senator Ron Wyden has said publicly that "[t]he current [territorial] relationship undermines the United States' moral standing in the world";[42] Senator Martin Heinrich has said that 116 years as an American territory is

---

38 A. W. Maldonado, *Luis Muñoz Marín: Puerto Rico's Democratic Revolution* (San Juan: Editorial de la Universidad de Puerto Rico, 2006), 183. According to Maldonado, "For the rest of his life, Muñoz pinpointed the precise moment he uttered the words as the turning point in his party's campaign, as 'the great decision' in his political career, and in Puerto Rican history." Ibid.

39 Trías Monge, *The Trials of the Oldest Colony in the World*, 107-18. Trías Monge, an unwavering Muñoz Marín supporter, conceded in his later years that the experiment had not resolved Puerto Rico's status problem and that, as the book's title suggests, Puerto Rico was "the oldest colony in the world."

40 American Presidency Project, "Democratic Platform of 1944," accessed Oct. 29, 2014, http://www.presidency.ucsb.edu/ws/index.php?pid=29598. The platform stated that "[w]e favor enactment of legislation granting the fullest measure of self-government for Alaska, Hawaii and Puerto Rico, and eventual statehood for Alaska and Hawaii." Ibid.

41 Consolidated Appropriations Act, Pub. L. No. 113-76, 128 Stat. 5 (2014); Eric Wasson, "In Spending Bill, A Path to Statehood," *The Hill*, Jan. 22, 2014, http://thehill.com/policy/finance/196059-spending-bill-includes-language-for-puerto-rican-statehood-vote.

42 "Opening Statement of Chairman Ron Wyden on Puerto Rico's Political Status, August 1, 2013," accessed Oct. 29, 2014, http://www.energy.senate.gov/public/index.cfm/files/serve?File_id=788c483c-92ba-4879-b3e1-637d655b7fa9.

"long enough";[43] and Senate Majority Leader Harry Reid has openly stated his support for Puerto Rico equality.[44]

The path is already there. It is the path that has been "accorded to all territories since the beginning of our government."[45] It is the path that the Democratic Party consistently and unambiguously supported for Puerto Rico—until the party took a detour—from the moment that Puerto Ricans became American citizens by birth. It is the path to which the Democratic Party must return with respect to Puerto Rico. The path is equality.

President Obama has done much for Puerto Rico. During his tenure, he has repeatedly sought to place Puerto Rico at the center of the American experience. In 2008, he campaigned personally in Puerto Rico, just as he did in the mainland states.[46] Once elected, in 2011, he became the first sitting president in fifty years to visit Puerto Rico and address its people. His address contained a signature phrase: "[E]very day, Boricuas help write the American story."[47] In 2014, at a bill-signing ceremony awarding a Congressional Gold Medal to the Borinqueneers, he opened by saying that "Puerto Rico became part of the United States in 1898,"[48] thereby distancing himself from the Insular Cases and their misguided view that Puerto Rico was "appurtenant and belonging to the United States, but not a part of the United States."[49]

---

43 Quoted in Michael Coleman, "Sen. Martin Heinrich Introduces Puerto Rican Statehood Bill," *Albuquerque Journal*, Feb. 13, 2014, http://www.abqjournal .com/352450/politics/sen-martin-heinrich-introduces-puerto-rican-statehood-bill.html. Senator Heinrich hails from New Mexico, which spent sixty-six years as a territory before gaining statehood—the longest of any state. According to Heinrich, "Puerto Rico has spent nearly 116 years as an American territory. That's long enough. The debate over Puerto Rico's status needs to be settled once and for all so that its people can focus on fostering a more prosperous future." Quoted in ibid.

44 "Reid: I've Always Been For Statehood," *Caribbean Business*, Nov. 19, 2013, http:// puertoricowow.net/news/reid-ive-always-been-for-statehood-91194.html.

45 American Presidency Project, "Democratic Platform of 1928."

46 Jeff Zeleny, "Obama Campaigns in Puerto Rico," *New York Times*, May 24, 2008, http://thecaucus.blogs.nytimes.com/2008/05/24/obama-campaigns-in-puerto-rico/?_php=true&_type=blogs&_r=0.

47 Barack Obama, "Remarks at a Welcome Event in San Juan, Puerto Rico" (Luis Muñoz Marín International Airport, San Juan, Puerto Rico, June 14, 2011), http:// www.whitehouse.gov/the-press-office/2011/06/14/remarks-president-welcome-event-san-juan-puerto-rico.

48 Barack Obama, "Remarks at Signing of the Water Resources Reform and Development Act and the 65th Infantry Regiment Congressional Gold Medal" (South Court Auditorium, June 10, 2014), http://www.whitehouse.gov/the-press-office/2014/06/10/remarks-president-signing-water-resources-reform-and-development-act-and.

49 Downes v. Bidwell, 182 U.S. 244, 287 (1901).

Today's crisis gives him an opportunity to do much more. He has an opportunity to fulfill a pending promise and to cement his legacy. When he became president, Obama promised to resolve Puerto Rico's status problem during his first term in office. He made that vow most publicly in a 2009 letter to Puerto Rico in which he acknowledged that prior administrations had kicked the can for years on this issue and said, "This time must be different."[50]

This time *is* different. For one thing, the current crisis urgently calls for a once-and-for-all resolution to the problem. More importantly, since the start of Obama's second term, the Obama administration has officially become the first administration in American history to confront a clear rejection of the territorial status quo from the people of Puerto Rico. The people have spoken, the promise is pending, and our crisis is urgent. The president can resolve it and make history.

President Obama also has an opportunity to cement his legacy. In his second inaugural address, the president spoke movingly about how "our journey is not complete" until we ensure, for example, that a little girl born in the bleakest poverty knows that she has a chance to succeed like anybody else, because she is an American citizen, she is free, and she is *equal*—not just in the eyes of God but also in our own.[51] I thought that was terrific. And yet I wonder if I was the only one who imagined that beautiful little girl being born in Puerto Rico and who thought that if that was the case, she would not have an *equal* chance to succeed. If we are to make these enduring and self-evident rights true for every American citizen, then "our journey is not complete" until we achieve full equality of citizenship for that little girl and everyone like her.

During his tenure, President Obama has been a strong advocate for equality. He has spoken out on marriage equality, using his second inaugural address to underscore that "our journey is not complete until our gay brothers and sisters are treated like anyone else under the law, for if we are truly created equal, then surely the love we commit to one another must be equal as well."[52] He again spoke out for equality in 2014, when the Civil Rights Act[53] turned fifty, hailing how the landmark law "brought us closer to making real the declaration at the heart of our founding—that we are all created equal."[54] He also spoke passionately in support of equality for Washington, DC, which he

50   Barack Obama, letter to Governor Luis Fortuño, Jan. 4, 2009 (on file with the author).

51   Barack Obama, "Inaugural Address" (United States Capitol, Jan. 21, 2013), http://www.whitehouse.gov/the-press-office/2013/01/21/inaugural-address-president-barack-obama.

52   Ibid.

53   Civil Rights Act, Pub. L. No. 88-352, 78 Stat. 241 (1964).

54   White House, "Statement by the President on the 50th Anniversary of the Civil Rights Act of 1964," press release, July 2, 2014, http://www.whitehouse.gov/the-press-office/2014/07/02/statement-president-50th-anniversary-civil-rights-act-1964.

defended as "absolutely the right thing to do," even while conceding that the politics of getting it through Congress can be "difficult."[55]

As President Obama reminds us, "giving our all to a difficult task . . . is the price and the promise of citizenship."[56] Indeed, Obama has championed the concept of American citizenship like few others. In his 2014 State of the Union address, he defended citizenship in a way that resonated deeply, especially among those citizens living in Puerto Rico, who are deprived of one of the most basic civil rights: the right to vote for their president. As he said, "Citizenship means standing up for *everyone's* right to vote."[57] Also in 2014, in the context of immigration, he said, "We don't want a situation in which we've got *two categories of people* in this country—folks who are full-fledged citizens and folks who are not."[58] That is exactly right—except we have that now, in Puerto Rico. As the president says, we should not.

We have all seen the seismic demographic change in the United States, as reflected by the growth in the Latino community. I firmly believe that the story of Latinos is the story of America. The story of America cannot be one where that little girl born in the bleakest poverty knows that she does *not* have an equal chance to succeed because she feels the burden of a second-class citizenship and suffers the consequences of that inequality every day. The story of America cannot be one where a president can send a young man into harm's way to defend our freedoms but where that young man is not free to vote for his commander in chief. And the story of America cannot be one where a citizen can be good enough to raise millions of dollars to help elect a president but not good enough to cast a vote for him. In the story of America,

---

55   Lucy McCalmont, "Barack Obama on D.C. Statehood: I'm for It," *Politico.com*, July 21, 2014, http://www.politico.com/story/2014/07/washington-dc-statehood-president-obama-109186.html#ixzz389YdH1bg.

56   Macon Phillips, "President Barack Obama's Inaugural Address," *The White House Blog*, Jan. 20, 2009, http://www.whitehouse.gov/blog/inaugural-address. As Obama said (ibid.):

> What is required of us now is a new era of responsibility—a recognition on the part of every American that we have duties to ourselves, our nation and the world; duties that we do not grudgingly accept, but rather seize gladly, firm in the knowledge that there is nothing so satisfying to the spirit, so defining of our character than giving our all to a difficult task. This is the price and the promise of citizenship.

57   Barack Obama, "State of the Union Address" (US House of Representatives, Jan. 28, 2014), http://www.whitehouse.gov/the-press-office/2014/01/28/president-barack-obamas-state-union-address (emphasis added).

58   Quoted in Aaron Blake, "Obama Suggests He's Open to Immigration Deal Without Path to Citizenship," *Washington Post*, Jan. 31, 2014, http://www.washingtonpost.com/blogs/post-politics/wp/2014/01/31/obama-suggests-hes-open-to-immigration-deal-without-path-to-citizenship (emphasis added).

no right is more central to citizenship, no right makes us more equal, than the right to vote. And there is the opportunity: President Obama has the chance to become the first president in American history to cast the issue of equal citizenship for Puerto Ricans as a moral imperative.

In 1963, President Kennedy did something that no other president—not even Lincoln—had done. He committed the country to assuring full equality for African Americans and declared that doing so was a moral imperative:

> We are confronted primarily with a moral issue. It is as old as the scriptures and is as clear as the American Constitution. *The heart of the question is whether all Americans are to be afforded equal rights and equal opportunities*, whether we are going to treat our fellow Americans as we want to be treated.[59]

President Obama should commit the United States to assuring equal citizenship for Puerto Ricans as a moral imperative. He should say that the US Constitution forbids the creation of second-class citizens. If he does so, in my view, he will cement his legacy with the Puerto Rican community, who hold few things as dear as their American citizenship. President Obama is uniquely equipped to make this case. He was born on an island that happens to be the last territory to become a state, and his family history shows that he understands all too well the soul-crushing effects of colonialism. In light of the 2012 vote from the Puerto Rican people rejecting the island's territorial status, and the 2014 crisis that is deeply rooted in the legacy of the Insular Cases, President Obama has the chance to bend the moral arc of history— which bends toward justice but does not bend on its own.

We now have an opportunity to complete our journey. Until we resolve the structural problem—really, the civil rights deficit—that has held Puerto Rico back, we will simply be placing Band-Aids on the real problem. At other difficult times in the United States' history, some have called for focusing on issues like the economy instead of on the structural problem at hand. But as the White House has established, our economic success *requires* resolving our status problem. In this moment of truth, Band-Aids just won't do.

The path for Puerto Rico is equality. It is the path that all previous American territories where American citizens live have successfully traveled. This country has *never* cast adrift a territory where American citizens live. After the 2012 vote, there can be no more delays—not even "for a time" or "temporarily." The people have spoken. The "third way" experiment is now officially over. We have an opportunity to change and a moral duty to lead. If we are to reconsider the decisions of the past, and if we are true to ourselves,

---

59   John F. Kennedy, "Report to the American People on Civil Rights," transcript, John F. Kennedy Presidential Library and Museum, June 11, 1963, http://www.jfklibrary .org/Asset-Viewer/LH8F_0MzvOe6Ro1yEm74Ng.aspx (emphasis added).

we know that we would not do it the same way again. As Bill Gates said recently, the way that the United States runs Puerto Rico "is just wrong."[60] We must make it right.

We have a fundamental choice. We can continue down our current path, and say again that status is not the issue, or we can have the courage to change. The people of Puerto Rico showed enormous courage in November 2012 when they rejected the status quo and said *we want change.* When Rosa Parks refused to sit on the back of that bus and changed the course of history, she did so because she got fed up and did something about it. The 2012 vote shows that Puerto Rico is fed up. The 2014 crisis requires that we do something about it.

Our time is now. Equality is the way.

El Futuro Es Nuestro.

---

60   Quoted in Jeff Goodell, "Bill Gates: The Rolling Stone Interview," *Rolling Stone,* Mar. 13, 2014, http://www.rollingstone.com/culture/news/bill-gates-the-rolling-stone-interview-20140313.

CHAPTER NINE

Puerto Rico and the United States at the Crossroads

Carlos Iván Gorrín Peralta

Puerto Rico has been a territory of the United States since the relation between the two countries began as an act of war in 1898. Under the Treaty of Paris,[1] which put an end to the Spanish-American War, Spain ceded sovereignty over Puerto Rico to the United States. Puerto Rico ceased to be a colony of Spain and became a colony of the United States.[2] For more than half of the constitutional history of the United States, the people of Puerto Rico have been subjected to the ignominy of colonial rule, which is a subversion of the original values on which the American Republic was founded. Furthermore, it contravenes international legal obligations acquired toward the end of the twentieth century. The colonial policy of

---

1 Treaty of Peace between the United States of America and the Kingdom of Spain, U.S.-Spain, Dec. 10, 1898, 30 Stat. 1754.

2 The term "colony" does not exist in US constitutional law. After all, the members of the Philadelphia Convention, whose newly formed "United States" had only recently ceased to be colonies, could not conceive that the new nation would acquire and rule colonies. Only the territory to the northwest of the original states existed. Hence, the constitutional term, derived from the text and later expounded in case law, is "territory." The United States would eventually acquire colonies, but they are still referred to as "territories," a less opprobrious word.

the United States has been constitutionally rationalized by the doctrine articulated in the Insular Cases, which is over one hundred years old.[3] And yet it is really a very well-kept secret, largely absent from the study of constitutional law in American law schools.[4] It has been an almost invisible part of "the law of the land," having been "relegated to the backburners of judicial concern . . . [and floating] in the penumbra of legal priorities considerably below the rule against perpetuities."[5] The time has come to address issues that for too long have been kept in the closet. Reconsidering the Insular Cases is a welcome and necessary development.

I have entitled this chapter "Puerto Rico and the United States at the Crossroads." In the singular, "crossroad" is a road that crosses another or

---

3   Some authorities employ the term Insular Cases to refer to the original string of cases decided by the Supreme Court in 1901, which mark the origin of the doctrine. The cases most pertinent to Puerto Rico are *De Lima v. Bidwell*, 182 U.S. 1 (1901) and *Downes v. Bidwell*, 182 U.S. 244 (1901). Other cases decided between 1902 and 1922, which actually developed the doctrine of territorial incorporation and gave it unanimous acceptance by the court, are also frequently included in the term. The most significant are *Hawaii v. Mankichi*, 190 U.S. 197 (1903); *Dorr v. United States*, 195 U.S. 138 (1904); *Rassmussen v. United States*, 197 U.S. 516 (1905); *Dowdell v. United States*, 221 U.S. 325 (1911); *Ocampo v. United States*, 234 U.S. 91 (1914); and *Balzac v. Porto Rico*, 258 U.S. 298 (1922).

   Thorough expositions of the cases can be found in Jaime B. Fuster, "The Origins of the Doctrine of Territorial Incorporation and Its Implications Regarding the Power of the Commonwealth of Puerto Rico to Regulate Interstate Commerce," *Revista Jurídica de la Universidad de Puerto Rico* 43 (1974): 259-94, 290-91; Raúl Serrano Geyls, "The Territorial Status of Puerto Rico and Its Effects on the Political Future of the Island," *Revista Jurídica de la Universidad Interamericana de Puerto Rico* 11 (1977): 385-448; Juan R. Torruella, *The Supreme Court and Puerto Rico: The Doctrine of Separate and Unequal* (Río Piedras: Editorial de la Universidad de Puerto Rico, 1985), 40-100; José Trías Monge, *Historia constitucional de Puerto Rico*, vol. 1 (Río Piedras: Editorial de la Universidad de Puerto Rico, 1980), 235-72; Carlos I. Gorrín Peralta, "Historical Analysis of the Insular Cases: Colonial Constitutionalism Revisited," *Revista del Colegio de Abogados de Puerto Rico* 56 (1995): 31-55; and Efrén Rivera Ramos, *The Legal Construction of Identity: The Judicial and Social Legacy of American Colonialism in Puerto Rico* (Washington, DC: American Psychological Association, 2001).

4   Sanford Levinson, "Installing the *Insular Cases* into the Canon of Constitutional Law," in *Foreign in a Domestic Sense: Puerto Rico, American Expansion, and the Constitution*, ed. Christina Duffy Burnett and Burke Marshall (Durham, NC: Duke University Press 2001), 122.

5   Torruella, *The Supreme Court and Puerto Rico*, 4.

the junction where the two roads meet.[6] The plural, "crossroads," is a crisis situation or point in time when a critical or fateful decision must be made.[7]

The relation between Puerto Rico and the United States stands at the crossroad of constitutional law and international law, particularly international human rights law and, more specifically, the collective right of all peoples to self-determination. This chapter will examine how the doctrine of the Insular Cases came into existence and how it contradicts the right to self-determination recognized in international law. Finally, it will examine how Puerto Rico and the United States are at the crossroads—at a point when a critical and fateful decision must be made.

From Self-Determination to Colonial Constitutionalism

The Declaration of Independence of 1776, which has been heard more clearly around the world than the shots fired at Lexington and Concord, states that

> Governments are instituted among Men, deriving their just powers from the consent of the governed. . . . [I]t is the Right of the People . . . to institute new Government, laying its foundation on such principles and organizing its powers in such form, as to them shall seem most likely to effect their Safety and Happiness.[8]

That seminal act of self-determination[9] was reaffirmed when "the people" adopted the Constitution of the United States, drafted by the Constitutional Convention and ratified by the state legislatures.[10] Blood had been spilled to secure that right of self-determination, and it has continued to spill since then throughout the world. Four score and seven years after independence, over the battlefield of Gettysburg, Abraham Lincoln would renew the proposition that a government *of* the people, *by* the people, and *for* the people should not perish from the earth.

---

6   *New Webster's Dictionary of the English Language: Deluxe Encyclopedic Edition* (1981); *Advanced English Dictionary and Thesaurus*, v. 5.2.40 (2014).
7   *Advanced English Dictionary and Thesaurus*; *New Webster's Dictionary of the English Language*.
8   THE DECLARATION OF INDEPENDENCE (U.S. 1776).
9   As shall be seen below, the US Declaration of Independence, together with resolutions adopted by the Assemblée Nationale during the French Revolution, is considered by the international human rights community as the first articulation of the right to self-determination.
10 "The express authority of the people alone could give due validity to the Constitution." James Madison, "The Federalist No. 43" (1788).

Yet, over the course of the nineteenth century, the nature of the Republic was transformed. What Thomas Jefferson had referred to as the republican ideal of "an empire of liberty"[11] somehow mutated into a very unrepublican regime that claimed the liberty to rule an empire. The territory clause of the Constitution,[12] which had been conceived as a mere property clause granting the federal government the power to dispose of and make all needful rules and regulations regarding the Northwest Territory and other property belonging to the United States, was reinterpreted as granting Congress the power to acquire new territories by purchase or conquest and to exercise sovereignty over them, even though their inhabitants were not allowed to participate in their own government.[13]

By the 1890s, dominant racist and imperialistic ideologies resulted in the infamous "separate but equal" doctrine of *Plessy v. Ferguson*[14] and in the colonial doctrine of territorial nonincorporation, enacted into law in 1900[15] and judicially constitutionalized in the Insular Cases. Since then, Congress has purported to exercise constitutional power over a new category of "unincorporated territories" that are not part of the United States but rather mere possessions.

As soon as the United States acquired Puerto Rico after the Spanish-American War, a debate ensued within US political and academic circles regarding what to do with the new possessions. On one side, the Republican Party—under imposing figures such as Henry Cabot Lodge, Theodore Roosevelt, and William McKinley—insisted on the latest brand of Manifest Destiny, which purportedly imposed the duty to civilize and christianize backward areas of the world. Besides, the new possessions presented a golden opportunity to turn the United States into a great imperial power, to improve its military capability and the protection of national interests (via bases and coaling stations overseas), and to increase the commercial potential of illimitable markets and sources of cheap raw materials. It was argued that the national interest required that these possessions be kept. But their alien nature required that they not be annexed as full-fledged territories or, eventually, as states.[16]

---

11 Brook Thomas, "A Constitution Led by the Flag: The Insular Cases and the Metaphor of Incorporation," in *Foreign in a Domestic Sense: Puerto Rico, American Expansion, and the Constitution*, ed. Christina Duffy Burnett and Burke Marshall (Durham, NC: Duke University Press 2001), 89.

12 U.S. CONST., art. IV, § 3, cl. 2.

13 Am. Ins. Co. v. 356 Bales of Cotton, 26 U.S. 511 (1828); Late Corp. of Church of Jesus Christ v. United States, 136 U.S. 1 (1890).

14 Plessy v. Ferguson, 163 U.S. 537 (1896).

15 Organic Act of 1900 (Foraker Act), ch. 191, 31 Stat. 77 (1900) (codified as amended in scattered sections of 48 U.S.C. (2013)).

16 Fuster, "The Origins of the Doctrine of Territorial Incorporation," 290-91.

On the other side of the debate, equally imposing figures such as Mark Twain, President Charles William Eliot of Harvard, President Jacob Gould Schurman of Cornell, William James, Samuel Gompers, Andrew Carnegie, Grover Cleveland, and William Jennings Bryan held a diametrically different view. The new possessions had to be relinquished. To maintain them as colonies would be tyrannical and a violation of liberty and democracy. To make them territories and eventually admit them as states would not be wise; they were culturally foreign and incapable of being states.[17]

The legal aspects of the debate were articulated in a series of articles published in the *Harvard Law Review* and *Yale Law Journal* in 1899. There were initially two sides to the debate. Some academics expounded what would come to be known as the democratic "anti-imperialistic" position, suggesting that the values that animate the American Republic prohibited the country from acquiring a foreign land and governing it indefinitely, without the participation of its people in the government.[18] Since "the Constitution follows the flag"—in other words, wherever the authority of the United States is exercised, the Constitution must apply in full—the new territories would have to be considered part of the United States. However, because the new possessions were truly foreign, populated by inferior races incapable of civilized government, it was unthinkable that they might eventually become part of the American people. The United States had to relinquish them as soon as possible; otherwise, the danger of compromising core national values and tainting the nation with inferior foreign races loomed over the land.

The republican "imperialistic" side of the debate argued that according to settled law, the United States could acquire new lands through military conquest or treaty. Furthermore, since the Constitution gave Congress "the power . . . to make all needful Rules and Regulations respecting the Territory or other Property belonging to the United States,"[19] there was no constitutional limit concerning what the government could do in the newly acquired foreign lands.[20]

A third, allegedly intermediate, theory emerged from the clash of the first two.[21] According to this view, the United States had the power to acquire

---

17 Ibid., 289-90.
18 Carman F. Randolph, "Constitutional Aspects of Annexation," *Harvard Law Review* 12 (1898): 291-315; Elmer B. Adams, "The Causes and Results of Our War with Spain from a Legal Standpoint," *Yale Law Journal* 8 (1899): 119-33.
19 U.S. CONST., art. IV, § 3, cl. 2.
20 C. C. Langdell, "The Status of Our New Territories," *Harvard Law Review* 12 (1899): 365-92; Simeon E. Baldwin, "The Constitutional Questions Incident to the Acquisition and Government by the United States of Island Territory," *Harvard Law Review* 12 (1899): 393-416; Simeon E. Baldwin, "The People of the United States," *Yale Law Journal* 8 (1899): 159-67.
21 Abbott Lawrence Lowell, "The Status of Our New Possessions: A Third View," *Harvard Law Review* 13 (1899): 155-76; James Bradley Thayer, "Our

new territories, Congress had the power to rule them under the territory clause, and the Constitution did not necessarily follow the flag. A newly acquired territory would not be part of the United States unless Congress so determined. In addition, only fundamental constitutional provisions would apply in those unincorporated territories. As a result, the dangers feared by the anti-imperialists were not real. The United States could constitutionally acquire territories without making them part of the nation. These new "unincorporated" territories could be ruled by Congress without limitations except those imposed by fundamental constitutional provisions. The first view was racist; the second was imperialistic. The third, so-called intermediate— or, rather, hybrid or composite—view was both.

In the Insular Cases, the Supreme Court elevated this third view—that is, the theory of territorial nonincorporation—to the rank of constitutional doctrine, part of the supreme law of the land. In a seminal concurring opinion in *Downes v. Bidwell*,[22] Justice Edward White articulated the first judicial formulation of the doctrine:

> [W]hile in an international sense Porto Rico [is] not a foreign country, since it [is] subject to the sovereignty of and [is] owned by the United States, it [is] foreign to the United States in a domestic sense, because the island has not been incorporated into the United States, but [is] merely appurtenant thereto as a possession.[23]

The doctrine of the Insular Cases and its interpretation of the territory clause pose a grave inconsistency with the founding values of the Republic. Based on political expediency, the doctrine defers to Congress and the president the governance of the territory, compromising the basic tenets of democracy, liberty, and self-determination of the people. The federal government is not a government *of* the people of Puerto Rico, nor is it validated *by* the people, nor does it rule *for* the people of Puerto Rico. Puerto Rico is subjected to the application of federal laws[24] without the real participation of its people in the Congress that enacts these laws. The federal executive administers such laws in Puerto Rico, despite the fact that Puerto Ricans do not participate in its election. The federal judiciary interprets and applies the laws in Puerto

---

New Possessions," *Harvard Law Review* 12 (1899): 464-85; John K. Beach, "Constitutional Expansion," *Yale Law Journal* 8 (1899): 225-34.

22   Downes v. Bidwell, 182 U.S. 244 (1901).

23   Ibid., 341-42 (White, J., concurring).

24   Section 9 of the Puerto Rican Federal Relations Act, as reenacted by Public Law 600 of 1950, 64 Stat. 319, states that "the statutory laws of the United States not locally inapplicable . . . shall have the same force and effect in Puerto Rico as in the United States." The same text has been in force since 1900.

Rico, despite the fact that the judges are designated by a president it does not elect and are confirmed by a senate in which Puerto Rico does not even have nominal participation.

A Mirage of Democracy

Supporters of the present status argue that between 1950 and 1952, the people of Puerto Rico consented collectively to the United States–Puerto Rico relation. In 1950, Congress passed Public Law 600.[25] According to its terms, it was adopted "in the nature of a compact"[26] and was submitted to the people of Puerto Rico for adoption or rejection. If accepted, the act would authorize the people of Puerto Rico to call a constitutional convention to draft a constitution, which would then need to be ratified by popular vote and sent to the president of the United States, who would submit it to Congress for final approval. The act was accepted by the people of Puerto Rico; thereafter, a constitution was drafted, ratified by popular vote, and approved by US Congress after significant last-minute amendments.[27] On July 25, 1952—the fifty-fourth anniversary of the United States' bombing of San Juan and invasion of Puerto Rico during the Spanish-American War—the Constitution of the Commonwealth of Puerto Rico was proclaimed; it has been in force to this day.

It has been argued that as a result of the process that evolved between 1950 and 1952, Puerto Rico and the United States entered into a mutually binding agreement "in the nature of a compact" whereby Puerto Rico acquired significant sovereign powers and thus ceased to be an unincorporated territory of the United States. The "compact" argument relies in part on the resolution

---

25 Act of July 3, 1950, Pub. L. No. 81-600, 64 Stat. 319 (codified at 48 U.S.C. §§ 731 et seq. (2013)).

26 Ibid. Section 1 of the act states:

> Be it enacted by the Senate and House of Representatives of the United States of America in Congress assembled, That, fully recognizing the principle of government by consent, this Act is now adopted in the nature of a compact so that the people of Puerto Rico may organize a government pursuant to a constitution of their own adoption.

27 Act of July 3, 1952, Pub. L. No. 82-447, 66 Stat. 327, conditioned approval of the new constitutional text by requiring that the Constitutional Convention of Puerto Rico declare in a formal resolution its acceptance of the following changes: article II, section 20 of the constitution, part of the document's bill of rights (social and economic rights), would be eliminated; compulsory school attendance would not be required for students receiving private instruction; and any future amendments to the constitution would have to be consistent with Public Law 447, the US Constitution, the Puerto Rican Federal Relations Act, and Public Law 600.

adopted by the United Nations (UN) General Assembly in 1953 in which Puerto Rico was removed from the list of non-self-governing territories. The US delegation's petition to the UN argued that through the 1950-1952 arrangement, Puerto Rico had consented to a new constitutional status and attained a level of self-government that exempted the United States from the duty of reporting annually on the steps taken to achieve self-government.[28] Furthermore, for several years after the creation of the commonwealth, some court decisions suggested that Puerto Rico had in fact ceased to be a territory of the United States. Although it was not a state, it was also not a territory— Puerto Rico had supposedly achieved a *sui generis* status and was "to be deemed sovereign over matters not ruled by the Constitution."[29]

This theory is a sham. The phrase "in the nature of a compact," which characterizes Public Law 600, was the result of deceitful and intentional ambiguity, a sort of "double speak" in Washington and San Juan. In his posthumously published memoirs, the late José Trías Monge—one of the legal artificers of the process, member of the Puerto Rican Constitutional Convention, former secretary of justice of Puerto Rico, and former chief justice of the Puerto Rico Supreme Court—recalls the moment in which the phrase was coined:

> With regard to the compact, [the then resident commissioner Antonio] Fernós had been one of the most vocal defenders of the idea in 1947 and 1948, but then tenaciously opposed any explicit reference to the idea in the bill to be introduced in Congress. In his judgment, the existence of a compact could be deduced from the process to be followed; its express mention would endanger the legislation. This brought about a meeting in Washington between Fernós, [Abe] Fortas, and the author [Trías Monge]. It was there that, at the suggestion of Fortas, a compromise was reached in which the law would only say ambiguously that it would be adopted "in the nature of a compact."[30]

In other words, an intentionally ambiguous text was necessary to argue before Congress that the legislation did not really entail a compact or mutually binding agreement that limited the exercise of plenary powers of future congresses over Puerto Rico. It had a form similar to a compact, but without the substance. At the same time, in the political discourse in Puerto

---

28   G.A. Res. 748 (VIII), U.N. GAOR, 8th Sess., Supp. No 17, at 25, U.N. Doc. A/2630 (Nov. 27, 1953).

29   See, e.g., Mora v. Torres, 113 F. Supp. 309 (D.P.R. 1953); Mora v. Mejías, 206 F.2d 377 (1st Cir. 1953); Cosentino v. Int'l Longshoremen's Ass'n, 126 F. Supp. 420 (D.P.R. 1954); R.C.A. Communications, Inc. v. Gobierno de la Capital, 91 D.P.R. 416 (P.R. 1964); Calero-Toledo v. Pearson Yacht Leasing Co., 416 U.S. 663 (1974).

30   José Trías Monge, *Cómo fue: Memorias* (San Juan: Editorial de la Universidad de Puerto Rico, 2005), 144 (author's translation).

Rico, the argument continues to be made that a mutually binding compact had been reached.[31]

In any case, the legislative record of Public Law 600 of 1950 is clear. The purpose of the enactment was to allow Puerto Rico a greater degree of local self-government and to obtain acquiescence of the colonized to the existing territorial relationship. The nature of the relationship and the sovereignty of the United States over Puerto Rico were to remain intact, as were the legislative authority of Congress, the executive power of the president, and the judicial jurisdiction of federal courts.[32]

The United States' 1953 petition to the UN General Assembly to be excused from submitting annual reports on measures to realize the right to self-determination of the people of Puerto Rico was granted by resolution.[33] However, the record shows that the resolution was adopted in view of misleading information provided by US representatives. Mason Sears, the US

---

31   Trías Monge would once again bear witness. Many years later, he wrote that during the campaign for the popular vote on Public Law 600, Governor Luis Muñoz Marín stated repeatedly that "Law 600 may only be amended by common agreement." José Trías Monge, *Historia constitucional de Puerto Rico*, vol. 3 (Río Piedras: Editorial de la Universidad de Puerto Rico, 1980), 58-62.

32   In his testimony before Congress, Muñoz Marín said that "if the people of Puerto Rico should go crazy, Congress can always get around and legislate again." Antonio Fernós Isern, the then resident commissioner, added: "[T]he authority of the Government of the United States, of the Congress, to legislate in case of need, would always be there." Later on, he reiterated that the bill "would not change the status of the island of Puerto Rico relative to the United States. . . . It would not alter the powers of sovereignty acquired by the United States over Puerto Rico under the terms of the Treaty of Paris." On the House floor, during the debate of the measure, Fernós stated that "the present exercise of United States authority over all matters of a federal nature, would continue undisturbed." A report submitted by Oscar Chapman, secretary of the interior, stated that "[t]he bill under consideration would not change Puerto Rico's political, social and economic relationship to the United States." According to the State Department report submitted to Congress on this legislation, "the Department of State believes it to be of the greatest importance that the Puerto Rican people be authorized to frame their own constitution . . . in order that formal consent of Puerto Ricans may be given to their present relationship to the United States." The Senate report recommending approval stated that the bill was "designed to complete the full measure of local self-government in the island by enabling the 2 ¼ million American citizens there to express their will and to create their own territorial government. . . . The measure would not change Puerto Rico's fundamental political, social and economic relationship to the United States." Raúl Serrano Geyls, *Derecho constitucional de Estados Unidos y Puerto Rico*, vol. 1 (San Juan: Colegio de Abogados de Puerto Rico, 1986), 488.

33   G.A. Res. 748 (VIII), U.N. GAOR, 8th Sess., Supp. No 17, at 25, U.N. Doc. A/2630 (Nov. 27, 1953).

representative to the UN Trusteeship Council, had incorrectly informed the UN that a referendum had been held in Puerto Rico in which the people had had three choices—full integration as a state, full independence, and association—and in which the people had opted for association. Such a referendum was never held, and the people never had any choice other than between maintaining Puerto Rico's territorial status under prior organic acts of Congress or maintaining the same territorial relationship but with the ability to elect the local government. Ambassador Henry Cabot Lodge, Jr., the United States' permanent representative to the UN, would later tell the General Assembly in an oral statement that any future changes to the relationship would require the mutual consent of Puerto Rico and the United States.[34]

Fifty-four years later, in an official report on Puerto Rico's status, the executive branch of the federal government asserted that the statement by the US representative had no legal import. This 2007 report was issued by the President's Task Force on Puerto Rico's Status, an initiative established by President Clinton in 2000. The task force's first report was published in 2005 and its second in 2007. With regard to Lodge's 1953 oral statement before the UN General Assembly, the 2007 report states the following:

> In its official request to the United Nations, the United States stated that Congress had given Puerto Rico the freedom to conduct its own internal government subject only to compliance with federal law and the U.S. Constitution. The official request did not state that Congress could make no changes in Puerto Rico's status without its consent. It is true that, prior to the submission of this official request, the U.S. representative to the U.N. General Assembly indicated orally that common consent would be needed to make changes in the relationship between Puerto Rico and the United States. Notwithstanding this statement, however, the Department of Justice concluded in 1959 that Puerto Rico remained a territory, and as noted above, the Supreme Court, while recognizing that Puerto Rico exercises substantial political autonomy under the current commonwealth system, has held that Puerto Rico remains fully subject to congressional authority under the Territory Clause. *See Harris*, 446 U.S. at 651-52.[35]

Of course, the principal importance of this report lies not in its appraisal of the legal significance of the statement of the US representative to the UN but in its main conclusion:

---

34 President's Task Force on Puerto Rico's Status, *Report by the President's Task Force on Puerto Rico's Status* (Washington, DC: White House, 2007), 6.

35 Ibid.

"Commonwealth" is used to describe the substantial political autonomy enjoyed by Puerto Rico[. T]he term appropriately captures Puerto Rico's special relationship with the United States. The Commonwealth system does not, however, describe a *legal* status different from Puerto Rico's constitutional status as a "territory" subject to Congress's plenary authority under the territory Clause "to dispose of and make all needful Rules and Regulations respecting the Territory . . . belonging to the United States." Congress may continue the current commonwealth system indefinitely, but it necessarily retains the constitutional authority to revise or revoke the powers of self-government currently exercised by the government of Puerto Rico. Thus it is important to recognize that, as long as Puerto Rico remains a territory, its system is subject to revision by Congress.[36]

The 2005 report had reached similar conclusions:

> For entities under the sovereignty of the United States, the only constitutional options are to be a State or territory. As the U.S. Supreme Court stated in 1879, "All territory within the jurisdiction of the United States not included in any State must necessarily be governed by or under the authority of Congress" (*First Nat. Bank v. Yankton County*, 191 U.S. 129, 133 (1879)). It is a general rule that one legislature cannot bind a subsequent one. For example, one Congress may repeal or amend the laws of a previous one, and Congress may pass laws inconsistent with treaties. Thus, one Congress cannot irrevocably legislate with regard to a territory (at least where the legislation is not part of converting the territory into a State) and, therefore, cannot restrict a future Congress from revising a delegation to a territory of powers of self-government.
>
> The Federal Government may relinquish United States sovereignty by granting independence or ceding the territory to another nation; or it may, as the Constitution provides, admit a territory as a State, thus making the territory clause inapplicable.[37]

These conclusions of the reports, which represent the official position of the federal executive, are in accordance with recent Supreme Court case law. Despite initial judicial decisions suggesting that a significant constitutional change had occurred in 1952, subsequent decisions have made it abundantly clear that Puerto Rico is still a territory of the United States, and Congress still exercises plenary powers over Puerto Rico under the territory clause of the Constitution.[38]

---

36 Ibid., 5-6.

37 President's Task Force on Puerto Rico's Status, *Report by the President's Task Force on Puerto Rico's Status* (Washington, DC: White House, 2005), 6.

38 The first indicia began to emerge as early as 1966 with *Americana of P.R., Inc. v. Kaplus*, 368 F.2d 431 (3d Cir. 1966). By 1976, the Supreme Court would decide that the process of 1950-1952 had not changed federal court jurisdiction in Puerto

The clearest expression can be found in *Harris v. Rosario*,[39] which addressed the question whether Congress has the power to establish a ceiling in federal transfers received by Puerto Rico under a social entitlement program:

> Congress, which is empowered under the territory Clause of the Constitution . . . to "make all needful Rules and Regulations respecting the Territory . . . belonging to the United States," may treat Puerto Rico differently from States so long as there is a rational basis for its actions.[40]

There seems to be no doubt remaining. Puerto Rico is an unincorporated territory of the United States, subject to the plenary powers of Congress under the territory clause. The end result of the 1950-1952 process was very limited in scope. In 1947, Congress had enacted legislation for the election of the governor as head of a government charged with purely local matters. In 1952, some changes were introduced in the structure of the local government. For example, the number of legislators increased in the Legislative Assembly; the judges of the Supreme Court would be designated by the governor, not the president; and the new constitution recognized new rights that limit only the local government. However, the relation itself, regulated in the organic acts of 1900 and 1917, remained intact in what would thereafter be known as the Puerto Rico Federal Relations Act.[41]

The initial illusions of some that a significant constitutional change had occurred and that Puerto Rico was no longer a territory—a colony of the United

---

Rico. Examining Bd. of Engineers, Architects & Surveyors v. Flores de Otero, 426 U.S. 572 (1976). Three years later, the Supreme Court relied fully on the theory of territorial nonincorporation articulated in the Insular Cases to decide in *Torres v. Puerto Rico*, 442 U.S. 465, 470 (1979), that
> Congress may make constitutional provisions applicable to territories in which they would not otherwise be controlling. . . . [B]ecause the limitation on the application of the Constitution in unincorporated territories is based in part on the need to preserve Congress' ability to govern such possessions, and may be overruled by Congress, a legislative determination that a constitutional provision practically and beneficially may be implemented in a territory is entitled to great weight.
Fortunately, the court decided that Congress had seen it "beneficial" to extend to Puerto Rico the Fourth Amendment's protection from unreasonable searches and seizures—not because the amendment must apply to Puerto Rico but out of the goodness of the congressional heart.
39 Harris v. Rosario, 446 U.S. 651 (1980).
40 Ibid., 651-52.
41 Jones Act, Pub. L. No. 64-368, 39 Stat. 951 (1917), *amended by* Pub. L. No. 81-600, 64 Stat. 319 (1950), now known as the Puerto Rico Federal Relations Act of 1950 (codified at 48 U.S.C. §§ 731 et seq. (2013)).

States—were just that: an illusion of having achieved a decolonizing solution to the colonial/territorial problem. It was a mirage of self-determination based on deceit and ambiguity. There was no option. The people were given the opportunity to symbolically consent to the territorial relation. In the unlikely event of a refusal to consent, the colonial relation would continue anyway. The claim of legitimacy through wholesale consent of the governed is tantamount to saying that a slave owner may validly maintain a regime of involuntary servitude so long as he asks his slave whether she prefers to adopt the rules for her household herself or whether she prefers that her master continue to dictate those rules. Colonialism, like slavery, violates inalienable rights that may not be validly abrogated or renounced. No individual may consent to slavery; no people may consent to colonialism. International law has proscribed it through the development of the right to self-determination.

Self-Determination as a Human Right

The history of the struggle for human rights is as old as recorded history because it is the struggle against domination and oppression. There have been clear invocations of human rights concepts since the most ancient legal codes. However, the most recognizably significant historical period in the development of modern conceptions of human rights is the Enlightenment of the seventeenth and eighteenth centuries, whose natural law ideas still influence contemporary legal thought and human rights literature.[42] The origins of the principle of self-determination are also traced to the important documents that resulted from that period. Most authors identify the 1776 Declaration of Independence of the United States of America[43] and documents considered and adopted by the Assemblée Nationale during the French Revolution[44] as the first articulations of the principle. However, the actual term "self-determination" is a product of the early twentieth century. Curiously, it came from opposing sides of the ideological and geopolitical

---

42 Carlos I. Gorrín Peralta, "Human Rights: Individual and Collective Freedom for the Satisfaction of Human Needs," in *Research in Law and Policy Studies*, vol. 3, ed. Stuart Nagel (Greenwich, CT: JAI Press, 1995), 111.

43 Antonio Cassese, *Self-Determination of Peoples: A Legal Reappraisal* (Cambridge: Cambridge University Press, 1995), 11; Joshua Castellino, *International Law and Self-Determination* (The Hague: Martinus Nijhoff, 2000), 111.

44 In 1792, the Assemblée Nationale declared its will to help support all peoples willing to fight for the cause of liberty elsewhere. Castellino, *International Law and Self-Determination*. A year later, the National Convention considered a draft constitution for the French Republic whereby the republic would renounce to annexing any foreign territory without the consent of its population. Unfortunately, the principle would not always be applied in practice, especially when the republic turned into an empire. Cassese, *Self-Determination of Peoples*.

spectrum. In 1916, Vladimir Lenin articulated the first compelling enunciation of the principle, as a prerequisite for the achievement of socialism throughout the world.[45] Soon thereafter, Woodrow Wilson, beginning with his famous 1919 Fourteen Points address, put forth the idea of self-determination as the logical corollary to popular sovereignty, synonymous with government based on the consent of the governed,[46] and as a pseudonym for the right to democracy.[47] The concept would become useful for restructuring Europe after the Great War and for the work of the League of Nations.[48] Three strands of the right emerged: (i) as a right of each people to choose their own form of government (internal self-determination); (ii) as a guiding principle for drawing up boundaries in Europe; and (iii) as a principle for settling colonial claims (external self-determination).[49] The third strand would not develop until after World War II, with a new emphasis on decolonization within the newly created United Nations.

From the convulsions of World War II, popular revulsion over Nazism, and the specter of massive human rights violations, the new international organization set as one of its principal goals the promotion of human rights standards. The UN Charter states that one of the purposes of the organization is "[t]o develop friendly relations among nations based on respect for the principles of equal rights and self-determination of peoples, and to take other appropriate measures to strengthen universal peace."[50] Articles 55 and 56 of the charter are particularly significant:

> Art. 55. With a view to the creation of conditions of stability and well-being which are necessary for peaceful and friendly relations among nations based on respect for the principle of equal rights and self-determination of peoples, the United Nations shall promote:
>
> > higher standards of living, full employment, and conditions of economic and social progress and development;
> >
> > solutions of international economic, social, health, and related problems; and international cultural and educational co-operation; and
> >
> > universal respect for, and observance of, human rights and fundamental freedoms for all without distinction as to race, sex, language or religion.

---

45 Vladimir Illich Lenin, *Theses on the Socialist Revolution and the Right of Nations to Self-Determination* (1916), cited in Cassese, *Self-Determination of Peoples*, 15.

46 Cassese, *Self-Determination of Peoples*, 18.

47 Castellino, *International Law and Self-Determination*, 13.

48 Cassese, *Self-Determination of Peoples*, 20.

49 Ibid.

50 United Nations Charter, art. 1(2).

Art. 56. All Members pledge themselves to take joint and separate action in co-operation with the Organization for the achievement of the purposes set forth in Article 55.[51]

This was the first articulation of the principle of self-determination in a multilateral treaty, conceived as a major piece of legislation of the new world community.[52]

The work was far from over. As soon as the UN Commission on Human Rights began to work, it decided to create an international bill of human rights composed of three parts: (i) a declaration; (ii) one or more conventions; and (iii) a machinery for implementation.[53] Two years later, on December 10, 1948, the UN General Assembly adopted the Universal Declaration of Human Rights.[54]

Great debates ensued after the adoption of the Universal Declaration on how to elevate its general principles into binding treaty provisions. Those debates were deeply influenced by the ideological and geopolitical concerns of the Cold War.[55] As a result of geopolitical competition in the General Assembly for almost two decades, in 1966 not one but two international covenants were approved, separating the civil and political rights of the liberal tradition from the economic, social, and cultural human rights emphasized in socialist theory and law. Interestingly, both the International Covenant on Civil and Political Rights (ICCPR)[56] and the International Covenant on Economic, Social and Cultural Rights[57] have a common article 1 that recognizes the right of all peoples to self-determination. The *travaux préparatoires* reveal the reasoning that before any rights are enjoyed, people must be masters of their own political destiny. Self-determination is thus the gateway for the full enjoyment of human rights, both economic, social, and cultural rights and civil and political rights.[58] The text of article 1 states:

---

51 Ibid., arts. 55-56.
52 Cassese, *Self-Determination of Peoples*, 41-43.
53 Peter Meyer, "The International Bill: A Brief History," in *The International Bill of Rights*, ed. Paul Williams (Glen Ellen, CA: Entwhistle Books, 1981), xxiii-xxiv.
54 Universal Declaration of Human Rights, G.A. Res. 217A (III), U.N. GAOR, 3rd Sess., at 71, U.N. Doc. A/810 (Dec. 10, 1948).
55 Gorrín Peralta, "Human Rights," 114-16.
56 International Covenant on Civil and Political Rights, G.A. Res. 2200A (XXI), U.N. GAOR, 21st Sess., Supp. No. 16, at 52, U.N. Doc. A/6316 (Dec. 16, 1966), 999 U.N.T.S. 171, *entered into force* Mar. 23, 1976 [hereinafter ICCPR].
57 International Covenant on Economic, Social and Cultural Rights, G.A. Res. 2200A (XXI), U.N. GAOR, 21st Sess., Supp. No. 16, at 49, U.N. Doc. A/6316 (Dec. 16, 1966), 993 U.N.T.S. 3, *entered into force* Jan. 3, 1976 [hereinafter ICESCR].
58 Castellino, *International Law and Self-determination*, 31.

All peoples have the right of self-determination. By virtue of that right they freely determine their political status and freely pursue their economic, social and cultural development.

All peoples may, for their own ends, freely dispose of their natural wealth and resources, without prejudice to any obligations arising out of international economic cooperation, based upon the principle of mutual benefit, and international law. In no case may a people be deprived of its own means of subsistence.

The States Parties to the present Covenant, including those having responsibility for the administration of Non-Self-Governing and Trust Territories, shall promote the realization of the right of self-determination, and shall respect that right in conformity with the provisions of the Charter of the United Nations.[59]

The third paragraph is especially important. Not only do all peoples have the right of self-determination, but colonial powers have a concomitant obligation to "promote the realization of the right"—in other words, to take "*positive action* to facilitate realization of and respect for the right of peoples to self-determination . . . [and to] refrain from interfering in the internal affairs of other states and thereby adversely affecting the exercise of the right to self-determination."[60] The implication is that state parties have an obligation to relinquish their powers to colonized peoples.[61]

In addition to its recognition in treaty provisions, the right to self-determination has evolved through customary rules expressed in UN General Assembly resolutions. Although these resolutions are technically not sources of international norms, they play an important role in the growing international consensus on self-determination as a part of customary international law.

The 1960 Declaration on the Granting of Independence to Colonial Countries and Peoples[62] was adopted unanimously by the UN General Assembly, with only nine abstentions. It is one of the clearest statements on self-determination within international law:

1. The subjection of peoples to alien subjugation, domination and exploitation constitutes a denial of fundamental human rights, is contrary to the Charter of the United Nations and is an impediment to the promotion of world peace and co-operation.

---

59 ICCPR, art. 1; ICESCR, art. 1.
60 Human Rights Committee, General Comment No. 12: Article 1 (Right to Self-Determination), *in* Compilation of General Comments and General Recommendations Adopted by Human Rights Treaty Bodies, at 183, para. 6, U.N. Doc. HRI/GEN/1/Rev.9 (Vol. I) (2008).
61 Castellino, *International Law and Self-Determination*, 33.
62 G.A. Res. 1514 (XV), U.N. GAOR, 15th Sess., Supp. No. 16, at 66, U.N. Doc. A/4684 (Dec. 14, 1960).

2. All peoples have the right to self-determination; by virtue of that right they freely determine their political status and freely pursue their economic, social and cultural development.

. . .

5. Immediate steps shall be taken, in Trust and Non-Self-Governing Territories or all other territories which have not yet attained independence, to transfer all powers to the peoples of those territories, without any conditions or reservations, in accordance with their freely expressed will and desire . . . in order to enable them to enjoy complete independence and freedom.[63]

Also in 1960, the General Assembly adopted the Principles Which Should Guide Members in Determining Whether or Not an Obligation Exists to Transmit the Information Called for under Article 73(e) of the Charter.[64] This resolution declares and reiterates states' obligation to transmit information with respect to territories whose peoples have not yet attained a full measure of self-government. Furthermore, the resolution defines what constitutes a "full measure of self-government": a decision made by the people to (i) constitute themselves as a sovereign state; (ii) associate freely with an independent state; or (iii) integrate with an independent state already in existence.[65] The second option, that of free association, must be viewed in the context of General Assembly Resolution 742 of 1953,[66] which describes the manner in which non-self-governing territories can subsequently be deemed "fully self-governing." Self-government is attainable primarily through full independence, but the General Assembly has also recognized association with another state if it is done freely and on the basis of absolute equality.[67]

Finally, the General Assembly's 1970 Declaration on Friendly Relations[68] proclaims a series of fundamental principles previously articulated in the UN Charter and in resolutions regarding the use of peaceful means to resolve disputes instead of the use of force, cooperation among states, the sovereign equality of states, the fulfillment of obligations assumed by states, and equal rights and self-determination of peoples. The consensus regarding this "restatement" of principles previously recognized was such that the

---

63 Ibid., arts. 1, 2, 5.
64 G.A. Res. 1541 (XV), U.N. GAOR, 15th Sess., Supp. No. 16, at 29, U.N. Doc. A/4684 (Dec. 15, 1960).
65 Ibid., annex, princ. VI; Castellino, *International Law and Self-Determination*, 27-28.
66 G.A. Res. 742 (VIII), U.N. GAOR, 8th Sess., Supp. No. 17, at 21, U.N. Doc. A/2630 (Nov. 27, 1953).
67 See Manuel Rodríguez Orellana, "In Contemplation of Micronesia: The Prospects for the Decolonization of Puerto Rico under International Law," *University of Miami Inter-American Law Review* 18 (1987): 457-90, 470-71.
68 G.A. Res. 2625 (XXV), annex, U.N. GAOR, 25th Sess., Supp. No. 28, at 121, U.N. Doc. A/8028 (Oct. 24, 1970).

resolution was adopted without a vote.[69] With regard to self-determination, the Declaration on Friendly Relations reiterates the right of all peoples to determine their political status without external interference and to pursue their economic, social, and cultural development. Furthermore, it reiterates the affirmative duty of colonial powers to facilitate self-determination and to bring a speedy end to colonialism, which is a denial of fundamental human rights and contrary to the UN Charter. The declaration recognizes the substantive options from which the people may validly select: full independence, free association or integration with an existing state, or "the emergence into any other political status freely determined by a people."[70]

International consensus (*opinio juris*) has evolved to characterize the right of self-determination as a fundamental, collective human right that must be respected by all states, even those not signatories to international instruments. The major role of this right since 1945 has been to provide a juridical foundation for decolonization. In this task, it has been remarkably successful.[71] There is no longer any doubt that all peoples subjected to colonial rule have a right to "freely determine their political status and freely pursue their economic, social and cultural development" as a sovereign independent state, as a freely associated state, or through integration into an existing state.[72] Self-determination is an inalienable right, a peremptory norm of

---

69 Castellino, *International Law and Self-Determination*, 35.
70 Supporters of the current status have construed this phrase to the effect that any arrangement, including the continued exercise of congressional power under the current territorial regime, may be a valid exercise of self-determination, as long as it is consented to by the people. This is a misconception of the international consensus embodied in the declaration. Its own preamble states that it is adopted "[c]onsidering the provisions of the Charter as a whole and taking into account the role of relevant resolutions adopted by the competent organs of the United Nations relating to the content of the principles." As a reiteration of principles previously adopted, this declaration must be construed within the framework of prior declarations and may not contravene them. It recognizes only those status options that are truly decolonizing—a people may not exercise their right to self-determination by consenting to colonialism. Far from being a valid exercise of the right, this would entail the oxymoron of renouncing an inalienable right. Rubén Berríos Martínez, Fernando Martín García, and Francisco Catalá Oliveras, *Puerto Rico: Nación independiente, imperativo del Siglo XXI* (Santo Domingo: Editora Corripio, 2010), 175-79.
71 Lee C. Buchheit, *Secession: The Legitimacy of Self-Determination* (New Haven: Yale University Press 1978), 16.
72 Cassese, *Self-Determination of Peoples*, 72-73; Allen Buchanan, *Justice, Legitimacy, and Self-Determination: Moral Foundations for International Law* (New York: Oxford University Press, 2004); Jaume Ferrer Lloret, *La aplicación del principio de autodeterminación de los pueblos: Sahara Occidental y Timor Oriental* (Alicante:

international law from which no state may derogate,[73] even with the consent of the colonized people. As a result, the International Court of Justice has recognized the evolution of the concept, acknowledging it as part of the *corpus juris gentium* and a binding legal norm.[74]

The new law of self-determination has not resulted in the invalidation of prior acquisitions of territory by conquest or through cession. But it has led to the emergence of legal obligations to enable the people of colonial territories to choose freely whether to opt for independent statehood, free association, or integration with an existing state. Those obligations do not produce an immediate legal effect of rendering the legal title over colonial territory null and void; they envisage a temporary legal regime that must lead to the eventual relinquishment of sovereignty and extinction of the legal title.[75]

Self-Determination and the Law of the United States

Under the presidency of Jimmy Carter, the United States signed both of the 1966 international covenants on human rights. And in 1992, the Senate approved the ratification of the ICCPR,[76] which entered into force for the United States on June 8 of that year.[77] The supremacy clause of the US

Publicaciones Universidad de Alicante, 2002), 19.

73 Cassese, *Self-Determination of Peoples*, 169-74.
74 Legal Consequences for States of the Continued Presence of South Africa in Namibia (South West Africa) Notwithstanding Security Council Resolution 276 (1970), Advisory Opinion, 1971 I.C.J. Reports 16, 31-32 (June 21); Western Sahara, Advisory Opinion, 1975 I.C.J. Reports 12, 31-33 (Oct. 16); Case Concerning East Timor (Portugal v. Australia), Advisory Opinion, 1995 I.C.J. Reports 90, 102 (June 30). See also José A. de Obieta Chalbaud, *El derecho humano de la autodeterminación de los pueblos* (Madrid: Tecnos, 1985), 106.
75 Cassese, *Self-Determination of Peoples*, 186-87.
76 U.S. Reservations, Declarations, and Understandings, International Covenant on Civil and Political Rights, 138 Cong. Rec. S4781-01 (1992).
77 According to the Vienna Convention on the Law of Treaties, an international instrument becomes binding on a state party after the state has expressed its consent to be bound. Such consent is expressed by signature, exchange, ratification, acceptance, approval, or accession. Vienna Convention on the Law of Treaties, Apr. 24, 1970, 1155 U.N.T.S. 331, arts. 2(1)(b), 11. "The United States has yet to ratify it, but the State Department has said that 'the Convention is already generally recognized as the authoritative guide to current treaty law and practice.' S. Exec. Doc. 92d Cong., 1st Sess. 1 (1971)." David Weissbrodt, Joan Fitzpatrick, and Frank Newman, *International Human Rights: Law, Policy and Process*, 3rd ed. (Cincinnati: Anderson, 2001), 113. See also Michael John Garcia, "International Law and Agreements: Their Effect Upon U.S. Law," *Congressional Research Service*, Mar. 1, 2013, n.7.

Constitution ordains that "all Treaties made, or which shall be made, under the Authority of the United States, shall be the supreme Law of the Land."[78] Consequently, the United States has assumed the obligation to facilitate, through positive action, the exercise of the right to self-determination by the people of any territory or colony under its sovereignty.

It has been argued that the ICCPR is not part of the supreme law of the land because it was ratified with a "declaration" proposed by the executive branch and approved by the Senate to the effect "that the [substantive] provisions of Articles 1 through 27 of the Covenant are not self-executing"[79] and thus not part of the supreme law of the United States until Congress and the president approve implementing legislation.

Even before the adoption of the Constitution, international agreements entered into by the United States were an integral part of its domestic law. As early as 1793, the Supreme Court indicated that "the United States [had], by taking a place among the nations of the earth, become amenable to the law of nations."[80] Three years later, the court indicated that "[w]hen the United States declared their independence, they were bound to receive the law of nations, in its modern state of purity and refinement."[81] That was the prevailing view of international obligations when the supremacy clause of the Constitution was drafted, declaring treaties part of the supreme law of the land.

However, early in the nineteenth century, a distinction was drawn between "self-executing" and "non-self-executing" treaties. Most authorities trace the origin of the doctrine to *Foster v. Neilson*,[82] which held that

> [treaties are] to be regarded in courts of justice as equivalent to an act of the legislature, wherever it operates of itself, without the aid of any legislative provision. But when the terms of the stipulation import a contract, when either of the parties engages to perform a particular act, the [agreement] addresses itself to the political, not the judicial department; and the legislature must execute the contract, before it can become a rule for the court.[83]

---

78   U.S. CONST., art. VI, cl. 2.
79   U.S. Reservations, Declarations, and Understandings, International Covenant on Civil and Political Rights, 138 CONG. REC. S4781-01, § III(1) (1992).
80   Chisolm v. Georgia, 2 U.S. 419, 474 (1793).
81   Ware v. Hylton, 3 U.S. 199, 281 (1796). See Garcia, *International Law and Agreements*, 1.
82   Foster v. Neilson, 27 U.S. 253 (1829).
83   Ibid., 314. *Foster* was overruled on other grounds by *United States v. Percheman*, 32 U.S. 51 (1833).

The modern articulation of the doctrine appears in *Medellín v. Texas*[84]:

> What we mean by "self-executing" is that the treaty has automatic domestic effect as federal law upon ratification.
>
> In sum, while treaties may comprise international commitments . . . they are not domestic law unless Congress has either enacted implementing statutes or the treaty itself conveys an intention that it be "self-executing" and is ratified on these terms.[85]

Still, the definition of "self-executing" is not clear.[86] Professor Myres McDougal said back in 1951 that "'self-executing' is essentially meaningless and . . . the quicker we drop it from our vocabulary the better for clarity and understanding."[87] Since then, an impressive chorus of scholars has criticized the doctrine.[88] However, as David Sloss writes, "despite repeated exhortations by scholars to either clarify or dispense with the concept of self-execution, courts continue to employ the term, and the ambiguity surrounding its usage has only increased with the passage of time."[89]

The doctrine has been relevant only in the judicial consideration of cases requiring treaty enforcement by a court. Thus, if a litigant seeks damages for the violation of a treaty but the instrument does not create a private right of action, the court will consider the treaty non-self-executing.[90] Similarly, a treaty that purports to achieve something for which the Constitution requires

84 Medellín v. Texas, 552 U.S. 491 (2008).
85 Ibid., 505.
86 Carlos Manuel Vázquez, "Treaties as Law of the Land: The Supremacy Clause and the Judicial Enforcement of Treaties," *Harvard Law Review* 122 (2008): 599-695, 628; David Sloss, "The Domestication of International Human Rights: Non-Self-Executing Declarations and Human Rights Treaties," *Yale Journal of International Law* 24 (1999): 144.
87 Myres McDougal, "Remarks at the Annual Meeting of the American Society of International Law (April 27, 1951)," *Proceedings of the American Society of International Law* 45 (1951): 101-2, 102.
88 For an incisive critique of the doctrine, see Juan R. Torruella, "The *Insular Cases*: The Establishment of a Regime of Political Apartheid," *University of Pennsylvania Journal of International Law* 29 (2007): 283-347, 335-43 and authorities cited therein, especially Jordan J. Paust, "Self-Executing Treaties," *American Journal of International Law* 82 (1988): 760-83; Louis Henkin, *Foreign Affairs and the United States Constitution*, 2nd ed. (New York: Oxford University Press, 1996), 201. See also David Sloss, "Schizophrenic Treaty Law," *Texas International Law Journal* 43 (2007): 15-27.
89 Sloss, "The Domestication of International Human Rights," 144.
90 Vázquez, "Treaties as Law of the Land," 629.

legislative action will also be construed as non-self-executing.[91] Likewise, treaties are non-self-executing if they impose an obligation that requires political judgments that are not justiciable.[92]

However, the doctrine of non-self-execution does not preclude a treaty from having the force of law. It only means that the treaty may not be judicially enforced.[93] No decision of the Supreme Court has stated that a non-self-executing treaty lacks the force of law. Since *Foster*, some treaties are seen as creating obligations addressed to the political branches and not to the courts; as a result, they may not be considered by the courts because the judicial department lacks the power to require the legislature to legislate. That is a strictly political prerogative that the courts may not usurp. Only if the legislature complies with the obligation imposed by the treaty may the court enforce it, since the treaty has become equivalent to a statute.[94] The most recent embodiment of the doctrine—*Medellín*—relies on *Foster* to state that a non-self-executing treaty may not be enforced judicially, but it never states that the treaty lacks the force of law. As Carlos Manuel Vázquez explains, "Such a treaty is . . . not judicially enforceable because of the particular nature of the obligation it imposes, not because it lacks the force of domestic law."[95]

Accordingly, if one accepts the continued recognition of the doctrine of non-self-executing treaties, two questions must be considered. First, what is the nature of the obligation imposed by a non-self-executing treaty? Second, is the right to self-determination, specifically recognized by the ICCPR, part of the law of the land?

The ICCPR provides that parties to the covenant "shall promote the realization of the right of self-determination."[96] Upon ratification, the United States assumed the obligation to take positive action to facilitate the exercise of this right. That obligation undoubtedly pertains to Congress, which is constitutionally empowered under the territory clause "to dispose of and make all needful Rules and Regulations respecting the Territory."[97] To assert that Senate approval of the non-self-executing declaration created a loophole for bypassing this obligation, which is so clearly stated in the text of the treaty, would be a travesty.

---

91   Ibid.
92   Ibid. See also Garcia, *International Law and Agreements*, 6-7.
93   "When a treaty is ratified . . . the United States acquires obligations under international law and may be in default of those obligations unless implementing legislation is enacted." *Restatement (Third) of Foreign Relations*, Section 111, cmt. h (1987).
94   Vázquez, "Treaties as Law of the Land," 648-49.
95   Ibid.
96   ICCPR, art. 1.
97   U.S. Const., art. IV, § 3, cl. 2.

Declarations do not create limits to the legal obligations emanating from a ratified treaty.[98] But even if they could, the Senate's approval process for ratifying the ICCPR reveals that the purpose of the declaration was not to deny the treaty's legal force. The text of the declaration, which was proposed by the executive branch, sought to "clarify that the Covenant will not create a private cause of action in U.S. courts."[99] The representative of the administration reiterated this in hearings before the Committee on Foreign Relations: "[T]he ICCPR provisions, when ratified, will not by themselves create private rights enforceable in US Courts; that could only be done by legislation adopted by the Congress."[100] In response to written questions submitted by Senator Jesse Helms regarding whether the treaty could change or supersede domestic law, as Sloss describes, "the Bush Administration appear[ed] to be suggesting that the ICCPR [would] be 'the law of the land,' and [would] supersede inconsistent domestic law, despite the fact that it is not self-executing."[101] Ratification was premised on these representations.

The right to self-determination is therefore part of the law of the United States on two accounts. First, it has been recognized by the UN Charter and

---

98 As Torruella points out, "The distinction between a declaration and a reservation is not one of mere semantics. A non-self executing declaration differs materially from a reservation." He continues by quoting two leading commentators on the issue:

> [T]he Senate lacks the constitutional authority to declare the non-self-executing character of a treaty with binding effect on U.S. courts. The Senate has the unicameral power only to consent to the ratification of treaties, not to pass domestic legislation. A declaration is not part of a treaty in the sense of modifying the legal obligations created by it. A declaration is merely an expression of an interpretation or of a policy or position. U.S. courts are . . . not bound to apply expressions of opinion adopted by the Senate (and concurred in by the President). . . . The treaty is law. The Senate's declaration is not law. The Senate does not have the power to make law outside the treaty instrument.

Stefan A. Riesenfeld and Frederick M. Abbott, "Foreword: Symposium on Parliamentary Participation in the Making and Operation of Treaties," *Chicago-Kent Law Review* 67 (1991): 293-312, 296-97, quoted in Torruella, "The *Insular Cases*," 341-42.

99 Senate Committee on Foreign Relations, *US Senate Report on Ratification of International Covenant on Civil and Political Rights*, US Senate Executive Report 102-23 (1992), 19, cited in Sloss, "The Domestication of International Human Rights," 166.

100 *International Covenant on Civil and Political Rights: Hearing Before the Committee on Foreign Relations, U.S. Senate*, 102d Cong. (1992), cited in Sloss, "The Domestication of International Human Rights," 166.

101 Sloss, "The Domestication of International Human Rights," 166-67.

the ICCPR, treaties duly ratified by and entered into force for the United States, and is thus part of the "law of the land" under the supremacy clause of the Constitution. Furthermore, the right is part of international customary law, which for more than a century has been considered federal law by the Supreme Court.[102]

All branches of the federal government have agreed that Congress, empowered by the territory clause of the Constitution, continues to exercise sovereignty and plenary powers over Puerto Rico. As a result, the international norms related to the right to self-determination are fully applicable. The present relationship, illegitimate under international law, can no longer be considered a valid option. Congress should now act to facilitate a process of self-determination.

Legislation has been introduced on several occasions since 1989 in the House and in the Senate, purportedly to allow for a process of self-determination, but Congress has failed to pass any enabling legislation.[103] The latest insubstantial gesture of congressional action was the approval of the executive's proposal for an appropriation of $2.5 million to educate the people of Puerto Rico about, and to hold a plebiscite on, options approved as constitutionally viable by the attorney general of the United States.[104] That, of course, could include the island's current territorial status, which has been constitutionally viable since the Insular Cases. It is a nonproposal, and it does not comply, even remotely, with the international obligation to promote self-determination.

Puerto Rico's territorial status activates a duty under international law to take positive steps to allow the people to exercise their fundamental collective human right to self-determination. As a matter of constitutional law, Congress has the power "to dispose of the territory." By refusing or neglecting to do so,

---

102 As the court held in *The Paquete Habana*,175 U.S. 677, 700 (1900):

> International law is part of our law, and must be ascertained and administered by the courts of justice of appropriate jurisdiction, as often as questions of right depending upon it are duly presented for their determination. For this purpose, where there is no treaty, and no controlling executive or legislative act or judicial decision, resort must be had to the customs and usages of civilized nations; and, as evidence of these, to the works of jurists and commentators, who by years of labor, research, and experience, have made themselves peculiarly well acquainted with the subjects of which they treat. Such works are resorted to by judicial tribunals, not for the speculations of their authors concerning what the law ought to be, but for trustworthy evidence of what the law really is.

103 Manuel Rodríguez Orellana, "Puerto Rico and the U.S. Congress: The Road Ahead," *Texas Hispanic Journal of Law and Policy* (forthcoming).
104 Consolidated Appropriations Act, Pub. L. No. 113-76, 128 Stat. 5 (2014).

the United States continues to exercise plenary powers over Puerto Rico, in violation of its international obligations.[105]

Options for the Future

Will Congress—should Congress—act to fulfill its legal, moral, and political obligations regarding the exercise of self-determination by the people of Puerto Rico? It should and it must. The relation between Puerto Rico and the United States stands at the crossroads. We are in a crisis situation in which a critical decision must be made.

First of all, the territory is in an untenable position. After 116 years under the plenary powers of Congress, colonialism has failed. The territory is broke. The current crisis can be traced to a period of more than forty years in which the territory's finances were kept artificially afloat through the emission of public debt. Now, after seven or eight years of recession and depression, the debt has been repeatedly degraded to the level of junk bonds, menacing even the stability of the bond market. The government of Puerto Rico has been forced to adopt severe measures that have affected public employees, reduced government services, increased taxes, and made it possible for public corporations to default on their obligations. The present depression of the colonial economy taints the prestige of the United States and looms over the Treasury, as some talk of a "federal bailout" to save the day. In fact, both the White House and the Federal Reserve have begun to examine the situation in search of solutions.

Second, the people of Puerto Rico have rejected the territorial relationship. For sixty years, the United States and supporters of the regime defended the legitimacy of the relationship by referring to the consent of the people supposedly expressed in 1952 upon the creation of the Estado Libre Asociado. That consent has evaporated into thin air. In a plebiscite held on November 6, 2012, a clear majority of 54% of the electorate rejected the current territorial status. Consent to a colonial regime is never legally valid, but now it has simply ceased to exist.

The third reason for urgent action is that the international community is observing and beginning to act. The UN Special Committee on Decolonization has kept the case of Puerto Rico on its agenda through a long series of resolutions since 1972. The committee's 2013 resolution characterizes the relation, for the first time ever, as one of "political subordination."

---

105 Torruella, "The *Insular Cases.*" "By continuing to patronize its continuing relationship to Puerto Rico, the United States not only degrades its image as a leader of the democratic world, but also places itself in clear violation of its international commitments, and thus concomitantly contravenes its own domestic 'Law of the Land.'" Ibid., 333.

Accordingly, the resolution calls on the US government to expedite a process that will allow the people of Puerto Rico to fully exercise their inalienable right to self-determination.[106]

And in Latin America, the Community of Latin American and Caribbean States has issued a unanimous declaration that takes note of the resolutions adopted by the UN Special Committee on Decolonization, commits member states to working toward the eradication of colonialism from the region, and creates a working group of four states to elaborate proposals for the advancement of the objectives of the UN resolutions on Puerto Rico.[107]

Two questions arise. What are the substantive options for the future status of Puerto Rico? What process ought to be put in place to reach a decision?

Three alternatives to the territorial regime have been proposed by political forces in Puerto Rico. The so-called *estado libre asociado soberano*, or sovereign free associated state, would require that Congress dispose of the territory and that a compact of free association be adopted, following the example of several insular communities of the Pacific associated with New Zealand and the United States. None of these communities is viable as an independent nation. Their populations range from 1,400 to slightly over 100,000. Their combined population is similar to that of the city of Ponce, on the southern coast of Puerto Rico. Of course, the option of free association, as a transitional status toward independence, cannot be summarily dismissed.

There is also the option of admitting Puerto Rico as a state of the union. Proponents of statehood insist that in 2012 their option obtained a 61% majority, when in fact only 45% of those who participated voted for that option.[108] Statehooders insist on a claim of equality for US citizens residing in

---

106 Special Committee on the Situation with regard to the Implementation of the Declaration on the Granting of Independence to Colonial Countries and Peoples, Decision of the Special Committee of 18 June 2012 concerning Puerto Rico, U.N. Doc. A/AC.109/2013/L.6 (2013).

107 *Havana Declaration*, II Summit of the Community of Latin American and Caribbean States, Jan. 28-29, 2014, paras. 38-40.

108 The plebiscite ballot contained two questions. In the first question, voters could vote "yes" or "no" regarding whether they wanted to maintain Puerto Rico's current territorial relationship with the United States. For the first time, a majority of the people rejected the territorial status, with 54% voting "no" and 46% voting "yes." In the second question, voters could vote for one of three options: statehood, independence, and *estado libre asociado soberano*. Here, 45% voted for statehood, 4% voted for independence, 26% voted for *estado libre asociado soberano*, and 26% did not vote for any of the options. During the campaign, the Popular Democratic Party had asked voters to cast blank votes in the second question. Half of the party's electorate did so; the other half voted for the *estado libre asociado soberano*. If the blank votes are factored out, statehood obtained 61%, independence 6%, and

Puerto Rico and try to evoke the struggle for civil rights and racial equality to appeal to liberals and moderates in the United States. However, the status of Puerto Rico is not an issue of individual civil rights but of the collective right of the Puerto Rican people to self-determination, an inalienable human right that, as a matter of law, cannot be renounced. Statehood is irrevocable. The people of an unincorporated territory or colony that constitutes a distinct nationality cannot exercise their right to self-determination by renouncing permanently their inalienable right to self-determination.[109] Although the principle has evolved primarily around colonial situations, it may also apply beyond the colonial context. It may not be used to justify dismantling a sovereign state, but it remains a crucial principle of the collective human rights of peoples or nationalities within a state.[110] Self-determination is consistent with the principle of territorial integrity, but it may legitimate secession from an independent state in some circumstances.[111] Thus, a people or nationality that opts for integration into another state does not extinguish its right to self-determination.

For Congress to make a statehood offer, it must consider whether a simple majority of 51% would suffice. Even if the statehood option obtained a "supermajority," the question would still be whether Congress should admit the territory with a substantial minority that would rather opt for separate sovereignty under independence or free association. Congress would have to revisit the political criteria that it has repeatedly employed in the process of admitting new states:

> 1. That the inhabitants of the proposed new State are imbued with and are sympathetic toward the principles of democracy as exemplified in the American form of government.
>
> 2. That a majority of the electorate wish statehood.
>
> 3. That the proposed new State has sufficient population and resources to support State government and at the same time carry its share of the cost of the Federal government.[112]

---

estado libre asociado soberano 33%. Needless to say, the blank votes can reasonably be interpreted as not favoring statehood.

109 Rubén Berríos Martínez, "Self-Determination and Independence: The Case of Puerto Rico," *Proceedings of the American Society of International Law* 67 (1973): 11-17, 17.

110 Malcolm Shaw, *International Law*, 4th ed. (Cambridge: Cambridge University Press, 1997), 216-17.

111 Ibid.

112 H.R. Rep. No. 85-624 (1957), *reprinted in* 1958 U.S.C.C.A.N. 2933.

In applying these criteria to Puerto Rico, Congress must understand that Puerto Rico is a Latin American nation. It should realize that nationalities cannot be suppressed and will reappear. We must remember the Soviet Union, Yugoslavia, Scotland, Catalonia, the Basque Country, and, closer to home, Quebec.

Finally, there is the option of independence, supported by a majority of the people seventy years ago. It has dwindled in recent decades as a result of repression and of economic and psychological dependence. And yet independence is the natural destiny of all peoples. Sometimes, critical events produce unexpected results. For example, in 1774, George Washington wrote with regard to independence, "I am well satisfied that no such thing is desired by any thinking man in all North America."[113] And some months prior to July 1776, none other than Thomas Jefferson stated that a happy and permanent relation with England was desirable and that no one was interested in separating from England.[114] Fortunately, those were not his last words.

An independent Puerto Rico would be free to pursue its economic development unhindered by federal limitations. It would be free to establish productive relations with other nations, including the United States, which would benefit much more from a free Puerto Rico than from a bankrupt colony. The route to independence would require a careful but very viable economic transition, such as that already negotiated by the Puerto Rican Independence Party with congressional leaders in 1989-1991.[115]

In fact, it now turns out that all three substantive options for the future status of Puerto Rico will require an economic transition from the current economic crisis to conditions of self-sufficiency and sustained economic development. In compliance with the legal obligation to promote self-determination, transitional aid under independence, for instance, must be

---

113 Quoted in Washington Irving, *The Life of George Washington*, vol. 1 (New York: G.P. Putnam, 1860); Charles A. Kromkowski, *Recreating the American Republic: Rules of Apportionment, Constitutional Change, and American Political Development, 1700-1870* (Cambridge: Cambridge University Press, 2002), 122.

114 Jefferson wrote a letter to John Randolph, a friend who had moved to England fearing that the colonies proposed to take arms against the king. "Believe me sir, there is not in the British empire a man who more cordially loves a union with Great Britain, than I do. But by the God that made me, I will cease to exist before I yield to a connection on such terms as the British Parliament proposes; and in this, I think I speak the sentiments of America." John Sharp Williams, *Thomas Jefferson: His Permanent Influence on American Institutions* (New York: Columbia University Press, 1913), 28.

115 For a synthesis of the advantages of independence for Puerto Rico, see Rubén Berríos Martínez, "Puerto Rico's Decolonization," *Foreign Affairs* 76 (1997): 100-114.

viewed not as a federal bailout but as reparations for more than a century of colonialism.

With regard to the process leading to a solution of the problem, Washington must "dispose of the territory"[116] to facilitate and promote self-determination. In San Juan, legislation should be enacted to allow Puerto Rico to determine its future through the exercise of the constituent power that resides in the people. [117]

Currently, there are several proposals. The New Progressive Party has proposed a bill now pending in Congress to authorize a yes-or-no vote on statehood. But this proposal does not solve the problem. First, its political possibilities are about as strong as those of the abolition of the papacy by the Catholic Church. But even if it were approved, what would happen if there is no majority, or if there is one by only a slim margin? The territorial status would prevail.

Some members of the Popular Democratic Party have proposed legislation for a constitutional status assembly whose elected majority would negotiate with the United States the terms of a new relationship not subject to the territory clause.

The Puerto Rican Independence Party has proposed legislation to call for a status assembly based on the constituent power of the people. It would be inclusive of all nonterritorial options—independence, statehood, and free association—and would demand a response from Congress to all three proposals. The end result would be a plebiscite in which the people of Puerto Rico would vote on options acceptable to the United States, with full knowledge of what each proposal really entails. What kind of free association? What conditions and concessions for statehood, if it were plausible? What terms for the new relationship between the United States and an independent Republic of Puerto Rico?

In the coming months, these procedural proposals will be discussed, and hopefully a decision will be made regarding a process of self-determination for the people of Puerto Rico. Such a decision will require overcoming the forces of inertia and immobility that have stalled the process for decades.

Reconsidering the Insular Cases is an indispensable prerequisite to solving the colonial problem. The doctrine of territorial nonincorporation

---

116 U.S. CONST., art. IV, § 3, cl. 2.
117 Emmanuel Joseph Sieyès, *Qu'est-ce que le Tiers État?* (Paris: Éditions du Boucher, 2002); Vladimiro Naranjo Mesa, *Teoría constitucional e instituciones políticas*, 8th ed. (Bogota: Temis, 2000), 361-62; Pedro de Vega, *La reforma constitucional y la problemática del poder constituyente* (Madrid: Tecnos, 1985), 15; Jorge Reinaldo Vanossi, *Teoría constitucional*, vol. 1 (Buenos Aires: Depalma, 1975), 277.

must be expunged from American law. We must rip out the academic pages containing the blueprint for the constitutionalization of colonialism by Congress and the Supreme Court, and read them only for the purpose of studying a shameful past that should never be repeated. The congressional exercise of imperial power must become a thing of the past.

As Rubén Berríos has written, "Colonialism denigrates the colonized, but it also demeans the colonizer."[118] The time has come to agree with Justice John Marshall Harlan when he dissented in *Downes* in 1901:

> The idea that this country may acquire territories anywhere upon the earth, by conquest or treaty, and hold them as mere colonies or provinces . . . is wholly inconsistent with the spirit and genius, as well as with the words, of the Constitution.[119]

It is also inconsistent with international human rights law and an insult to human dignity in this day and age.

---

118 Berríos Martínez, "Puerto Rico's Decolonization," 112.
119 Downes v. Bidwell, 182 U.S. 244, 380 (Harlan, J., dissenting).

Contributors

Tomiko Brown-Nagin is the Daniel P.S. Paul Professor of Constitutional Law at Harvard Law School and a professor of history at Harvard's Faculty of Arts and Sciences. The co-director of Harvard Law School's Program in Law and History, Brown-Nagin is an award-winning legal historian and expert in constitutional law and education law and policy. Her 2011 book, *Courage to Dissent: Atlanta and the Long History of the Civil Rights Movement*, won the Bancroft Prize in American History. Brown-Nagin currently is at work on a biography of Constance Baker Motley, the famed civil rights lawyer, politician, and judge.

Rafael Cox Alomar is an assistant professor of law at the University of the District of Columbia David A. Clarke School of Law in Washington, DC. He is the author of *Revisiting the Transatlantic Triangle: The Constitutional Decolonization of the Eastern Caribbean*. He holds a BA, *magna cum laude*, from Cornell University, a JD from Harvard Law School, and a DPhil from the University of Oxford.

Carlos Iván Gorrín Peralta is a professor of law at the Inter-American University of Puerto Rico. Prior to his academic appointment, he occupied several positions in Puerto Rico Legal Services. He has authored numerous publications on legal education, human rights, and constitutional law, particularly the constitutional relations between Puerto Rico and the United States. Since 1989, Gorrín Peralta has served as a consultant and attorney for the Puerto Rican Independence Party. He is a former president of the Inter-American Bar Association. He holds a BA from the College of the Holy Cross, a JD from the University of Puerto Rico School of Law, and an LLM from Harvard Law School.

Chimène Keitner is the Harry and Lillian Hastings Research Chair and a professor of law at the University of California Hastings College of the Law. She has also taught at the law schools of Berkeley, the University of Southern California, and Tel Aviv University. She is the author of *The Paradoxes of Nationalism: The French Revolution and Its Meaning for Contemporary Nation Building*, and dozens of shorter works on the relationships among law, communities, and borders. Previously, she clerked for the chief justice of the Supreme Court of Canada. She serves on the Executive Council of the American Society of International Law and is an adviser for the American Law Institute's *Restatement (Fourth) of Foreign Relations Law*. She holds a BA in history and literature from Harvard College, a JD from Yale University, and a doctorate in international relations from the University of Oxford, where she was a Rhodes Scholar.

Andrés W. López is an accomplished attorney with extensive involvement in the Latino community in the United States. For the past eleven years, he has led his own law firm focused on complex litigation. Prior to that, he worked for two top-tier firms and two federal judges in Boston and San Juan. During the 2012 presidential campaign, López served as national chairman of the FuturoFund, an entity led by national Latino leaders to raise funds for President Obama's reelection campaign. López has served on President Obama's National Finance Committee since 2007, and he served as an adviser to Obama's 2008 and 2012 campaigns. Recently, Obama appointed López to the Board of Trustees of the John F. Kennedy Center for the Performing Arts. López is also a presidential appointee and co-founder of the effort to create a Smithsonian American Latino Museum on the Washington, DC, National Mall. In 2012, *PODER* magazine selected López as one of the "100 Most Influential Hispanics in America." He is a graduate of Harvard College and Harvard Law School.

Gerald L. Neuman is the co-director of the Human Rights Program and J. Sinclair Armstrong Professor of International, Foreign, and Comparative Law at Harvard Law School. He teaches human rights, constitutional law, and immigration and nationality law. His current research focuses on international human rights bodies, the transnational dimensions of constitutionalism, and the rights of foreign nationals. His prior writings on territorial issues include "Whose Constitution?" (*Yale Law Journal*); "Anomalous Zones" (*Stanford Law Review*); "Constitutionalism and Individual Rights in the Territories" (in *Foreign in a Domestic Sense: Puerto Rico, American Expansion, and the*

Constitution, ed. Christina Duffy Burnett and Burke Marshall); and "Closing the Guantanamo Loophole" (*Loyola Law Review*). From 2011 to 2014, he served as a member of the United Nations Human Rights Committee.

Christina Duffy Ponsa is the George Welwood Murray Professor of Legal History at Columbia Law School. She is the co-editor of *Foreign in a Domestic Sense: Puerto Rico, American Expansion, and the Constitution* and the author of several articles and essays on the constitutional implications of American territorial expansion. She is currently working on a constitutional and international legal history of American empire in the late nineteenth and early twentieth centuries. Before joining the Columbia faculty in 2007, she served as a law clerk to Judge José A. Cabranes on the United States Court of Appeals for the Second Circuit and to Justice Stephen G. Breyer on the United States Supreme Court. Ponsa holds a BA and PhD from Princeton University, an MPhil from the University of Cambridge, and a JD from Yale University.

Efrén Rivera Ramos is a professor of law and former dean at the University of Puerto Rico School of Law. He is the author of *The Legal Construction of Identity: The Judicial and Social Legacy of American Colonialism in Puerto Rico* and of numerous book chapters and articles on a range of topics, including the relationship between the United States and Puerto Rico. He holds a BA in political science and a JD from the University of Puerto Rico, an LLM from Harvard Law School, and a PhD in law from University College London.

Rogers M. Smith is the Christopher H. Browne Distinguished Professor of Political Science and associate dean for social sciences at the University of Pennsylvania, where he founded the Penn Program on Democracy, Citizenship, and Constitutionalism. His books include *Political Peoplehood*; *Stories of Peoplehood*; and *Civic Ideals*, which received six "best book" awards from four professional associations and was a finalist for the 1998 Pulitzer Prize for History. Smith was elected a fellow of the American Academy of Arts and Sciences in 2004 and of the American Academy of Political and Social Science in 2011.

Bartholomew Sparrow is a professor of Government at the University of Texas at Austin. His books include *The* Insular Cases *and the Emergence of American Empire; From the Outside In: World War II and the American State; Uncertain Guardians: The News Media as a Political Institution*; and, most recently, *The Strategist: Brent Scowcroft and the Call of National Security.*

He has been a fellow of the Woodrow Wilson International Center for Scholars; the Shorenstein Center on Media, Politics and Public Policy; and the Harry S. Truman Library Institute.

Juan R. Torruella was born in San Juan, Puerto Rico, and has sat on the United States Court of Appeals for the First Circuit since 1984. He served as chief judge of that court from 1994 to 2001. After working in private practice, he was appointed to the United States District Court for the District of Puerto Rico in 1974, where he served as chief judge from 1982 to 1984. Judge Torruella has written extensively on the Insular Cases and has published over 1,500 opinions during his career as a federal judge. He holds a BS in economics from the Wharton School of the University of Pennsylvania, a JD from Boston University School of Law, an LLM from the University of Virginia, an MPA from the University of Puerto Rico, and an MSt from the University of Oxford.